S Phillips

The Naked Rower

The Naked Rower

How two Kiwis took on the Atlantic — and won!

Rob Hamill

Hodder Moa Beckett

ISBN 1-86958-766-9

Published in 2000 by Hodder Moa Beckett Publishers Limited [a member of the Hodder Headline Group]
4 Whetu Place, Mairangi Bay, Auckland, New Zealand

Produced and designed by Hodder Moa Beckett Publishers Ltd
Writers: Rob Whyte and Michael Wall
Film by Microdot, Auckland, New Zealand
Printed by Publishing Press, Auckland

Phil

You were the strength supporting my dream

You were the builder of our boat

You were the one, the only one

Who I could reminisce with

In 5Ø years' time

Grandchildren on lap

And truly understand

To Kerry and John

You are with me always

Sponsor's Message

Rob Hamill's *Kiwi Challenge* typifies what it means to be the underdog. With nothing but a vision to get to the start-line of a rowing race, Rob begged, borrowed and pledged his way from Hamilton to the Canary Islands. The commitment to win was absolute — how could he return without victory? Victory made all that much sweeter by the financial shoestring that held it together and the comradeship of Phil Stubbs.

In reading this book, some will be inspired to follow their dreams — irrespective of the odds — and win on the world stage. This is the legacy of Rob Hamill, Phil Stubbs and *Kiwi Challenge*.

Chris Dunphy
Managing Director, LEP International
February 2000

Contents

Acknowledgements

My thanks go to Rob Whyte for helping flesh out the story. To Michael Wall and Julie "Coming of Age" Collier, thank you for making me feel at home in every way. Michael, your guidance and humorous observations were illuminating and inspiring.

To our families, many thanks for your unwavering support throughout our journey.

Nothing in the world
is as soft and yielding as water.
Yet for dissolving the hard and
the inflexible, nothing can surpass it.

Tao Te Ching

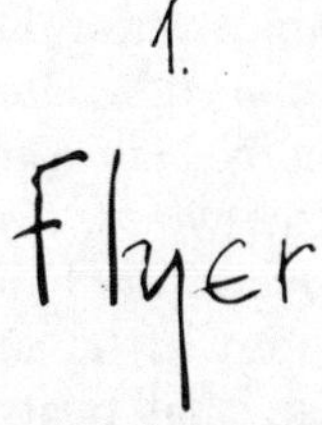

1. Flyer

Make voyages. Attempt them. That's all there is.
Elaine Dundy

ALL JOURNEYS BEGIN AT some crossroads in time and most involve many a traveller. This one began in July 1996 in a locker room in Charlottesville, Virginia, on the banks of the Rivanna River. The New Zealand rowing team was at a training camp two weeks prior to competing in the Atlanta Olympic Games. On the locker room wall, amongst the local club notices, a plain flyer caught my eye. Somebody wanted a partner to row in a race across the Atlantic Ocean.

Unknowingly, I was standing at the crossroads.

The ensuing journey would come to encompass the efforts of hundreds of people without whom it could never have happened. That said, it will, I guess, be remembered as the story of two men. I was privileged to be one of them and to be in the position to tell our story as I experienced it. I will do so as honestly as I am able, but I am under no illusions here. I know that, had things turned out differently, the tale would have been more complete and may well have been told differently.

That cannot be.

*

On that day I was 32 years old, single, had no regular girlfriend, was employed by the Waikato Polytechnic as a liaison officer and had never been to sea. I was a World Championship silver medallist in the lightweight double sculls, had won Commonwealth gold and held a world record on the ergometer or indoor rowing machine. Given our recent successes, my rowing partner and I were given a chance of taking the gold medal at the Atlanta Olympics in a couple of weeks' time. Financially, I was on the bones of my bum.

All of this notwithstanding, the flyer had planted the germ of an idea in my mind. For the next five days I found myself pausing each time I passed the notice board. It occurred to me that this was something I could possibly do when the Olympics were over. I could almost see the headline in the

Waikato Times: "*Olympic Gold Medallist to Row the Atlantic!*"

What I didn't know then was that the trans-Atlantic race would involve the exploration of unknown territory; both figuratively and literally. Far more people had climbed Mount Everest than had rowed the Atlantic, or all the oceans in the world combined, for that matter.

In 1896 the Norwegians George Habro and Frank Samuelson had made the first crossing and startled the world, covering the distance in 55 days and arriving in Le Havre from New York half-dead: a record for a two-man crossing that still stood a century later. Since then only 29 people had succeeded in rowing an ocean in small boats anywhere on Earth.

At least six ocean rowers had died in the attempt to row the Atlantic. In August 1966, David Johnstone and John Hoare's boat *Puffin* was found overturned at sea in the northern Atlantic. They had disappeared after rowing for over 84 days. Just two months before I saw the Atlantic Rowing Race flyer, Peter Bird, perhaps the greatest ocean rower of all time, had crossed the Pacific — a journey of 5211 nautical miles — and disappeared off the coast of Alaska after 69 days at sea.

Most successful attempts at the Atlantic crossing — such as Chay Blyth and John Ridgeway's well-documented 91-day crossing (also in 1966) — had involved rowing the northerly route to gain assistance from the Gulf Stream current sweeping west to east from Cape Cod to the British Isles. But the northern route was subject to storms and a heavy traffic flow with both fishing boats and cargo ships.

The flyer informed me that the race route would be across the mid-Atlantic, north of the equator in mid-autumn. Competitors could expect reasonable weather, rather similar to that of March in New Zealand. At this latitude the north-east trade winds would assist over the second half of the journey, providing both a following sea and wind.

Given the paucity of attempts in the past the race idea was highly ambitious. Thirty boats would attempt the journey from the Canary Islands to Barbados. This meant that, in this one event, 60 people — twice the number of all previously successful voyagers — would attempt the same feat at the same time and they would be racing competitively. If history was anything to go by, some would die in the attempt.

But I was blissfully unaware of all of these things that sunny day in Charlottesville. What instinctively appealed about the Atlantic race was the thought of a Kiwi crew cleaning up the event. That was how the adventure began.

*

Steger (Antarctica 1989) quoted in Ranulph Fiennes, *Mind Over Matter*

"What separates me from most men is that I rarely see boundaries or limits. If I want to do something I do it. As a result there is no profound answer as to why I love this kind of life or why I want to cross Antarctica. I simply want to."

At the start I didn't say anything about my new enthusiasm. I was there on a different mission with a different agenda. When I eventually did mention the race to my rowing partner Mike Rodger, it didn't even raise his pulse rate. He was not the slightest bit interested and suspected I might be a couple of kumara short of a hangi. I then brought the flyer to the attention of several other rowers; suggesting this race might be an awesome follow-up to the Olympics. They were universally uninterested so I crossed my fellow Olympians off as potential candidates and concentrated on the immediate challenge. Glory awaited — or so I thought at the time.

*

Later, among the shattered hopes and dreams that had been Atlanta, the thought of the Atlantic race was constantly playing in my mind. Our Olympic performance was the slowest Mike and I had ever rowed in an international regatta. I was gutted, in no small measure because I knew exactly what we had done wrong.

In difficult circumstances we had qualified for the Olympics nine weeks earlier. On the flight from New Zealand to Europe I had caught a bug which I tried to train through but I ended up with pneumonia. Mike, too, became ill and we both landed in bed for several days. Neither of us was fit to compete at that level by the time the qualifying rounds took place, and yet we had qualified. We thought we were invincible and that was the way we trained. From that point on every training session was an Olympic final. By the time we got to the real thing, we were physically exhausted. It taught me a lesson I'll never forget.

*

The Olympics had been the low point in my rowing career. A week later, in September of 1996, I was flying to the World Rowing Championships in Scotland. A major segment of the in-flight entertainment was Olympic highlights. This was too much. I stared out of the window seeing nothing, tears in my eyes. What a loser! Nor did the humiliation end there. At the championships we again performed dismally.

Afterwards I was in Nottingham, staying with a friend, Gary McAdams.

Gary knew a little about the Atlantic Rowing Race and he informed me that all the boats were kitset jobs that had to be assembled by the contestants. That seemed feasible to me, and furthermore he knew that there were already a few being put together in Britain and gave me some advice on how to contact the organisers. Another friend, Ken Atkins, was aware that I was thinking about rowing the Atlantic race.

Ken offered some advice, "You should read Ranulph Fiennes' *Mind over Matter*. Read that and then see if you still want to row the Atlantic, mate."

That was very sound advice indeed. I read this and Chay Blyth's

A Fighting Chance. Both were chilling, sober statements of the mental toughness required to succeed in supreme tests of endurance. In Ranulph Fiennes' and Mike Stroud's case it was an unassisted Antarctic trek by foot hauling all their equipment and food. It quietened, but didn't silence my enthusiasm; rather it proved a much appreciated reality check.

*

I was influenced by rowing from the tender age of two. The story goes that my parents put me in the family dinghy, a 7 ft plywood creation with a cut-off bow similar to that of an Optimist yacht. They launched it into the swimming pool at the river mouth of the Whakatane Heads then threw an anchor overboard and placed one oar handle in my tiny hands. Apparently I managed to splash the oar in the water enough to propel the dinghy and eventually completed a half circle.

Throughout my childhood to the end of my teenage years I rowed that dinghy back and forth across the Whakatane River at least 3000 times (I never exaggerate), by myself, with friends or family — whitebaiting, setting the flounder net, pitching a tent on the sandhills for an overnight camp or simply swimming in the surf. I loved getting in that little boat and paddling as fast as I could.

Occasionally I rowed out into the surf and nearly paid dearly for that one time when a wave picked up the boat and flipped it over, sandwiching my body between the upturned boat and the sandy ground. A pocket of air trapped under the boat enabled me to take gulps of air while I wrestled the boat off me.

*

With the competitions in Europe over I returned home to Hamilton and continued to think about the race, uncertain how to proceed. Then one night on impulse I rang The Challenge Business office in the United Kingdom. The Challenge Business was set up by Chay Blyth to promote high profile nautical challenges. The office manager, Teresa Evans, was efficient and very helpful.

"Certainly Mr Hamill, I'll get an information pack out to you immediately."

Now that was a good start. I couldn't recall when I was last addressed as Mr Hamill.

"Three questions, Teresa. When is the race scheduled to begin? What are the costs to enter? And to purchase the kitset?"

The kitset was simply a set of 23 sheets of pre-cut plywood which competitors around the world would then assemble, producing theoretically identical boats. As with so much else about this race, the theory and the practice would turn out to be quite different things.

"All that information is in the package, Mr Hamill. The starting date of the race isn't fixed yet, but will be either October or November next year."

Make it November please, I need all the time I can get, I thought.

"The kitset costs are included in the entrance fee. The entrance fee is $27,000 which includes $16,000 for the kitset. That has to be paid up front. Is there anything else I can help you with at the moment?"

"No not just at the moment.... "

"Well, the package will be on its way today, and thank you for your interest, Mr Hamill."

I don't know how long I stood still holding the phone, my mouth agape. I suppose it was only a second or two, but the ardour in my belly hit the floor, splat! $27,000! God. For a race! A race with no prizes!

I walked once around my flat thinking at a furious rate before I picked up the phone and called The Challenge Business back, this time to speak with its Director, Sir Chay Blyth, about the size of the entrance fee. It was that amount, he informed me, primarily because of the safety requirements. Two mother ships would be required to monitor and assist the fleet which would quickly disperse over the mid-Atlantic. I understood. Then I talked about my situation as an amateur sportsman and he understood.

We discussed a number of rowing-related issues while I gathered my nerves. Then I put my proposal: could I pay over a period of time? I needed the boat first, then I could aspire to equip it and eventually pay the remainder. To my enormous relief Chay accepted my offer, saying that he would be in New Zealand in January and would like to meet me then. Some warmth returned to my belly, my spirits rose, I could again feel the passion. This could indeed be a goer. I went out that night as happy as a rower with a new skiff.

I decided that my first target was to raise $20,000.

*

Cameron Bell, New Zealand representative rower, August 1999

For a start Rob Hamill is a sculler. I always deem that to be a rower with no friends. A wide-eyed young lad from Whakatane who proudly proclaimed down at the Wairau Rowing shed in Blenheim, way back in1986, that he was "Irish". A keen man who had a mild affliction of acne and a tendency towards bogan music – I well remember the genuine disbelief and aggrievement he displayed when, driving his red Torana, he was firmly instructed to turn his favourite AC/DC anthem OFF.

During our training in Blenheim no one ever doubted his commitment or ability, but as with us all we were untried in competition. I'll never forget that first race of his at Barrington in Tasmania. His Aussie opponent was a Goliath. When the Colts singles came into sight of the finish line, here was this little eccentric dynamo leading the Aussie's much-vaunted champion giant. The Aussie support was gobsmacked while the rest of the Kiwi team screamed like lunatics. Rob's victory provided a real boost to the team.

Eccentric. I could not believe some of his antics. Especially his ritual of removing his rowing shorts and underpants after winning that race, wrapping a towel around his waist and trundling off to retrieve his blades from the water's edge. The situation begged for someone to remove the towel.

*

One night I went out to a dinner party at a friend's flat. The dinner was superb, the company charming, the conversation interesting. Among the guests was a delightful blonde named Carolyn McNabb — an intensive-care nurse at Waikato Hospital — who will appear again in our story. There was a lull in the conversation and I heard myself say, "I'm going to row the Atlantic. There is a race from the Canary Islands to Barbados and I'm going to enter."

I sat there thunderstruck by what my mouth had confessed. Up until that point I hadn't actually decided. Sure, I wanted to be in the race, but wanting to and deciding to are very different propositions. I was appalled by what I had blurted out. People were interested in the project, but all thought I was mad, and thankfully the conversation soon changed to more manageable subjects. I sat transfixed by what I had done. Mr Hamill was committed.

When the race entrance form arrived I filled it in, went to the bank and then sent off my $200 deposit with the entry form. I was determined to win that race. But I still had only a hazy idea of the extraordinary obstacles to be overcome before I even reached the starting line-up. I knew nothing of raising finance, media exposure, building ocean-going craft or blue-water rowing. Nor did I have a clue who (if anyone) might partner me in this seemingly dubious venture. Most people who learned what I was up to thought I was involved in the ultimate folly.

I was determined to prove them wrong.

2.
The Ali Way

The follies which a person regrets in his life, are those which he didn't commit when he had the opportunity.
Helen Rowland

MUHAMMAD ALI HAS ALWAYS been my idol. His skill, athleticism, courage, arrogance and self-belief all had a huge influence on me as an 8- to 12-year-old. He was the epitome of a champion. The more I learned about him, the more I admired him. Long before I was aware of sports psychology, I was fascinated by his statements such as, "I am the greatest!"; his self-characterisation, "Float like a butterfly, sting like a bee"; and his pre-match psychology, "If he even dreams he can beat me, he had better wake up and apologise."

Arrogant, yes, but having made those statements he had committed himself to perform, to deliver, to discharge his obligation. It was his ability to deliver on his proclamations that excited me. He was exciting, he was committed and his commitment captured my imagination. I saw Ali at the Olympic Games opening ceremony and I was inspired. Later I met him in the games village and again I was awestruck. It was the Ali approach that I would apply in my bid to win the first trans-Atlantic rowing race.

*

I received notification of the starting date, October 12, 1997. Unfortunately it was not the November start I had been hoping for. I had just 12 months before the starting gun would be fired, a pitifully short time considering all that had to be done. I was alone and at sea. What the heck, I was committed, now I had to deliver. December 1, 1996 was the target date I had set myself to come up with the required money for the boat kitset to get the whole project under away.

The Challenge Business only placed orders for kitsets on the first of the month. Thus a January order would jeopardise my schedule. I figured that it would take two to three months to build and completely outfit the boat. That would allow me a couple of months towing the boat around to raise the finance, a couple of months for training and a couple of months to get it to the Canary Islands. I definitely didn't want to leave the ordering any later than December 1, 1996.

*

I first went to the media in October 1996. I naively believed that if I obtained wide enough exposure, someone somewhere would think, "Gosh, what a great opportunity. I must support this guy." I sought help from Peter Montgomery and was interviewed on Sportstalk ZB. Next I went on Coast-to-Coast television with Buck Anderson. Deep down I knew I was being unrealistic but I had to give the fairy godmother a try. That done, the reality set in. I knew I was in for a real battle to get the sponsorship I sought.

The radio media were very good to me. Peter Montgomery took an instant liking to the project and, much later, came to check the boat during construction. Sportstalk presenter Murray Deaker was also supportive and had me in his studio for an hour. We took questions and talked a lot about the race: what the objectives were, why I was doing it and the fact that I was looking for a partner. But at this point my primary concern was getting the money.

I had started on an incredible learning curve needed to gain corporate sponsorship. In the months that followed I would approach in excess of 250 companies and organisations, and 90 per cent of those approaches were unsuccessful. Yet, there would also be a significant number of people and companies who assisted to the limits of their capacity to do so. The education of Rob Hamill had begun.

*

Sunday Star-Times, November 3, 1996

The race is almost a year away but it is already consuming Hamill's brain waves. Even when the New Zealand rowing representative is asleep, the event is present.

The nightmare is the terror experienced by many small-boat sailors who sail the world's oceans. It's the fear of being mowed down by a giant ship as Hamill and his partner sleep in their water-tight compartment.

Hamill jokes that he will have a lighted Christmas tree on top of the boat to act as a beacon, but the rowers will be allowed a wide range of safety equipment, including radar.

"You can plan for many things, but if a whale wants to roll you, it will," he says.

*

Now let's be up front here. I am not one given to airs and graces. I was a frequenter of the outdoors, unfamiliar with the indoors, atrium fashions and canyons of offices. All my life I had practised the doctrine that actions speak louder than words and I prefer casual dress. I didn't possess a suit as I had no need of one, and the only shirt, tie and jacket that "went together" was my Olympic outfit from Atlanta. Thus equipped I felt ready to tackle serious fundraising.

When I mentioned to a friend that I was thinking of going to the bank and getting a top-up on my house mortgage, she said, "Don't do that, Rob. As soon as you fall into that mind-set, you will get trapped into accepting that that is the only way you can raise money. It will become a self-fulfilling prophecy. Think, you have to get the money from somewhere else, you have to get a sponsor. Think sponsorship, Rob."

But by the middle of November, I had received nothing. So I went to the bank. I was driving in my car when I heard on the radio that my bank at that time were offering up to $10,000 lifestyle top-up loans on existing mortgages. I simply rang up the bank, gave them my account number, asked for $10,000. "Yes, it's in the account." Simple, easy and the transfer was complete.

Now I'd really done it — I was financially committed. I simply had to get started somewhere. I had been going nowhere raising money and certainly not the additional $10,000 that was required by December 1. I was very disheartened. Without a boat I would have nothing solid to point to and say, "In this boat a partner and I are going to row the Atlantic. With your assistance we are going to win this race!" Without at least $10,000 in sponsorship to enable me to buy the kitset I had no boat.

*

My calendar told me it was November 26. Five days to the first deadline and I had nothing but my own mortgage. That evening I had been out training on Lake Karapiro and arrived back home at 8.30 p.m. Worried, I went back to work at the Waikato Polytechnic and finished off a letter that I had begun earlier in the day. As a desperate measure I was turning to one of those obvious businessmen who gets hit up for money all the time. Perry Holdings are fantastic backers of local recreation and sports in the Waikato and Brian Perry had always been in the back of my mind. But I had thought I could get sponsorship without treading the well-trodden path to his door. No, so it seemed.

I checked the telephone directory for Mr Perry's address and was genuinely surprised to find it was listed. Finishing the letter I sealed it and around 10.30 that night drove to his address, put my letter in the letterbox and walked away. Then I hesitated, thinking, "Hell, he is not going to get this until tomorrow after coming back from work and that will be another day wasted." I could see the light was on in what was probably the lounge, as the room was facing the river.

I retraced my steps to the mailbox and carefully extracted my letter, then I nervously walked up the path, expecting two starving Doberman

Pinschers to attack me at any second. My vital parts shrunk. The heavy door was right in front of me and no dogs had arrived. I knocked. Presently I saw a figure slowly come into the hall and start to open the door. This time I was thinking, "Oh God, here we go." I introduced myself, nervously blurting words in rushes. I could hear myself being too loud, trying to convey my sincerity with a stream of "reallys".

*

"G'day Brian, I'm Rob Hamill. I wonder if I could have a quick word with you please?"

He was rather taken aback. "Rob who?"

"Rob Hamill. I really do apologise for the inconvenience and being so late at night, but things have really got out of hand. I really need to show you something I'm doing. I'm going to row the Atlantic and I really need your help."

He looked steadily at me and seemed very relaxed about the situation. He wore a dressing gown and slippers. Deliberately, he opened the door wide and said, "Come on in, Rob."

I told Brian that I would be entering a race later next year and I wanted to be the first New Zealander to row across the Atlantic Ocean. Just as importantly I wanted to win the first ever rowing race across the Atlantic. I needed $10,000 and was wondering if I could borrow it off him. Well that is what I meant to say but I know I was far more meek, pathetic and feeble than that. Nevertheless, quite a reasonable request at a reasonable time, don't you think?

Brian Perry turned out to be the most humble guy and somehow reminded me of my father, a retiring, patient gentleman. He gave me the time of night and talked to me for about 15 minutes. He inquired about the race and who was organising it and to help I told him a bit about my past. At the end of our discussion he said, "Look, I have a charitable trust. I assist those who wish to attempt things out of the ordinary. I'll consider what you have given me, and I will have a meeting with my fellow trustees tomorrow."

He phoned me the next day saying he would support the campaign with a $10,000 interest-free loan. I was over the moon. The relief was enormous. I could literally feel my blood pressure drop. I could probably have got the money from somewhere within my family, but I wanted to spare the institution of final resort. Alternatively I could have sold my dinged-up 1987 Holden Barina and the 1970s orange-and-brown floral lounge suite that would have gone for at least $100 had I needed it.

*

Around this time something else was going on my life. The attractive blonde from the dinner party a few months back where I had blurted out my intention to row the Atlantic had now become my girlfriend, confidante and unpaid secretary. She would also soon move in with me. Carolyn McNabb was many things to me in those months and later, but her most important influence was forcing me to keep my feet on the ground and to remind me that there was more to life than rowing the Atlantic.

There is a story they tell about Muhammad Ali. He is settling into his seat on a plane before take-off when the air hostess notices that his seat belt is not fastened.

"Excuse me, Mr Ali, can you do your seat belt up please?"

"Superman don't need no seat belt," Ali replies.

The hostess is not fazed: "Superman don't need no airplane, either."

Carolyn was like that.

3.

Wanna Row the Atlantic?

A silly question is the first intimation of some totally new development.
Alfred North Whitehead

NOW THE PROJECT WAS under way in earnest, I knew I had to do something about finding a rowing partner. None of my fellow Olympians had shown the least interest when I had spoken to them in Atlanta, so I assumed I'd have to look elsewhere. A friend suggested two people. The first was rower Chris White, and the second was mountaineer and adventurer Graeme Dingle.

Chris White is one of the icons of New Zealand rowing, a bull of a man who often spoke about a person having the rage to win. He had competed at the Atlanta Olympics — in the four without coxswain. Like me, he had failed to win a medal. Oddly enough, I hadn't discussed the race with Chris when in Charlottesville so I gave him a call. He thought about the idea, but decided against it for several reasons.

First, to Chris winning a rowing race of this nature would have seemed like second prize. His focus had always been on Olympic gold and anything else was simply not good enough. If he were to commit to rowing again, it would be with a view to an Olympic gold and not rowing some unknown race in a big puddle on the other side of the world. Second, domestication beckoned. He was looking to establish a career and family; a difficult combination if you also wish to win an ocean-rowing race. I respected Chris' viewpoint and moved on.

Though never having met Graeme Dingle, he seemed to me an interesting suggestion. He had the reputation as one of those wiry characters who could take a few knocks and keep going. Graeme was very interested but ruled himself out of contention due to his other commitments.

I then considered two other candidates. Richard Newey, an old rowing friend from Whakatane rowing days, indicated that he might be interested in joining forces. We rowed together in 1984 and were part of a Whakatane crew that won the novice eight title at the national champs. Richard had gone on to represent New Zealand in the single scull but, in his own words, "had had an unceremonious departure from the sport making way for Rob Waddell — as ya do". Although interested, he had overriding financial commitments.

*

At that stage Waddell was not the international figure he has now become. Indeed I think I can claim to be the first "journalist" to predict his coming fame. At the time I was putting out a news sheet designed to keep my friends up with the progress of my bid and convince sponsors that I was deadly serious about what I was doing. In one edition, reporting on my efforts at the New Zealand Championships, I wrote:

> I combined with Rob Waddell to win the double scull. Rob is to rowing what Tiger Woods is to golf. I reckon he will be the next New Zealander to win a world championship gold medal (you heard it here first, folks!)

A year later my prediction came true.

*

Another contender to row with me was Ian Wright, also an Atlanta Olympian, who finally put up his hand and contacted me. He had thought about the race for some time and decided that he was the right man for the job. At first, I was taken back by Ian's desire to do the race because his wife Wendy was four months pregnant. I spoke with Ian and Wendy and although we had a few laughs about the situation they realised there was an element of real danger and that the unborn child might never meet its father, something that I suggested might not be a bad thing! Nevertheless they both agreed in principle and I added Ian's name to the list of candidates, bringing the total to one.

Following the radio interview with Peter Montgomery, I received a phone call from Graham Dalton who said he was very interested in doing the race. It was a bizarre coincidence in that two days prior I had phoned his younger brother Grant, the outstanding Whitbread sailor. I left a message on Grant's answer phone, "Grant, would you be interested in a slight deviation from your current occupation?"

I had figured Grant would be ideal in that he was physically strong and had valuable sea experience. I remembered hearing a story about a potential yachting mishap. Apparently, when one of the stays holding the mast in place had broken, Grant had caught and held the stay until help arrived and disaster was averted. Whether the story was true or not, or even physically possible, didn't matter to me. Grant returned my call but informed me he couldn't entertain the idea as he was preparing *Merit Cup* for the Whitbread Round the World yacht race.

Grant's older brother Graham is around 1.90 m with a lanky frame insulated by a layer of padding; the result of several years in journalism.

He admitted to being 44 years old but had a history in rowing, having picked up the sport at the age of 20. After being nominated for a Colts trial he took up single sculls, as the results reflected his input alone, and not that of a team. An advantage Graham possessed was his sea experience. He had many hours of ocean sailing behind him, including a solo trans-Tasman race.

Graham and I discussed the race and the surrounding issues I needed to resolve. He was the first to mention some of the dangers at sea, including a rogue wave that can be disproportionately large and come in from a different angle to the prevailing swell.

"At night, if you're lucky, you can hear the thing coming and brace yourself," warned Graham. "But that might not matter because that is the very wave that could easily capsize a craft of this nature."

I was always aware that safety would be an issue. I wasn't yet thinking about it as much as I would as the venture progressed; nevertheless I didn't sleep well that night. The consolation was that at least Hamill's list had two names.

*

Graham Dalton, journalist, publisher, July 1999.
I first heard of Rob's ambition to row the Atlantic when listening to Peter Montgomery interview him on Newstalk ZB.

What struck initially was that here was a guy who was going public with a project when he had no money, no partner nor anything else other than his dream. Conventional wisdom would dictate this as not very clever. But I knew Rob Hamill had already achieved internationally in one of the toughest of tough sports, rowing. The enthusiasm and passion that blasted forth from my radio immediately captivated me and I phoned him within the hour.

We all do some smart things and dumb things in life, but my immediate call to Rob I rate in hindsight as one of the smarter. Not only did it provide an association with what turned out to be a piece of New Zealand sporting history, but also I made a firm mate.

The first call most people make on someone who seeks to do the unconventional (like row the Atlantic) is that they're mad. But in talking to many such characters like Rob the contrary is true. Inevitably they're stable, secure, both-feet-on-the-ground individuals. Those who aren't never get past go or fail to live and tell the tale.

*

A few weekends later, Andrew Sanders from the *Sunday Star-Times* wrote an article on what I was hoping to achieve. To me it seemed the article was huge, half filling the front page of the sport section and completely filling another page in the middle of the section. He covered all aspects of the race including my history, Chay Blyth's history, the race concept and a number of interesting anecdotes. The article was to spark another.

In Wellington at the time there was a passing fad where pubs and restaurants posted pages of the day's paper above the urinal in the men's toilets, thus enabling male patrons to catch up on the latest news while relieving themselves. And it just so happened that some unknown bar worker — a sports fan perhaps — chose to post the *Sunday Star-Times* story there for the edification of patrons. A seemingly minor act, but one which would change both my life and that of an off-duty policeman who already knew about the race, but until then had no idea any other Kiwi was interested.

A couple of days later I returned to my apartment in Hamilton to find a message on my answer phone. It simply said that the caller had read the *Sunday Star-Times* article and that he'd be interested in rowing the Atlantic with me. But it wasn't what was said that intrigued me — any nutter could have read the article, found my number and made the call — but rather the voice. It was as if I had been called by Forrest Gump himself (the movie was screening in New Zealand at the time). Instinctively I felt that this man was interesting. Just how interesting was something that I did not learn until later. Be that as it may, I was about to meet Phil Stubbs.

*

When it was all over one of Phil's numerous girlfriends would send me a poem she had given him at a crucial point in our story:

> I feel embarrassed sending this to you (Rob) but, believe it or not, the hard old man actually said how great it was and that he had seen lots of dolphins in the last few days. So here goes …
>
> *when the dolphins shoot silver trails*
> *between the sunset and the dawn*
>
> *when they chuckle*
> *at the strange flukes you row*
>
> *when a dolphin breathes beside you,*
> *a sudden friend*
>
> *when she leaps naked and sensual*
> *in the Atlantic sun*
>
> *imagine that I come to be with you*
>
> **Anon** (I'm too embarrassed to sign it)

*

I picked "the hard old man" up at the airport. He had flown himself down in a plane that looked as if it belonged to the Red Baron. He was 36 years old, had rugged good looks, an engaging smile and a natural confidence. He struck me as a knock-about kind of guy who was physically strong and might well have the endurance qualities I was looking for. He had first been told about the race in England by a former girlfriend who had thought it would be just the challenge for him.

I took him to a popular café in town. We sat outside under the canopy and started chatting about his sporting background. He had competed in various events including the Coast-to-Coast endurance race, an ironman triathlon and a marathon. But the good news didn't stop there. Phil had represented New Zealand in surfboat and dragon boat racing, raced kayaks and had tried to break into the New Zealand kayak team. In particular he was fond of white water kayaking, having paddled rapids including Aniwhenua and the Huka Falls!

He also had varied blue-water sailing experiences, having sailed with his father to exotic South Pacific destinations such as Tonga, Fiji and New Caledonia. While I was in Atlanta competing at the Olympics, Phil was delivering a friend's yacht from America to Denmark and in the mid-Atlantic ended up doing battle with the outer edges of hurricane Bertha. I realised this guy had had considerable experience in many diverse endurance-type sports.

As our conversation moved along, the temperature was just as rapidly dropping. It was becoming a chilly spring afternoon. I put on my sweatshirt. I could see Phil was chilling, his skin a slightly blotchy red and blue. He sat in jeans and T-shirt getting colder as we talked, acne-sized goosebumps forming on his arms. We spoke for over an hour and not once did he complain about the temperature. I was impressed with his ability to withstand the discomfort. This I felt was a good sign. The Atlantic row would cause considerable physical distress and any athlete wishing to join up needed a high, almost masochistic tolerance to pain.

As we spoke I soon realised that Phil had some strongly held opinions. This didn't concern me so long as there was also reason and an ability to change those opinions in the light of new information when necessary. The overall impression he gave was one of hardness, determination, a proven track record and skills in ocean crossing and navigation that I didn't possess. He appeared to be a pretty good bet if I really wanted to win this race. But I needed to know more about him before I made my decision.

At the end of our meeting we stood up to leave and in a lighthearted, joking manner I inquired, "You know, two blokes stuck in a little boat could be a bit of a worry. You're not batting for the other side, are ya?"

"No worries there, mate."

*

Sir Peter Blake, November 22, 1996

Team selection is difficult and you can make mistakes. Conventional approaches lay the groundwork for sound selection. You must have your criteria, a firm idea of the type of person you are seeking; of course you examine the candidate's CV for strengths and weaknesses, how these fit with your criteria and the rest of your team. You interview the person, but at the end of the process you must trust your own intuition, your own gut feeling. Have confidence in your instincts.

*

I was still on the lookout for other candidates. Sir Peter Blake suggested Angus Buchanan, one of the crew on *ENZA*, the yacht that won the Jules Verne Trophy for the fastest non-stop circumnavigation of the globe. Unfortunately Angus was based in England and although he was keen, he could not get out to New Zealand early enough to help with preparations. Besides, he was a Pom and, with the greatest respect to Angus, deep down I really wanted a New Zealand challenge.

So I had three candidates to consider. At the time I was working for the Waikato Polytechnic as a sports liaison officer and George Duncan was my immediate boss. George was amazed at my willingness to throw away the shackles, burdens and responsibilities of adult life to pursue a dream, something he felt very few people did in today's pressurised world.

George and I talked about the pros and cons of going to sea with a friend as opposed to a complete stranger. He questioned whether the human friendship cycle might be similar to the human life cycle. He offered the analogy of friendships as being born, going through adolescence and maturing to a ripe old age until eventual and inevitable death. He suggested that being stuck in a boat could accelerate this process and speculated that taking a friend to sea might send the friendship into old age and premature death. Conversely, the relationship with a complete stranger could develop and mature into an enduring friendship by the time the project is completed. His musings certainly made me think carefully.

*

Graham Dalton, Ian Wright and Phil Stubbs.

Although Graham had reasonable sea experience I felt he was ruled out for two reasons; age and lack of recent hard physical activity. The speed of an individual's physical recovery during the race would be crucial to a sustained effort on the oars. His age might have been okay had he been competing in endurance events on a regular basis, but this was not the case.

*

Ranulph Fiennes, *Mind over Matter*

To take *friends* on stressful expeditions has always seemed to me to be foolish since I can think of no easier way of marring a friendship forever. I look for professional and dogged people and treat any friendship resulting from an expedition as an unexpected bonus.

*

Ian Wright was an Olympic and World Championship bronze medallist and was one of the strong men in the New Zealand rowing team. Aside from that he was a good friend, had a great sense of humour and enjoyed hard training. Ian's biggest bogey was the fact that he, like me, had little sea experience. Still, the fact that Ian was a good mate had me thinking.

Since I knew very little about Phil Stubbs, I had made a number of enquiries, the result being a wide range of comments from outside and within the police force, some complimentary, some not so. Phil, it was said, could be very difficult to get on with (not an uncommon character trait among elite athletes) and prone to irrational tantrums (again, quite common). One former pupil at Phil Stubbs' driving instruction course was still smarting from a seemingly irrational bawling out that Phil had given him that he believed was definitely not called for.

There was equally warm praise given. One comment in particular, from the multiple kayaking Olympic gold medallist Ian Fergusson, impressed me. "Phil is the type of guy who would be cut and bleeding, but if there was a race in progress or a target in mind, he would keep going regardless. He'll come through for you." Given that the compliment was coming from Ian Fergusson, it spoke volumes to me.

I was leaning towards choosing Phil because it seemed to me that — of all the candidates — he best complemented my own strengths. He was highly confident of his seamanship skills, he had the ability to make a major contribution to the boat building and he was so naturally gregarious that I thought he would be great at raising finance.

Nevertheless I was still undecided when I returned home to my parents' place in Whakatane for Christmas. There I spent many hours chewing the fat with my father. We went over the strengths and weaknesses of the three remaining contenders. He was emphatic that it had to be Phil Stubbs. When Mum came in and expressed the same view, I knew that he must be right. The decision was made and a great weight was lifted off my shoulders.

It looked like I had the answer to my silly question.

4

Building a Boat

And whatsoever you do, do it heartily.
Colossians 3: 23

THE KITSET ARRIVED ON January 15, 1997. At the time I knew nothing about boat building, I knew little about the ocean, and even less about the two in combination. I asked myself where do I get the best possible advice and assistance? The Whitbread and America's Cup boats — the best in ocean racing — all came from Auckland. That advice had to be in Auckland.

Before Christmas I talked to Bruce Lodder who was the co-designer of the black rowing skiffs that Philippa Baker and Brenda Lawson had rowed in Atlanta. He had recommended that I talk to Steve Marten of Marten Marine on the Tamaki Estuary who had a reputation as long as your arm for building fine boats. As he spoke, I became convinced that Marten's would understand what I was seeking. They were professional boat builders and they were builders of racing craft that won!

Steve Marten was the firm's principal and the driving force. Nervously I rang Marten Marine, and asked the receptionist, "Could I speak to Steve Marten, please?"

"Certainly. He is on a call at the moment — would you like to hold?"

"Yes please."

No music, no radio, just a thought-provoking silence. I was unusually nervous; damn it, this was important. I needed help, big time. Steve Marten was a passionate professional and I felt that, if I could get some time with him to talk through the concept, he might come on board.

"Steve Marten here."

I briefly explained I had this exciting project and needed a boat builder. Could I come and see him to explain it in greater detail? Frankly, he didn't sound very enthusiastic and said he was very busy. Nevertheless we agreed to meet late in the day, early the next week. Whew, I had reached first base and I was chuffed. When that afternoon finally arrived I was still nervous. I wanted Steve to share my vision and excitement about this great adventure that I was sure I knew how to win.

It is always amazing how two people can view things so differently.

Steve Marten, boat builder, Auckland, August 1999

Rob's concepts were awry. At that time, for example, he was listening to someone who was talking about an auto pilot steering you the whole time. I could see instantly it wasn't going to be necessary.

They weren't going to be moving if they weren't awake, rowing. If you were rowing it was going to be a piece of cake watching the compass. So during these initial arguments I could see I was meeting with a blank because I could visualise doing it but he couldn't even see what I was talking about!

He also had the notion of communicating every day via satellite communication with e-mails. That was part of the little picture that I got. I thought, "Well, okay, there is a bit to learn here!"

Getting the grand vision out of his head to a more practical version to achieve the win he obviously wanted, was, hmm … well … Now, what he took with him when he went was great. Rustic and basic.

To me the concept of keeping the boat light was obvious from the very beginning and I couldn't overemphasise this. It was so important you needed to be obsessional about it, and we did this all the way through the project.

As far as I was concerned, it was more about not being disadvantaged by being too heavy, rather than striving to gain an advantage by being lighter. I thought I was only making him the same as everybody else.

*

Well, I got the message! I was aware of the fact that the boat should be light — that was a consequence of skiff rowing — but I wasn't aware of the extremes to which we needed to go. In spite of my naïvety Steve did agree to assist us, he offered his time and expertise, and space in his shed when that was available. At the time, however, Marten's were flat out and there was no space in the yard for us to work in. So he suggested that we begin down the road at Firebird Marine with Alf and Dave Pinker, a great father-and-son team who made us welcome.

*

Dave Pinker, boat builder, August 1999

The kit was interesting. About 20 sheets of plywood arrived with a plan similar to one you might get if assembling a kitset table purchased at The Warehouse, plus a picture of a finished boat. We removed all of the sheets of ply but had some difficulty in understanding why the sheets varied from 6 mm to 7.5 mm and 9 mm, especially when you consider that these sections were all supposed to blend into the lines of a rowboat. There were no measurements or datum lines to work from and the straightforward project started looking more complicated. After contacting the UK manufacturer, we were told that what you see is what you get and the final result should look like the colour photo.

*

To Steve's exacting and perfectionist mind, this was not a well-designed kit. As there were no detailed plans, Alf and Dave couldn't construct a lofting, that is, a full-sized replica. This would have shown exactly what size the boat would be at any particular point. I knew Steve was a little concerned because with racing craft the hull often has to be forced to conform to the designer's specifications, but for this to happen the specifications and measurements need to be exact.

Steve made sure the boat was "true". That meant that when viewed from the bow, each half of the boat was a mirror image of the other and the keel alignment was precise so that the boat went straight through the water. At one stage the hull had to be broken back down and the framing readjusted to ensure this was indeed the case. The guys at Firebird Marine suspected many boats made from this kitset mould would have turned out to be not "true". They might well have had some funny bumps and wobbles in them, resulting in decreased hydrodynamic efficiency.

Having constructed the basic plywood, we then had to make a decision on whether or not to add a layer of fibreglass to the entire shell before painting. We rigged up a sling off the rafters in Steve's workshop, attached scales and winched the boat off the ground. In its naked form, the boat weighed in at a little under 200 kg. We were all slightly confused by the boat rules which stated the boat would be weighted in a dry condition. We assumed this meant that the 150 litres of water ballast we had to carry during the race was not included in the basic 410 kg minimum weight specification.

To confirm this I rang Teresa Evans from The Challenge Business in England.

"Rob, your assumption is incorrect. The 150 litres is to be included when the boat is weighed. The 410 kg minimum is the combined weight of the boat and the water ballast and fixed items of equipment."

That seemed to clarify the situation, for me at least. We had 200 kg of bare boat, 150 kg of water ballast, meaning that we had only 60 kg of paint and equipment to add before we met the 410 kg minimum requirement. What I didn't know then was that Phil harboured serious doubts about my understanding of what Teresa Evans had actually told me. But these he kept to himself.

The self-imposed limit of 60 kg immediately ruled out putting a layer of fibreglass to completely cover the shell. Designing a boat for catastrophes was not possible, according to Steve Marten; besides, you could never make a race boat strong enough to row into a metal channel marker or a half-submerged container. The reality of the oceans, yachties tell me, is that there are not many containers out there and those are fairly well spaced. Our chances of rowing the Atlantic and confronting a container were very low. To try and plan for the unexpected was futile.

The boat we built could drop off a 7 m wave and survive — that was our design and construction limit. An effective, adequate mid-Atlantic boat was all it was expected to be.

*

Now that our boat was starting to take shape it definitely needed a name. Initially I had started calling it *Kiwi Attitude*. Chay Blyth, who thought New Zealanders had their own approach to life, heartily agreed with the name. It came from a well-known advertising campaign that was being run for Instant Kiwi — a "scratch and lose" game — at the time. I had hoped that the organisers would become a sponsor. Unfortunately they couldn't see the potential for themselves in what we were doing. Eventually we settled on *Kiwi Challenge* until we found a naming sponsor. We never found one, so *Kiwi Challenge* it was.

*

In March we tried a few working bees: Richard Newey, Phil and a couple of others. Our job was to cove the internal joints of the hull, including the confines of the front and rear bulkheads. We had to mix Q-cell sanding powder which fills the gaps with Aerosol glue mix. You need seven parts of Q-cell to three parts Aerosol, then you mix that in with the resin mix which is in the ratio of four of epoxy to one of hardener. Now tell that to three big rowers, a policeman and me! It wasn't chaos. It was good fun, great camaraderie and an excellent way to speed the project along. But it wasn't really the best way to build a racing boat. We needed someone to help finish the craft.

We had hired the services of Nick de May, a former employee of Steve Marten. Ironically, Nick increased our dependence on the company's tools, materials, boat yard workers' knowledge and the fact that "we" were there every day, all day long. Steve Marten had agreed to give of his time and knowledge and space in his shed, but here we were using his tools and materials. We didn't have much money and Steve was bemused as to how he had unwittingly become a de facto sponsor. Steve also recognised that for the boat to eventuate he had to carry on or the project could end up on a rocky shore.

*

Phil was putting in a full day's work enforcing the law, as well as working nights on the boat. For several weeks Nick would set things up before going home and Phil would come in and work until the small hours of the morning. He was great at doing all the nasty little jobs that others shied away from, and at tying up the lose ends.

These jobs included resin sealing in restricted places such as in the horrible little bow cabin. Sanding inside both the sleeping cabin and bow cabin, making up the small attachments for the solar panel, fitting the slides on which the seats rolled, fitting the compass, log and hatches — the list went on. Later, in mid-May, he would take leave from the force so that he could work full-time on installing the equipment.

All of this did not come without some penalties in his personal life. Phil never had any trouble meeting up with women; indeed, to say that women were a big part of his life would be something of an understatement. Anyway, at this time, he had a Canadian girlfriend named Candice who had flown down and moved in with him. She could have saved herself the airfare. While she was waiting in their love nest, Phil was caressing the immaculate curves of *Kiwi Challenge* and lovingly rubbing her down with 400 grit sandpaper. Pretty soon Candice had had enough and flew home to Canada.

Candice was not the first woman who had lived with Phil and left him. Another was Kate Cumper, from England, whom he met in Penang in 1988 at a dragon-boat festival. They had lived together in Paremata, north of Wellington, close to the national police training academy. I mention her for several reasons. First, because it was she who told Phil about the Atlantic challenge while he was in England. Second, because when he spoke of the women he had known it was she he always came back to. And finally, because she will appear — albeit tangentially — in our story again.

*

Nick de May thought *Kiwi Challenge* was "a bloody ugly little boat!", but he crafted it with superb care and attention. The hull, inside and out, had to be resin sealed to exclude any moisture getting into the ply, the joints smoothed out by being coated with a high-fill undercoat, sanded, epoxy urethane undercoated, sanded, sanded and sanded, painted with a gloss coat, sanded, painted, sanded.

The boat was then turned over. The floors were carefully sanded, fitted, sealed, sanded, painted, sanded. Putting in the cabin floor meant working in such a confined space that you banged your head on the centre joist, sealed your elbows, sanded your knee and managed to get paint in your earhole and everything down the back of your neck. The face, eye and nose guards made Phil and Nick look like nuclear holocaust survivors!

After one working session I found a coin lying in the boat, beside the keel under the deck flooring. We agreed to let it remain there, loose. It is still there somewhere today, a two dollar coin, a free flowing spirit, the magnificent kotuku or white heron facing up. Kiwis could and would fly.

5

Exposure

Get your facts first, and then you can distort them as much as you please.
Mark Twain FROM SEA TO SEA

BEFORE THIS STORY WAS through, I would be exposed in more ways than I would have dreamed of. But, back in late 1996, what I figured I needed was maximum exposure and this meant television. I would soon learn that obtaining it was rather like being a squash ball on a squash court: bouncing frequently between vertical and horizontal surfaces and every now and then getting a push in another direction before winning a point.

I also had the idea that Waikato Polytech, for which I worked, would become some kind of sponsor of the effort. I went to the principal and explained the great opportunities that I saw in the teaching institution becoming involved; after all, we were very proud of our growing reputation in sports science. I was in for a rude shock. Not only was the polytech unwilling to stump up the money I was seeking, I was also politely but firmly told that if I wanted to row the Atlantic I'd better find myself another job. Bugger!

It was a great disappointment, tempered by the wonderful support I received at the time from the staff. One of them was dietitian Jeni Pearce who not only wished me well, but made it her personal mission to get us across the Atlantic in the best possible shape.

She had worked with Whitbread crews for over eight years. From her first Whitbread she had developed energy equations based on current data and research available. It was from those early equations in addition to the specialist work she completed over the intervening years that she was able to work out how much food we would need based on our height, weight, body type (frame size and muscle mass) and age.

Jeni's estimations were a compilation and a refining of eight years of work with 30 or so endurance athletes. Gut instinct plays a minor role as there is never the chance to verify, in a race situation, that what she does, actually works. That the crews who have used Jeni's dietary advice have won, have stayed reasonably healthy, and been pretty close to the predicted weight loss was vindication enough to me that she was right far more often than she was wrong.

*

The fact that I no longer had a paying job made the raising of my profile and the sponsorship money just that much more urgent. I desperately needed more publicity.

Rowers are not natural publicity seekers and they often resent those who they see as pushing themselves into the public eye. I don't know why this is. Maybe it has something to do with the sheer discipline of the sport. The perfect rowing team would probably be a set of clones. Individual flair is not something that is going to win you any points on the water; it's more likely to capsize the boat.

It's a sport that doesn't produce Muhammad Alis or Jonah Lomus. Rowers let their actions speak for themselves. This is a unwritten convention that I had to break if I was to have a chance of success. What I didn't understand then was that this would eventually lay me open to charges that I was an egotistical publicity hound. Perhaps they were right!

*

I approached Communicado and through them, TVNZ. A meeting with general manager Neil Roberts was arranged. Like many other New Zealanders, I was in awe of television and radio presenters and commentators. I quickly noted how staff showed respect in his presence. Unfortunately I let their attitude affect me, making me even more nervous. Outside it was a blustery day, threatening rain, but was still warm and humid. I had a big knee-length jacket on that was both waterproof and warm.

To meet Neil I decided to leave the jacket on. My thinking was that it might make me look a little bigger in the hope that he would not think, "This guy is too small to do this." My mission was to impress him and I thought size was going to help. In reality he wasn't looking at size at all; he was interested in personality and character. I sat next to his desk and began to perspire, gently at first and then with a vengeance. I was so damned hot from the lousy raincoat I had on.

After a couple of discouraging rebuffs followed by silence from TVNZ, I again attempted to contact Neil Roberts. That was the first of many secretarial and personal assistant deflections, stalls and refusals I encountered. Personal assistants and secretaries are a sponsorship hunter's worst nightmare. They seem to have a contractual clause in their job descriptions to deny sponsorship hunters access rights to decision makers. So from this time on I decided to use the tactic of obtaining either their home number or mobile number.

I sent Neil an egg timer, a photo of the boat and a caption saying, "Time is running out." Then, through a friend, I managed to get his home phone number and carefully plotted what was the best time to call without either offending him or catching him at a time where he would be too busy.

The evening I phoned him he was asleep, exhausted. I rang again at about 7.30 the next morning and spoke to him. I apologised profusely for contacting him at home and reminded him who I was. He remembered and when I asked him if he thought TVNZ might again be interested in looking at the sponsorship proposal he responded, "Yes, of course. I will always be looking at proposals if they are warranted, but I think we will have to wait until our new documentary specialist arrives."

Two weeks later I got a TVNZ letter saying the proposal was a no go again. They had re-examined it, but they didn't think it was suitable for their programme structure. The fairy godmother's wand did not wave, but Kim Webby from "60 Minutes" did approach me and was interested in a story.

I'm sorry I never got to work with Neil as I admired his creative, gung-ho approach to life. I was saddened when I later heard about his death from cancer. I sent a card of condolence to a close friend of Neil's and asked her to pass it onto the family. Much later I discovered she had used it in her eulogy to him.

*

Through the Waikato Rowing Club I knew a publican's son who was also a student at the polytechnic and so I gave him a call when I was at home in Whakatane.

"Dennis, do you mind if I come and talk to you about this rowing race I'm doing?"

"Yeah, yeah, Rob, sounds a great idea, yes, come out and see us."

I was at the Pinelands Motor Hotel at Kawerau in a flash! He was a really nice guy. We had a chat then I explained where I was financially; I had the $20,000 only at that stage. I had been with him for less than a quarter of an hour when he said, "Well, Rob, our community trust has a little money just at present and I would like to be able to help and get the project under way. We would be willing to contribute...."

Dennis mentioned a significant four-figure amount! I was floored; a very unusual situation for me. Regaining my composure a second later, I said in an equally quiet tone, "Well, thanks Dennis, that is really generous."

That money arrived on Christmas Eve and it was the first operating finance we had received; the campaign could now pay some of its housekeeping bills. It was a great Christmas present. We thought we were really under way.

*

It was at this time that Power and Marine agreed to provide the campaign with equipment to a substantial value. Theirs was an intelligent, sympathetic and wonderfully adept sponsorship.

The patience of their staff in educating Phil and me, and their expertise and ability to understand what we were trying to do with our boat was simply top class. I had been advised to contact Allan Dickinson. He was direct and responsive. If I would furnish him with a list of equipment up to a value, which he specified, Power and Marine would provide that equipment for the boat. I followed this up with a list of prioritised items. Allan vetted our list and forwarded it to Power and Marine.

Over the construction of the boat we found that we needed a little more, and more, and more. It was hardly surprising when Power and Marine came to us one day and said, "Hey guys, you have spent more than we had agreed to. You are over budget and frankly the arrangement is getting a bit out of hand. You'll have to go back and see Allan Dickinson as we're not prepared to let you have any more materials until you do."

I phoned Allan. "Could you please tell us where we are with our account with Power and Marine? I only have the retail figures and have no idea what the cost figures are."

I heard Allan shuffle papers, selecting the relevant sheet.

"You're over budget by $8000, cost."

"Good God. I'm sorry about that Allan. We still need some more materials and your staff have been outstanding. Would it be okay if we use Power and Marine and pay for the remaining materials?"

I held my breath, "Yes. That is okay." Agreed sponsorship, plus an overrun of $8000! Like every company that provided us with either services or product, we certainly got more than our share of value from them. But Power and Marine were exceptional. Go and ask your bank for an $8000 overdraft, then three months later ask them not only to forgo their interest but would they mind if we called it quits and wrote off the OD? I think they would tell you where to go.

*

The next stage in the media campaign was to attempt to secure interest from Paul Holmes. It was Holmes I really wanted to get on board in some way and I particularly wanted him to take the boat for a row. In early December I sent him a *Mission Impossible*-styled proposal. Each page had several words blown up to be eye-catching. It read:

"Three thousand miles
Two people
One boat
Your mission, Paul Holmes, is to row this boat."

I waited and waited. In mid-January I made contact with the producers of the "Holmes" programme. They had no record of my dynamic approach; it had simply been filed with the multitude of numerous other proposals. As always, getting hold of the right man was difficult. So after ferreting around

I obtained Paul Holmes' mobile phone number. When I made the call he was obviously busy, very busy, and said, "Look, Rob, can you call me back later this afternoon, about 3 o'clock?" When I rang at three the phone was switched off. I rang at 3.30 with a similar result and at four, ditto.

The following day I tried at roughly the same time, "Oh, Rob, please don't think I was fobbing you off. I wasn't. I was just so busy and I ended up accidentally turning my phone off. So tell me what you were talking to me about yesterday; what was it again that you are doing?"

"I'm going to row across the Atlantic. I am going to be the first New Zealander to row across the Atlantic, and I am going to win the first ever race to be rowed across the Atlantic. I would like you to row the boat that we are going to use."

After a brief information exchange he said, "Look, Rob, I could be tempted to have a look at it. I am definitely interested, it sounds like an incredible project. Send me a proposal will you?"

"I did, December last year."

"Oh, look, all right, well, could you send another to my secretary?"

Experience was fast teaching me that a verbal acceptance didn't necessarily mean action was going to happen very quickly. It still required follow-up phone calls, letters written and faxes sent before anything eventuated. On the day that we were to shoot I got the message that Paul was unable to come; he was off to Hong Kong to cover the hand-over celebrations. In his place Simon Mercep did a very good job of the story.

My problem was that all through this period I was telling potential sponsors, and current sponsors, that Paul Holmes was definitely going to take the boat for a row on the "Holmes" show. Naïve, I know, but some coverage was there and it certainly helped the effort.

*

I was learning that the real sponsorship money I needed was with the major corporates and that it was they I was going to have to talk to if I was to get anywhere. In this context the airlines were an obvious target. Not only could they make use of the global exposure that the race would generate, but they were also able to come in with free travel which — while cheap for the airline — was damned expensive if we had to pay for it ourselves.

A meeting was arranged with Air New Zealand. On January 15 — the same day the kitset arrived — I travelled, with a little trepidation, up to Auckland. David Beatson was another person I was in awe of. It was my third presentation. I began confidently. Soon I thought I had him in the palm of my hand. I was feeding him morsels of information about the project and explaining how this race was a great opportunity to publicise Air New Zealand in the United Kingdom.

Beatson was interested, so I continued enthusiastically, telling him about myself. Olympic rower, World Championship medallist, world record holder on the ergometer — it sounded great. It was flowing well. I was taking the bull by the horns. I wasn't going to sit back and be intimidated by high profile people in high rise places. I was the boss here, and they were listening to me. I was the one in control. I got down to what I was having to raise in total to do the whole project. Then I got to the question of how much I wanted from Air New Zealand.

The proposal I had been speaking to had been printed and then expanded out to an A3 size format on a self supporting stand. To make my point I flipped over to the last page. It was the finale where I offered the opportunities that Air New Zealand would reap from this huge opportunity. The bold-coloured title leapt out ...

"OPPORTUNITIES FOR QANTAS!"

I felt my face go crimson. We had bombed out with Qantas the week before. Beatson roared with laughter and said something about "just as well we are not Qantas, isn't it?" He then outlined what he would like to see in a proposal stating what we could offer. The meeting finished with him requesting that I put some finer details together and meet again the following week. I did so, but when I rang to set up another meeting, I discovered that David had had a major heart attack and was in hospital. I was sure it had something to do with the wild bold heading, "Qantas!"

Subsequently he made a complete recovery.

*

Graham Dalton, July 1999

It's just that Rob's Rob.

Take a meeting we had with David Beatson at Air New Zealand. I've always been a believer that you dress for the occasion and turned up in a suit. Rob, on the other hand, arrived as buoyant as ever in collar, tie and jeans – held up by a cowboy belt. And the funny thing was that on this and other occasions his wayward dress style seemed to add an indescribable something to the meetings we had with corporates.

Money and lack of time could very easily have sunk the project before it left our shores. I, for one, thought Rob and Phil were rank outsiders, such was the lack of campaign preparation, but in hindsight that's what gave them the edge. I now believe the ingredient many potential sponsors failed to fully appreciate was the passion or fire in the belly of both Rob and Phil. For example, Kim Webby from TVNZ phoned me. She was making a programme on the pair for "60 Minutes" and candidly admitted to me she hadn't expected them to get out of Auckland International Airport.

*

The meeting with Sir Chay Blyth that had been canvassed when I had first rung him in the UK was set for January 17. The "in awe" factor kicked in once again. I was so nervous. I left work at 4.30, leapt into the Barina and roared off to Taihape. The Blyths had been taking a brief break from the BT Global Challenge yacht race that was having a stop-over in Wellington at the time, and wanted to get out into the back-country fresh air.

Halting in a brisk fashion at the Blyths' Taihape motel, I grabbed my folder and quickly went to the unit where they where staying. I arrived feeling like a third former in the principal's office. I was bumbling around, bloody hopeless; my voice wouldn't stay normal, it would quaver and I was terrified it might suddenly go up an octave.

Sir Chay was great, quickly putting me at ease, and soon it was Chay, Felicity and Rob, but the steely and imperious personality that is unaffectedly Chay was always present. I was just in time to go to a restaurant with them. If my friends knew I was about to go to dinner they would have struck their panic button as some unfairly maintain they can always tell what I have had for dinner by what is on my shirt. I was mindful of the splatter factor.

"Would you like to follow us in your car to the restaurant, Rob?"

"Certainly, no problem."

I grabbed my folder and followed them out to my car. My keys were in my left jeans pocket so I plonked the folder down on the car roof and got the keys but fumbled in the fading light for the lock. Chay and Felicity gracefully got into their car, started the motor and backed out behind me, waiting.

Finally I managed to get the door open, leapt into the car, reversed out in front of the Blyths, changed into first gear, hit the gas and the folder hit the gravel behind me. I leapt out, grabbed all the white sheets of paper that were decorating the drive, completed an action replay of the leap into the Barina and nonchalantly drove away. Bloody Nora, what a start. When we arrived at the restaurant, Chay got out smiling and chuckling.

"Never again, Hamill," I thought, "you're a rower not a slapstick comedian."

At the restaurant Chay gave me a lesson in exacting quality service.

"There's no water on the table."

"Can I have the cork? I wish to smell the cork, before I taste the wine."

"I ordered medium rare, not alive and wild."

We talked for some considerable time. I wanted to know the answers to a thousand and one questions. Questions from all compass points; questions on the race and its organisation, what I could offer sponsors, how others were raising sponsorship money, did he know of any potential sponsors who might want to help us?

My questions were answered. I now understood much more about the realities of the race. This in turn lead to a discussion of our finances. I answered his questions and he, too, understood.

Chay was happy to take up cudgels on our behalf with politicians, organisations and private companies when he returned to Wellington. I drove on to Rotorua that night for a regatta in a much calmer frame of mind.

*

It is difficult to explain to people outside rowing the depth of support NZ Rowing received from ECNZ. When I "resigned" from my job at the Waikato Polytechnic, I contacted ECNZ to see if I could use the office Rowing NZ had occupied up until the Atlanta Olympics. The general manager was consulted and the company's support grew in very practical ways. I was provided with an office, an old computer that could still outpace my typing and publishing skills, paper, a phone and access to a photocopier; a great home base.

It was a prefab office with a full-frontal view of a bloody great cable drum complete with black cabling and a little sun at 4.30 sliding through the window. Old, spartan, entirely functional. Of even greater assistance was the company culture that accepted me, knew what I was attempting to do and expected me to get on and do it. This was a huge assistance to *Kiwi Challenge*'s chances of success.

Just before we left New Zealand, the sponsorship manager from ECNZ's head office would ring, totally out of the blue. "Look, Rob, we have been impressed by what you have achieved so far, the attitude and tenor of your campaign. We would also like to assist financially. We can offer you ... (a most acceptable four-figure sum)." I was absolutely delighted. I knew it — ECNZ would not let us down.

*

There were five kids in the family and I was the youngest. Three brothers, Kerry, John and Peter and my sister Sue. My parents' home fronts onto the heads in Whakatane. In front of the house there is the road, then the river; from front door to river's edge would be no more than 30 m.

I don't remember this but when I was five, Kerry, John and I were playing in the family dinghy in the Whakatane River upstream from home. It was an ebb tide. John quietly walked back home and went upstairs on the verandah adjacent to and overlooking the river. Mum had some friends there and they were having a cup of tea, chatting away. Back at the river bank Kerry rowed the boat out into the river and lay down flat, hidden from view.

"Your turn to row, Rob."

So I picked up the oars and rowed. The tide was carrying us down the river towards the heads. "Look, Mum, there is Rob in the dinghy!" cried

John, now on the verandah with the tea party. There was silence in Mum's group of friends. All they could see from shore was the dinghy floating along with a five-year-old happily playing at rowing, heading towards certain disaster at the river bar 200 m away!

Mum went absolutely spare! There was total pandemonium: her youngest child was in mortal danger! Then up sits Kerry, waves to the panicking tea party which by then had spread from verandah to shore. Kerry picks up the oars and nonchalantly rows the boat ashore. Kerry and John went to bed early that night.

*

On January 22 the *Sunday Star-Times* reported that Phil Stubbs was to be my partner in the venture. That night I dreamed that I was training overseas for the world rowing championships. Then I was walking back from training with a heavy pack on my back. The next thing I was climbing a rope ladder when I was hit by a train. The combination of the rope ladder *et moi* stopped the train in its tracks.

Phil played his part in raising funds. Through police work he had contacts with a number of publicans and he felt sure that through these contacts he would be able to raise some money for the campaign from the profits of the poker machines in the pubs. A number of pubs supported us, through the Lion Foundation, and so a large number of ordinary Kiwis unknowingly contributed towards our project. Pubs from Twizel to Auckland were involved. Their help was greatly appreciated.

*

While all of this was going on, both Phil and I were also competing at a fairly high level in our chosen sports. In January he went to Australia with the Titahi Bay Surf Boat team and won the Bass Marathon — a five-day endurance event. In March I would compete in the National Rowing Championships in Twizel.

While I was flying down — we were over the ocean at the time — I heard a loud comment from Rob Waddell who was sitting a couple of seats back. "I can't see any boats down there but the Hampster (a nickname he gave me) is down there somewhere." Then a pause and follow-up. "Blow that for a joke!"

6.
True Colours

Each extra kilo in weight is one more litre of water you have to shift.
Steve Marten, boat builder, Auckland

"GREY?"

"Yeah, grey."

"Aw, come on guys, grey is for reconstructions not originals. A light pink would go really well with this deck," responded Nick.

"No. That will calm us down. The police cells are pink. We don't want to be calmed down. We need to be stimulated." Obviously Phil had strong opinions on this, but a vigorous discussion took place over the paint colour for the decking. An original compromise was settled on, a light blue semi-gloss finish. Then a coat of non-skid, the non-skid being tiny little plastic balls that Nick mixed in with the Epiglass paint. Steve Marten hated the colour.

His riposte was curt. "A complete and utter stuff-up. Why do you want blue?"

Steve's opinion was understandable, but it was the only colour in the store at Marten's that day.

*

Before starting and also during the construction of the boat we really did a lot of research on different equipment needed to set up the boat, in particular the electrical system. I spent many hours researching, telephoning, asking questions and writing to people. I phoned around New Zealand, I phoned Europe and then Australia. A fortune was spent on telephone bills investigating this particular aspect.

Eventually we had to settle for the best commercially produced system. So we returned to established New Zealand companies. We wanted to get enough solar power to recharge the main battery so we could run the water-maker and a few other bits and pieces such as the Global Positioning System, the navigation lights, the compass back light, the recharger for the VHF radio and the cabin light.

The water-maker — which is a unit which extracts salt from sea water making it drinkable — was the major concern. It was the single most important piece of equipment in the boat. No water meant no drink and no food which would mean no rowing race — that equation was simple. We had to have enough electricity to power the water-maker.

Part and parcel of this power dilemma was how much battery power to carry on the boat. We settled for one rechargeable marine battery weighing 25 kg. Possibly this was a risk, not taking a back-up, but this was to be a significant factor in keeping the boat light. The electricity was to be provided by a solar panel firmly affixed to the top of the stern cabin, and more flexible but less efficient Unisolar panels clipped to the stern cabin side and on the deck of the forward cabin.

Phil had made an adjustable mounting for the more fragile solid stern panel so it would angle to the sun as it crossed the sky on our port side. The bow panel would be better placed to generate peak potential power in the middle and later parts of the day.

This seemed to provide enough for our needs. However, given the importance of the water-maker, we were concerned that in the trade wind belt we may not receive enough sunshine because of the expected cloud cover. We agreed to carry a back-up system in case the solar energy unit did indeed prove inadequate or failed. This would be an Aerogen demountable wind-driven generator, our luxury and it weighed 10 kg. When required it would be mounted in a housing located on the starboard stern, just out of harm's way if you stuck your head out the rear hatch.

*

In an attempt to improve my knowledge of seafaring I had approached the New Zealand America's Cup team in November 1996. They had been tremendous and one of the pieces of information freely offered was the choice of water-maker. Peter Blake said, "For your water-maker you'll need a small Power Survivor." Our Power Survivor 35 was housed on the starboard side of *Kiwi Challenge*, close to the rear cabin bulkhead. Opposite the water-maker was the battery, balancing the water-maker. Well, sort of. In the centre hold, under the rowing seats, were the 16 compulsory fresh water plastic containers.

Of course we started off with fresh water, but in the event of not being able to replace that fresh water with enough processed fresh water from the water-maker, we would have to replace it with sea water. This was because the water pottles had a dual purpose, firstly to aid the boat's self-righting capacity by providing 150 kg of ballast at the bottom and secondly for drinking water, both vital. Four pottles were connected to the water-maker and it, in turn, was connected to the battery: a bit like that traditional ditty on the connection of the bones, and just as important.

The water-maker operated off our 12-volt battery supply and when operating efficiently could produce four litres per hour. The unit could be manually operated in the event of a power failure. We initially estimated a requirement to drink 20 to 30 litres per day, therefore we needed to operate the unit for six to eight hours each day to maintain our stock of fresh water.

The water-maker worked by pressurising the salt water to 800 lbs per sq. inch, forcing the salt water through a special membrane. This removes virtually all viruses, bacteria and 98.4 per cent of the salt. The unit needed to be in daily use once operating, otherwise a build-up of bacteria would occur on the membrane. While installing the unit we had an accident. We managed to break a $500 part (it literally pays to read the instructions). The importer of Power Survivor units to New Zealand at that time, Bruce Robertson, had to come to our assistance to work through the installation, and even with his help, the unit was "sucking air" and was not producing as it should.

After several hours of hole cutting, sealing and fibreglassing, Phil had shifted the inlet to the lowest point on the keel to avoid air getting into the system.

*

We had yet to decide whether to take a communication system. Whatever system we settled on would cost money and would add extra weight. It could also require us to beef up the electricity-producing capability. Possibly more solar panels, but definitely bigger batteries. With advice from David Stubbs, Phil's father, we settled on a 2 kg, battery-operated, hand-held commercial short wave radio receiver. This would keep us in touch with the world, but, alas, not the world with us.

The thinking here was simplicity itself. The world did not need to hear from us, unless of course we got into serious trouble, in which case we could use our emergency beacon system. All we really needed from the world was our position in the race. This we hoped we might get from BBC sports news broadcasts. Mind you, I'm not sure that either of us had ever actually listened to one. Anyway, we would go on debating this one for weeks, before deciding on a minimalist approach.

The radar reflector was a piece of Kiwi ingenuity that did work. A reflector was needed because the plywood construction of the boat could not be picked up on radar. Again it was Phil, along with a couple of blokes from Marten's, who came up with a lightweight solution. The reflector had to be between 1.5 and 2 m above the fully laden static waterline. The solution was a narrow carbon pole the diameter of your little finger topped by a glued globe covered in gold reflecting tinfoil material. The reflector itself was basically three circular pieces of hardboard, two vertical, at right angles to each other, and the other horizontal. It was cheap and effective.

*

The rear cabin was tiny for two, but comfortable for one, giving an incredible — albeit false — sense of security. When both hatches were locked it felt like one of the original US space capsules: hot as hell, smelly, cramped but virtually indestructible.

The cubby cabin was 2.1 m long, 1.5 m wide and 800 mm high at the entrance, narrowing to 850 mm wide by 500 mm high at the stern. There was a well just inside the midships hatch which gave a little more height. While in training I kept banging my head on the roof, especially the main mini beam coming down the centre of the cabin. So the roof and floor of the cabin were covered in head, knee and elbow-protecting foam. Blue-coloured foam, of course.

The walls either side of the cabin had netting holders fixed for charts and clothes. On my side I had velcro hook straps glued to the *Kiwi Challenge* hull, for three of the four bean sprout germinating plastic containers.

In constructing the cubby cabin, we had a lively discussion over ties for sleeping. I suggested sleeping ties for two reasons. I found that even on training runs around the east coast of the North Island the boat rolled like a witch. I thought tie-down straps rather like a seat belt arrangement would stop my body rolling from side to side in the cabin when we were resting. It would swaddle us, allow us to relax and not have to brace ourselves, even subconsciously, for rolls, pitches and yaws.

I thought this movement, over a long time, would be tiring and not really permit our bodies to relax. Second, if the boat did capsize we would be held securely and wouldn't be thrown around the cabin like dolls. Being held higher, I argued, that extra weight above the water line would assist the boat to right itself more easily. I had the straps made up and was ready to install them.

Phil was against this idea. Steve Marten laughed. I gave it away.

*

Kevin Hessell, secondary school principal, September 1999

I played basketball with Rob Hamill in Whakatane. At this time – in the late 1970s, early 1980s – there were four good teams in the local men's competition: one based on Wairaka Marae in the town, players with very talented ball skills, another the Young Farmer's Club with fit, hardened young men. The rowing club was the third, with a couple of gold medal winners from Munich and an average height that seemed about 6 ft 6 in., and the high school made up the fourth team. Well … I had played basketball for New Zealand before I had gone to Whakatane. I was in reasonable shape but found the games tough. You needed a few boys to be there with you. Rob would be right there. He gave 110 per cent every time, and he just loved it. He came up smiling and laughing each time. He took defeat hard, but he didn't dump it on other people. He came back the next week and tried again, a little harder, a little more thoughtful. He learnt from our defeats.

*

Throughout this time I was getting a great deal of support and advice (not all of it welcome) from my mates. At the end of March 1997 Gary McAdams came back from England to visit family in Whakatane. I had a beer with him and Richard Newey and all the shit-stirring came out. At one stage he got down on his knees and said, "I'm not on my knees Rob, I'm on my heels, but please Rob, don't do it!" He was dead serious. He then went on to make jokes about Phil asking if he would be taking his guide dog with him on the boat — implying that Phil must be blind to be doing this thing with me. A case of the blind leading the blind! They also reckoned that if we got into trouble the rescue plane would only need follow the caramel trail with all our hundreds of Moro bars (I'm a bit of a chocolate monster).

7.
The Sponsorship Game

After the final NO, there comes a YES, and it is on that YES that the future of the world depends.
Wallace Stevens

IN MID APRIL I was in Wellington, visiting sports organisations and businesses in an attempt to secure sponsorship. On a personal level the visit was fine, as I knew many of the personnel involved in the organisations. However I was up against a brick wall in obtaining sponsorship money. I had a spare half-hour in the morning and, sitting at my sister's computer, I quickly tapped out a letter to Sir Robert Jones. I was in a hurry. I don't think well at the keyboard, but I nevertheless managed to squeeze out a letter in quick time. I was attempting to be lighthearted and funny. Some attempt. I'm not at all proud of this letter, but the response elicited was rapid, pointed and electrifying.

*

Sir Robert Jones
Robt. Jones Holdings Limited
WELLINGTON

Dear Sir Robert
I need your help and support. This does not mean to say that I am incapable of doing something myself. On the contrary, I am a Kiwi who is going out of the square to try and achieve something unique in New Zealand's sporting history.

On 12 October 1997 I will line up as the only New Zealander (and only entrant from the southern hemisphere) in the inaugural Atlantic Rowing Race. Leaving from Tenerife, Canary Islands, the 3,000 mile race to Barbados is expected to take 55–90 days.

Not only is this a daunting journey into the unknown, just as daunting is the need to raise the capital required. In November last year I raised $20,000 in loans to purchase a boat kit (standard to all entrants) and had it flown from the United Kingdom. Construction began in mid-January of this year and the boat will be ready for launching in three weeks' time.

I have been in Wellington this week raising funds with limited success.

To say I'm not fired up about this would be like saying Frank Nobilo makes a flamin' good wine, Andrew Galota has a brain and Winston Peters avoids mirrors! I could bore you with a screed of written material but why bother sending it when I can bore you in person? If it is convenient I would like to meet with you and bleed your brain (not your wallet) of information.

I am returning to Hamilton tonight so this short notice may rule out a meeting today.

If it is inconvenient today I can return to Wellington at a time that suits.

Regards,
Rob Hamill

Sir Robert's response:

11th April, 1997
Mr Rod Hamill
3/89 Tristam Street,
HAMILTON

Dear Mr Hamill,
I refer to your undated letter I found on my visit to my Wellington office today.

The reason you have encountered difficulty in attracting financial support may well lie in the possibility that, while rowing across the Atlantic attracts you, it has no similar appeal to others. Certainly from my perspective I cannot think of a more unpleasant way to waste 55–90 days of my life. It would be a lot cheaper to stay home in Hamilton and thrash yourself from dawn to dusk with a barbed wire whip, for which no sponsorship would be required.

Andrew Golota's name is not spelt "Galota".

Yours faithfully,
RE Jones

I noted that he had spelt my name incorrectly.

*

In January there was a Global Challenge cocktail function in Wellington. One of the guests was Warren Hodgson, a director of Serco. Chay Blyth, who was hosting the event, gave him a bit of a rough time on my behalf.

"Be a shame if *Kiwi Challenge* failed because of lack of funding," said Chay as Warren reduced his wine glass to a level that he thought might entice the waiter back to top it up.

"I know you've done a lot with the yacht race," Chay persisted, "but do you think Serco might throw in a bob or two to help?"

"Bloody Hell, Chay. This Save the Children thing is taking more time than I ever imagined. My staff have been tied up with your bloody yacht race for months now. Furthermore I'll never be able to get my fellow directors, who are all Australian, to understand why the hell we should get involved with something as lunatic as a New Zealander pushing a bloody rowing boat across the damned Atlantic. Now, where's the wine waiter?" That is what he meant to say but what actually came out was, "Sure, get him to give me a call."

I did and Serco were damned helpful.

*

I was working in the ECNZ office in Hamilton, buried at the computer frantically typing out letters to possible food sponsors. Food? Sure, we had to obtain food. Companies were willing to assist with product rather than cash and we were perfectly happy to accept food parcels for the Atlantic. So there I was feverishly writing letters — letters destined for all over New Zealand. I was on my fourth letter of the morning, sitting back, thinking of something a little more stimulating, a little more enticing. My eyes strayed to the bottom right hand of the screen on the computer. The clock showed 11.20 a.m. Shit!

We were due to present to LEP International in Auckland at 1 p.m. Quickly I gave the "save" key a prod. Where were all the presentation documents? I grabbed the black presentation folder and gave it the quick check. Everything appeared to be there so that was okay. Where the hell had I placed those tubes, the ones containing the drawings showing the logo on the boat? They weren't in the room. Damn. I left them standing up beside the photocopier. I zoomed down the corridor. The loose-leaf folder was next. It was on top of the filing cabinet, no problem. My jandals were at the office door, so I slipped those on and snatched the car keys from my top drawer and I was off. It was 11.40 a.m.

Ripping out past Te Rapa I had time to take stock. I still had yesterday's T-shirt on and my faded, frayed blue jean shorts. I had fully intended to zip home before I left, but not to worry, I was clean and at least we were on the way. I had everything I needed, but how did time slip by like that? I checked my watch, it stated all too clearly 11.50 a.m. and I had to be in Penrose by 1 p.m. That should be a piece of cake. I slipped quickly into the car park at Mainfreight's head office, got out and plonked the loose-leaf folder on the roof of the car and bent down to grab the presentation folder and tube files.

No! A gust of wind flipped open the loose-leaf folder and the spare sponsor's benefits gained, along with the financial figure sheets, floated gently off towards Great South Road. Dang! I raced across the car park and rescued those and was trotting back to the car when I had to dodge a flash new arrival coming into the park. A well-dressed young man slipped out of the car and walked assuredly towards the office building.

By now I had collected all my material and I ran past this corporate dude and up the stairs.

Blast! The tubes slipped out from under my arm and clattered back down the stairs. In trying to re-grab them I completed a half pirouette going upwards while the blasted tubes were taking off downwards. I quickly put the loose-leaf folder on the stairs and, while I was busy collecting all my pieces, the corporate dude strides past again. With a few leaps up the stairs I made the reception area just in time, whew. Thank God for Phil. Cool, calm, easy charm, immaculate in his police sergeant's uniform, five minutes to spare.

The receptionist asked us to come into the managing director's office. By this time I was all organised, all systems were go and — my God, the managing director was the guy from the car park!

The presentation went quite well considering the shambolic start. The managing director was Chris Dunphy and he appeared genuinely interested and asked perceptive questions. The meeting felt positive. They said they would consider our request and let us know. As he escorted us through the reception area he absolutely floored me.

"Whakatane boy made good, eh Rob?"

How on earth did he know I was from Whakatane?

I would later learn that he was a Bay of Plenty boy himself, and proud of the fact. The connection did us no harm at all.

*

This was only the second time I had seen Phil in uniform. In fact, previously he had hardly struck me as a uniformed kind of guy. I was wrong. Phil in uniform looked like he had stepped straight out of a police recruiting poster; a sharp, lean, clean-cut, blue-eyed, quick-witted young officer who had "future Commissioner of Police" written all over him. The sergeant from Central Casting.

The first time I was really taken aback. Where was the rough-and-tumble guy I'd been building a boat with? And which of these men was the real Phil Stubbs? I've never figured that one out for sure, but it seemed to me at the time that Phil was not a real policeman. That "Sergeant Stubbs" was a role he played. That he didn't actually put on a uniform when he went to work, so much as don a costume. Or maybe that's just what I wanted to believe.

Be that as it may, he had the reputation of being a damned good cop.

*

Chris Dunphy, Managing Director, LEP International, Melbourne, Australia, July 1999.

I met Rob Hamill and Phil Stubbs in unusual circumstances.

Rob had called on several occasions with bubbling enthusiasm for Mainfreight to sponsor a rowing race — or so I thought. This was not exactly a thrilling proposition for getting our name recognised as an international business. Rob told me that he had these GREAT ideas as to how we would benefit from the "investment" – to which I replied in the lukewarm affirmative.

After several unsuccessful attempts to meet and pitch this GREAT idea we finally settled on an afternoon meeting at Mainfreight's Penrose offices. This was more due to Rob's unfailing pestering efforts to secure a meeting, rather than any real interest on our part.

Arriving at our reception I met a uniformed Sgt Phil Stubbs. My immediate reaction was to mentally recount traffic convictions and other encounters with the law for which I may be still accountable and liable for prosecution (the misuse of a fire hydrant during Capping Week in 1986, etc). I needn't have worried, as Phil's disarming smile soon made me forget the uniform phobia and settle into a discussion of multi-sport events.

The sound of tubes bouncing down stairs, a rustling of papers and an expletive or two heralded Rob Hamill's arrival. Here we have chalk and cheese – a clean-cut policeman and a unshaven jandal-clad athlete. What chance of these two actually "clicking", let alone living and working together in an endurance event?

We settled down to a discussion, to find out the obvious – these two Kiwi battlers were on the bones of their sponsorship backsides. Yes, they needed money, but even more imperatively they needed to finish their boat, train in it and get it to the starting line.

Fortunately this was not as daunting as it seemed. A Mainfreight subsidiary, LEP International is a large airfreight mover and it seemed to be fitting that an international forwarder would support a race of Atlantic proportions – hence the LEP involvement in the *Kiwi Challenge*. We undertook to fly the boat and trailer from Auckland to London rather than sea freight it, as this would give the guys an additional eight weeks of sea-going training.

What was more interesting than the race was Rob and Phil. Their individual dynamics, backgrounds and sense of purpose were very easy both to relate to and to feel comfortable with. Both Rob and Phil have strong ties to the Bay of Plenty – my birthplace – and we easily struck up a rapport.

One afternoon in July I got a call from Rob and Phil "around the backside of White Island" – the cellphone reception was clear, and I could actually hear that these guys were enjoying themselves! Truly inspiring stuff – build a boat then sit in it and learn to make it go.

The boys were in regular contact with me leading up to the official launching ceremony at the Auckland Boat Show and other media gatherings. It was clear that Rob was expecting a glitch – that somehow LEP and Mainfreight would let him down at the 11th hour as other sponsors had. Well, we didn't.

*

The *Kiwi Challenge* was ready for the Auckland Boat Show. We were to be part of the Power and Marine stand the following morning. However, before that began I had to rush back to Hamilton to check on a couple of jobs. By 7.30 p.m. I was at Hamilton's Stitch-it Embroidery to see how the manager had got on with embroidering 150 polo shirts that were to be ready for the next day. They had yet to start them!

My offer to help was readily accepted and I was given a crash course on machine set-up and trimming techniques. As the evening wore on staff slowly drifted off home and by midnight Steve (the manager) and I were left alone trimming frayed edges on embroidered logos. Early on our conversation was bouncy and full of energy but as the night wore on we became mute figures hunched over our workbench, scissors flaring, while machines clackety-clacked into the small hours of the morning. By 5 a.m. we were both exhausted. Half an hour later, I loaded the wagon full of freshly embroidered shirts, drove home and slept fitfully until 9 a.m.

That day and over the weekend Phil and I did shifts at the Auckland Boat Show talking to the many passers-by and answering the myriad of questions one would expect. Which end is the front? Are you crazy? Why are you doing it? Don't you like girls?

Phil was equally sarcastic, "Mate, the only reason I'm doing this race is to meet girls after we win."

The inquirer muttered under his breath something about losing the plot and that there were much easier ways to meet girls.

In fact he was wrong about that. Phil could meet girls anywhere including — as it turned out — on a stand at the Auckland Boat Show. Pretty soon afterwards I became aware that he was having a relationship with a journalist who had been working on another stand at the show. When we met I had explained who we were and what we hoped to achieve. Phil had no doubt done something similar, but his pitch must have been somewhat different.

*

The Boat Show did not prove a great success. We had tried to drum up financial support by selling T-shirts, handing out flyers with information on the Supporters' Club and sponsorship opportunities. And what was the result of that weekend's frantic efforts at raising financial support from ordinary New Zealanders? We gave away 25 T-shirts, sold 12, and did not get a single sponsor or Supporters' Club member signed up. However, God loves those who try. We raised about $300 from our Donations Welcome box. And Phil got the girl!

8. Fine Tuning

Light, lighter, lightest.
Steve Marten, boat builder

EVEN THOUGH WE NOW had a boat, the building job was far from over. Take the question of where we would rest our bums. The technicalities of seat construction may have seemed a small matter back then, but they would eventually take on damned near life-or-death proportions.

The grooved track on which the little seat bogies travelled forward and back all those countless times was set onto aluminium joists. Phil cut circular holes to get rid of weight in both the starboard and port track joists. The seats were moulded foam coated with epoxy, very light indeed, the bogies' plastic wheels (no ball bearings thank you, ball bearings and salt water don't mix) and stainless steel axles going right through under the seat to the wheels on the joist opposite.

The seats were an example of an interesting psychological phenomenon. I had moved far in my thinking, I had changed many of my concepts about how we should and could do things. Then came the seat. Steve Marten suggested that we have individually designed seats, as the distance between the bones of our bum would be different.

Now this was my field of expertise. I was the rower. I had rowed in regular rowing seats for many hundreds of hours over 15 years, but I didn't walk around with my rowing seat under my arm. Our seats on the first row were normal rowing seats bolted to a piece of ply to which the wheels were attached. Now the call was for moulded foam seats. What self-respecting Kiwi rower required such individual attention? These would look like a large inverted Tupperware container with wheels. Now, I ask you, would you go to sea sitting on a Tupperware container? This was unnecessary. Forget about it. I guess you could say I was highly resistant to more change, particularly when I knew better.

So Steve got us to squat down, knees high, bum low, on a piece of wood. We then felt as the bones of our arse made contact with the wood, put our fingers on the spot and marked two spots. I was amazed to find that Phil's bum bones were 10 mm wider than mine. Using that distance measurement, a block of foam was scalloped out a little. We did the sitting test, more scalloping and so on until the seat felt comfortable. The seats were much superior. I knew that! I knew that! I was just kidding, Steve and Phil.

This was in fact quite a revelation for me, even if I didn't let on. It would have been a disaster to have gone to sea with the old style seats, anybody could feel that! After a few days we would have had sore bums, irritation and blisters; bumps and lumps would have followed. I still maintained I was just testing Steve and Phil and was really glad to see that they passed with flying colours. Now onto the next problem.

*

After testing we decided to adjust the position of the gates holding the oars, to lighten the gearing. We moved them 100 mm outward to the side of the hull.

Hardwood was used to strengthen the edge of the gunwale where the stern set of gates was fixed. For the bow set, a rigger had to be built to counter the boat's taper further forward. Mark, the engineer from Marten's, built a chunky but light aluminium rigger that suspended the gate out from the side of the gunwale. The oars now had a strong and light fulcrum at which to rest. Simply awesome.

Actually I still wasn't 100 per cent certain on the gearing of the oars in relation to the angle imposed by the length of the oar. The gunwales, onto which the rowlocks were secured, were higher than in any boat I'd rowed before. The conundrum was this. For efficient rowing it is preferable for the oar handles to move on a horizontal plane at the upper stomach/lower chest height of the seated rower.

If you have long oars, they will cross over at a lower height, as they enter the sea further from the boat and the angle coming back to you, the rower, is lower. If the oars are shorter, they enter the sea closer to the boat, therefore the angle is sharper and the crossover is higher up on your chest. Long oars create a lower angle which is good but they increase the leverage, therefore the loading is higher, which is not so good.

The opposite is true for shorter oars. The key is to get the balance. Then there is the factor of waves, and ocean rowing as opposed to rowing on calm, still, fresh water. Shorter oars are more effective in disturbed water with waves coming at you from differing angles and at differing heights on either side of the boat. Longer oars are more effective in calm, flat conditions. How short, how long, how efficient would each be? What effect would this have on our bodies? We chose two sets of oars each, one short and one of medium length.

*

Toilet paper was the next issue to be dealt with. Initially I had advocated that we should take a dozen rags. Phil would have six blue rags and I would have six red rags. This would save the weight involved in taking toilet paper: one of my more hair-brained ideas that thankfully Phil vetoed. After much testing and discussion we settled on 20 standard pieces each, per bucket visit, once a day, for 70 days. Vacuum packed, sealed, solved.

I recalled the interview I had given the *Sunday Star-Times* six months earlier, where I had spoken of all the safety technology we would have on board. That was before I understood the crucial importance of the weight issue. Radar? Lighted Christmas trees? I must have been dreaming.

*

The Sony Sports Walkman was another weight issue. Was it worth it? Alfred Pallas, a German professional living in Pauanui, thought so. Alfred mentioned that an ultra weight-conscious organisation, NASA, recognised the value of music as a relaxant and motivational tool, permitting astronauts to carry Walkmans and a limited number of personal tapes with them into space. This was enough for me; I needed my tapes. We settled on a Walkman and five tapes. I was happy.

Phil elected to take nothing.

*

Generally speaking, with safety issues we sought advice. An example here was deciding what equipment we would need when we were being pushed backwards. Both David Stubbs and Lloyd Klee from Safety at Sea insisted on taking a large sea anchor that would be deployed from the bow.

Nick de May was particularly concerned about the strength of the safety line attachments at each bulkhead. He felt that the attachments were weak. If the rower was knocked overboard by a wave he thought the attachments would rip out and the rower would be lost at sea. The three of us (Nick, Phil and myself) discussed this issue. Phil felt that the existing structure would do the job. In retrospect, I can see that we were very cavalier with regard to this issue.

"Look, mate," he said, "If you start looking for areas to strengthen the boat, add a bit here, another bit there, before you know it we will be carrying another 50 kg." Likewise there were worrying opinions on the length of rope we carried with our sea anchor. Originally we were advised 120 m would be the correct length. We reduced it to 70 m to save weight, tested it in 3–4 m seas and passed with flying colours. And we both agreed not to take the chain that helped to hold the sea anchor under water. We found large connection shackles worked like a charm.

*

Perhaps the two most contentious safety/weight issues were the policies of no spares and spartan communication equipment.

I was not completely happy with the decision to take no system to communicate with the outside world. Clearly there were weight reasons. Also, using the equipment would cause a distraction from rowing. Steve Marten was really very strong on that. To win we needed to row. To row we needed to concentrate solely on rowing. If we needed to communicate the reason would be that our race was over. We would then use the EPIRB (Emergency Position Indicator Radio Beacon) for rescue.

Against that I was aware that having a detailed knowledge of where our competitors were and how fast they were going could be very useful information. This we would not have. It would also have been great to communicate with Carolyn, as well as my family and friends back home. Eventually we decided to stick with the original decision to do without it.

The other major decision was to take few or no spares.

There were two exceptions: we took spare electrical fuses and spares for the Power Survivor water-maker. The instruction manual indicated that if something went wrong a spare filter and set of O rings (gaskets) would be needed. It was a similar philosophy that Phil had used with the safety harness: if we were to take any spares, what then would these be, where do you begin to cover equipment failure, where do you stop? No, I fully agreed, no spares. We didn't even take a spare 10-watt light bulb. In the event, it blew in the second week at sea, leaving us with no navigation lights.

By keeping the boat low-tech on board and by taking obsessive care in its construction the builders felt sure it would last at least two months in the mid-Atlantic.

*

It was now June 1997. The new steering system was proving particularly difficult, until finally we had a breakthrough. The original system was based on a cross between a surf ski and a rowing skiff set-up. During our training rows *Kiwi Challenge* confirmed what we had already suspected: the system was unsuitable for the job. Easy and effective control of the rudder with minimal added weight was deemed a high priority and Phil experimented with various concepts. A simple lever arm was positioned on the deck in front of the stroke, or stern, seat that pivoted at its centre point. To one end of the lever were attached two cables that split and ran out perpendicularly to each side of the boat, then ran down the side to the rudder.

The other end of the lever needed an adjustment mechanism. Jonathan, a Marten Marine employee, suggested using a hatch adjustment arm from a yacht. Phil attached the end to the side of the well and it worked perfectly: simple, effective and lightweight. We could adjust the rudder with relative ease, then lock it off so that the rudder acted more like a trim tab. One minor disadvantage was that we would not be able to make quick adjustments while surfing down the face of a wave. To set up a system to do this would have created a lot of additional weight which we felt was not warranted.

Meanwhile I was working on the final preparations for the official launching of the boat the following weekend. Graham Dalton and Virginia Wright from Serco helped set up and co-ordinate that function: one less job, thanks team.

*

June 8 was cool, overcast and drizzly. The boat hovered a foot above the water. Chris Dunphy, the master of ceremonies, invited local kaumatua Dick Taniwha and his whanau to perform the blessing. Having the boat correctly blessed was one of our more intelligent moves in the campaign. Dick gave his blessing in Maori, his whanau singing a waiata in support. At the end of their blessing every member of the whanau, young and old, filed past *Kiwi Challenge* touched her gently and whispered quiet prayers to the spirit world asking for guidance and protection for the little boat. That was so cool. The hair lifted on the back of my neck as I watched and I thought, "Mate, we need all the assistance we can get!"

Reverend Pauline Law performed a simple blessing. Chris then asked my mother to pour the champagne over the bow of the boat. The "60 Minutes" crew from TVNZ hovered as mum whispered, "I name this boat *Kiwi Challenge*," her soft Irish lilt barely audible even to Phil and me standing alongside.

The Boat Haulage mobile crane lowered *Kiwi Challenge* into the water and we took her for a quick row. Some commented on how fast it moved through the water. Don Rowlands, a Rowing New Zealand stalwart, watched as we rowed out the Viaduct Basin and returned. He was tsk-tsking, half muttering under his breath when Steve Marten, standing alongside, politely inquired as to whether anything was wrong.

Don replied, "When I rowed I would do over 2000 miles a year. These guys are going to row nearly 3000 miles in two months!" He added, "Steve, you've got no idea how annoying it can be if a team mate exhibits poor technique, even for just one session. When you are striving for perfection it can drive a man crazy."

"Is it really that bad?" Steve asked.

"Yep," he frowned and changed his voice in mock imitation of either Phil or myself, "I've had enough. You've been late at the catch for two weeks now — it's time you sorted it out!" The two men laughed.

*

That Sunday I was brought up to speed with the media's concept of a scoop. The television news media were generally very supportive of the *Kiwi Challenge* campaign. Exposure for the sponsors was crucial so I offered an exclusive on the launch to "One Network News" and they readily accepted. To help generate a larger crowd on the day the *Sunday Star-Times* agreed to run an article announcing that the boat would be launched that day. The article was tucked away at the bottom of page 8, with a black and white photo and small accompanying article.

Apparently, "One Network News" was annoyed by the article and decided not to do the story. If I had known that would be their attitude I would have made contact with TV3; or perhaps I should have communicated better with TVNZ and told them about the impending article. To me it seemed rather immaterial. It was a good sports story that for a change had nothing to do with rugby, cricket, netball or league.

9. Training

It's all to do with the training: you can do a lot if you're properly trained.
Queen Elizabeth II

THROUGH ALL OF THESE distractions, there was one matter that we could not ignore. The business of getting fit enough to row the Atlantic faster than all other comers! It was a task in which I was going to run into unexpected difficulties. I was already a rower of Olympic stature, but the problem was that they don't row the Olympics at sea, but rather on inland waterways that are, ideally, as calm as the proverbial millpond.

So how do you train for an ocean rowing race? Frankly, we didn't know. Nobody did. We had to go on our own past experiences and those of others. Back in 1977 New Zealander Colin Quincey rowed solo across the Tasman Sea from the Hokianga Harbour to Marcus Beach well north of Brisbane. Researcher and author Nobby Clark had advised Colin Quincey before he began preparation for his voyage, "Nearly all failures are because the job's been rushed."

Taking this advice to heart, Phil and I were not going to go away underprepared. Well, that was the theory. Training around the coastal waters of the Hauraki Gulf and Bay of Plenty would allow us to explore our boat's capabilities and idiosyncrasies and experiment with life at sea and the differing patterns and techniques of rowing on an ocean.

Friday night began quietly enough with a few gins and a glass of wine with friends but rapidly became a raucous night at the local. The morning after, May 24, 1997, I drove to Auckland extremely hungover for our first outing in *Kiwi Challenge*. I felt a little better by the time I met Phil at Marten Marine and finished off a few minor jobs on the boat, such as fitting an outboard motor and a couple of 50 litre petrol tanks. Just kidding, but the way I was feeling it would have been a great idea on that day.

We filled all the 10-litre containers with water just as we would have in the Atlantic and hooked *Kiwi Challenge* onto the Nissan Patrol that I had borrowed from ECNZ. I was as excited as a school kid having his first competitive row. I checked the boat and trailer, then the towing connection, and we were off to the briny. I could see onlookers doing double takes as we cruised to Bucklands Beach and this heightened my expectations and excitement. I backed down a ramp a discreet distance away from most people launching their boats, eased the boat off the DMW trailer and, being as nonchalant as I could, parked the wagon.

This was the moment we had both worked for. Phil sat ready in the rowing position with his oars locked into the gates, backside firmly positioned on the prototype seat. I pushed off and hauled myself up onto the side of the deck. The boat rolled violently to starboard as my weight took effect. "This thing is pretty damned tippy."

"Hmm," Phil responded in a non-committal way.

It was easy to tip the boat from one chine to the other. Only a slight shift in weight to one side and the boat responded accordingly. It was immediately obvious that we would have to pay attention to our boat's fine balance, as to row with the boat out of trim would alter its hydrodynamics and impede our progress.

Phil dipped the oars into the water, "touching" and gently moving the boat into the Tamaki Estuary. Once we were well away from the ramp we filled an additional 17 10-litre water containers. This brought the total water on board to 330 kg and that plus our body weight and that of the boat would have brought us up to about 750–800 kg. We wanted the boat close to our predicted race weight to give us an accurate idea of how it moved.

We were now ready for our first row.

*

Brad Lewis, (1984 Olympic gold medallist), *Assault on Lake Casitas*.
Sculling is a remarkably simple discipline. To learn the basics of the sport, head down to Sears and buy a 12 ft aluminium boat and a pair of oars. Toss the boat into the nearest lake or river, set the oars in the locks, and blast off.

Immediately you'll notice a problem – you're facing backwards. Like the tug-of-war, an Olympic sport in the early 1900s, and the backstroke in swimming, a sculler needs an intuitive sense of direction. Some scullers twist their heads around every stroke to check for watery obstructions, while others simply point their boat down the course and hope for the best. In theory, all scullers must keep the land on their starboard side so boats going in opposite directions will pass like cars on a freeway. Unfortunately, no center divider exists on a winding river. Every practitioner of the sculling game eventually collides with something – a bridge abutment, a navigational buoy – pray it's not another sculler.

After a few minutes, your arms and lower back will begin to tire, and a small blister will form on the palm of your hand. Welcome to the world of sculling. But unlike your Sears rowboat, a competitive scull has wheels mounted underneath the seat. The seat rolls on a pair of grooved, 30-inch tracks. The addition of the rolling seat allows you to power each stroke with your legs, the strongest muscles in your body.

The stroke is divided into two complementary segments, the drive and the recovery. The drive propels the boat through the water. The recovery allows an oarsman to move from the end of the stroke, the release, to the beginning of the stroke, the catch. The drive is all muscle, strength and eye-popping effort. The recovery is cool, subtle, a chance to take a breath and prepare for the next drive.

The driving effort is carefully quantified in the psyche of every practising oarsman. Half-power is like walking up a flight of stairs; three-quarters power is the same as a steady jog up those stairs; full-power is the equivalent of running to the top of Mt. Whitney. Then comes race-power. This is a special category, reserved for the ultimate in physical expression. At the completion of the final stroke of a close race, an oarsman should collapse over his oars, having spent every possible ounce of energy. Fainting from exhaustion at the finish line, although rarely seen, is greatly respected among competitors.

*

So now you know how to row.

I placed my oars in the gates, locked down the pin preventing the oar from popping out again and announced that I was ready to go. We took our first strokes pulling *Kiwi Challenge* through the water. She felt relatively sluggish; our strokes laboured and slow. It was little wonder it felt this way considering an Olympic class double scull rowing skiff weighs in at just 30 kg, compared to this 630 kg of boat weight! I noticed a cry from my legs, back and arms at the unusually heavy load I was placing on them. It felt as though a vertebra might pop out of the back of my spine with the load of each drive.

Damn. In my excitement I had missed out on a toilet stop before I left home, but not to worry, only a quick day trip. We rowed out around the southern end of Brown's Island, scooting around shallow reefs to avoid damage to the rudder. Almost immediately we found the steering system was suspect and the seats were too low, making us draw the oar handles too high to the finish of the stroke.

Uh oh! My lower bowel was suggesting that a quick trip to the dunny would be most appreciated. I hadn't even thought about that before we left and we had no toilet paper, nor paper of any description, not a single thing that could be used as a wiper. So I had no choice; I had to keep on rowing. The Tamaki Estuary was to our left, and further left I could see the Waiheke ferry belting back from the island to Customs Quay in the city. Uh oh.

"Look Phil, I'm sorry mate, I'm absolutely bursting I just have to go to the dunny. I'll have to hang out over the stern."

"Okay, if you must. Hang out as far as you can and don't drop any on the boat!"

I dived into the cabin, up with the rear hatch, down with the shorts, bum out as far as possible, down as close to the water as I could. My fingers were clinging to the edge of the hatchway but I was maintaining my position mainly by hanging on to the inside of the cabin with my legs.

A little ... hmm ... more than a little human by-product was sitting on the transom. The territory between the cheeks of my buttocks felt pretty slippery, too. Damn, damn, damn. "Phil, I'm just going to wash myself. I'll slip down the stern!"

"Hold it a minute mate, I just saw a stingray and school of barracuda go past while you were hanging two."

I leant over and washed the transom, scooping up water and rubbing the surface clean.

"There was a guy fishing here last weekend, caught a shark on his line, but unfortunately it got away."

I lowered myself into the water, bum to the rear, careful not to crush the crown jewels on the rudder or get hung up in the steering wires. God, it was cold.

"Isn't that the *Pride of Auckland* afternoon tea cruise coming from port?"

"Shut up, Phil! Concentrate on the rowing."

I dangled, literally, in the water.

"I'm going to have to turn to starboard, Rob, give that passing ferry a better view."

"Yeah, whatever."

"Oh, must have been the shark's dorsal fin that caught the corner of my eye."

While the banal banter continued from the solo rower, here was I, one hand clinging to the hatchway lip, the other washing my buttocks clean. The job completed I grasped the hatch lip with two hands and gently pulled myself up into the cabin.

"Just joking about the sharks, Rob. Thought it might help to focus the mind!"

*

I remember one significant event in my early years at school, one that had a huge effect on my development as an athlete. In form one, my teacher, John Featonby, took the class across to the hall to do a series of exercises. He made a competition of it by seeing how many full and correct press-ups we could manage in 30 seconds. I won with 28. Then we did the same with sit-ups and again I won again with 23.

It was a revelation for me. It seemed I was stronger than all the other boys and I wanted to be even better. I set what I think was my first conscious goal in life, to do 30 press-ups or sit-ups in as many seconds. Most evenings before I went to bed I would do as many press-ups and sit-ups as I could until I failed. Occasionally I would repeat the dose in the morning.

Once a week I would test myself to see if I had made any improvement. It wasn't long before the 30-in-30 barrier for press-ups was broken. The sit-up 30 in 30 took a little longer but that too was broken and so the test was extended to 35 in 30 and so on. I then developed different length tests from 10 seconds to 5 minutes, each time with the view of doing more repetitions than previously.

I was always strict on technique, never allowing my body to sag in the middle for press-ups and making sure my elbows touched my knees in the sit-ups (the traditional version with feet tucked under a bar and knees bent.) This was fun!

I kept up this consistent routine reasonably well throughout my school years and as a teenager found it no trouble to do 200–300 press-ups and sit-ups in one hit. For some reason those were the only exercises I did like that.

When I was 15, I added another exercise when one of the senior players in our volleyball team, Paul Barr, confided in me that most nights he held text books in his hands and with straight arms would lift them sideways as if trying to fly. Good for the "lats", he reckoned. The fact that it did nothing for the "lats" but lots for the shoulders didn't matter. I added it to my repertoire regardless. The result of this activity, I think, is one of the reasons I have a very good power-to-weight ratio.

I always believed I was better than most people thought me to be. Maybe even when people thought I was good at a sport I thought they thought otherwise. Confused? Anyway, I think this is partly what drove me in many of the sports I pursued and was certainly part of the equation for the Atlantic crossing. There were so many doubters that I had to prove them wrong.

*

The next morning saw our first serious row out to Rangitoto Island, that landmark symmetrical volcano. This time I rowed in comfort past Brown's Island and we continued on to Rangitoto. The row took us only 50 minutes so we anchored near the jetty and went for a run up to the top of the volcano, which produced a fair bit of heavy breathing from the pair of us. Phil's breathing was in fact so loud that I called him "Clyde"(Clydesdale) as he lumbered up the hill.

While rowing back to the boat ramp Phil received a phone call from his personal trainer and fellow police officer Steve Farrell, informing him that another officer, Rob Nicol, had been shot while on duty. The prognosis was good, he would survive but the call reaffirmed the risks and difficult situations the police get into. Phil rowed back without talking. We pulled into the boat ramp just as the sun began to disappear over the horizon. It was quiet and peaceful. As we cleaned the boat I had a sudden but overwhelming feeling of pride and joy. I couldn't think of anything that I would rather do right now than clean the boat in which we intended to row across the Atlantic.

My spine tingled and my scalp prickled. I slapped the boat: "You know what, mate, this is our project and nobody else's. We are the only New Zealanders and the only entry from the Southern Hemisphere," I enthused. "We are on the bones of our arse yet we have created this campaign from nothing but a dream. Isn't that great?"

"Yeah, it's pretty good, mate. I tell you what, this is going to be a great adventure. It'll be a great race too and I reckon we can win it," replied Phil.

"Damned right, dude!"

On that note we chortled to ourselves as we loaded the boat onto the trailer. I drove back to Hamilton with *Kiwi Challenge* in tow on an incredible high, feeling like a million dollars.

*

I was also absolutely delighted with *Kiwi Challenge*'s allocated race number, 25. My Dad, Miles Hamill, had been the General Motors dealer in Whakatane. Therefore I'm sure you can understand that I'm a Holden fan and a Peter Brock fan. Peter Brock's second racing car carried the same number as *Kiwi Challenge*, 25. I'm not superstitious but 25 was the nearest thing to a good omen for me.

*

Later that week we tested the Global Positioning System (GPS). On our run to Rangitoto it had told us that while rowing together we could tick along at three to four knots quite comfortably. Phil was a little doubtful and suggested the equipment might be inaccurate at low speeds but when we later fitted a log (or speedo) it confirmed that GPS estimate to be accurate. The GPS could easily be described as the lazy sailor's navigation tool as it saved us having to learn how to use a sextant, which in turn saved having to take calculation sheets, calculators and of course, a sextant.

Then it was time to try a longer row. We left Okahu Bay at 3 p.m. on a black Friday, June 13, and headed for Great Barrier Island, 55 nautical miles out to sea. On leaving Auckland, Phil thought it would be great public relations to drop in, unexpectedly, on one of the sponsors if he was home on Rakino Island.

*

Brian Corbett, Lion Foundation, Auckland

I have a holiday home in the Hauraki Gulf and had gone there one weekend for a bit of R&R. On Friday evening towards dusk I heard a voice hailing me as I was scrabbling under the house for some piece of equipment.

Engineering an awkward under-house U turn, I saw Stubbsie grinning from ear to ear.

Knowing the ferry was not due for some time I remember saying, "How the hell did you get here?" "Well," he said in that laconic manner of his, "me and Rob decided to row to the Barrier for a practice."

Now anyone who is familiar with Auckland will appreciate that throwaway line! Anyway we all walked back down to the bay to see Rob holding the boat in position and with that they turned about and rowed off to the entrance of the bay and set off for the Barrier.

As we climbed back onto our deck we could see the rear light of the boat as it moved at a very fast clip across the water and eventually out of our view. I guess at that moment the enormity of the task they were about to undertake hit me and I remember sitting in the dark for about an hour reflecting on the sheer magnitude of what they were about to do.

*

We rowed together for three hours in good conditions, then Phil dropped out to prepare dinner. I had brought all sorts of bits and pieces to supplement the staple of Alliance and Nutrazeal freeze-dry. One of the items purchased was a kilogram of dried apricots, the biggest bag of dried apricots I'd ever seen.

"Yum! Dried apricots. My favourite," said Phil.

He opened the packet and was into them like a gannet. His primary focus was to prepare the freeze-dry meal so, while it was soaking for 15 minutes, Phil sat back and ate dried apricots. He tossed me half a dozen. Before I knew it he had demolished the packet. I was amazed and a little disappointed with the rapid demise of the apricots and the very few that had come my way. However, in addition to the kilo of apricots the meal was cooked and eaten, no worries. Now I was impressed. I had just witnessed an incredible "human Insinkerator" functioning.

Of course for me eating freeze-dried food for the first time was like taking the Muhammad Ali of laxatives. It worked a treat.

*

At 7 p.m. we changed over. I ate my meal and hit the pit. Phil rowed till 9 p.m. and all was well, then I rowed till 11 p.m. The next two shifts were planned for four hours each at the oars and Phil was first up. About two hours into my sleep I was woken by a crashing of oars against the deck, an almighty thump and suddenly the boat keeled severely to one side. I rolled into the side of the cabin, my face pushed against the plywood shell. A few moans and groans emanated from outside.

"What's going on Phil?" I yelled, "Are you okay?"

"Oohhh MMMate!" came an anguished cry, "I've just had the most wicked stomach cramps and I've been holding on and holding on — ya know how we are not allowed to stop rowing during our shift for anything?"

"Yeah ... and ...?" I inquired.

"Well, I hung on but suddenly I just HAD to go, and I didn't have much time!"

"I see." I couldn't, thankfully. But I did understand.

"Sorry to wake you up, mate, but I didn't have much choice."

Eventually Phil got rowing again and I giggled myself back to sleep. Been there, dunny that. About 90 minutes later I was awoken by a good-natured yell from Phil,

"Wake up Hamill ya scurb, get on the oars!"

"Yeah, righto."

Bleary-eyed, I changed into my rowing attire and pushed open the hatch. There being little moonlight I was enveloped by darkness with my eyes not yet adjusted to the meagre starlit visibility. As I clambered out of the hatch, fumbling about trying to secure a hold by which to keep my balance, my hand came to rest upon the shaft of an oar. I knew the oar was held in place by the gate, so I attempted to grab hold of the oar while I worked my way out of the cabin. Unfortunately, my hand slipped off the shaft, which was extremely greasy. I fell out of the cabin onto the deck.

Feeling sheepish for my clumsy fall, I stood up rubbing greasy slime between my fingers and raised my hand to my nose for an inquiring sniff. I nearly gagged! Immediately it became apparent that during the emergency earlier on, the bucket was not handy so Phil had made a dash for the side of the boat. Unfortunately, by the time evacuation began he was still moving into position. I launched myself half over the side to wash my hand clean. As I did so I rested my free hand on another little pile of muck, which nearly sent me overboard.

Phil was in hysterics as he watched this drama unfold, which included all manner of shrieks, yelps and curses on my part.

"Bloody Nora, Phil, it's everywhere!"

Phil sat back and in his typically casual manner replied, "Yeah." He paused, then continued whimsically, "Ya know, mate, I thought I could smell something."

Needless to say, the few packets of dried apricots we took on board during the race were rationed.

*

I rowed from 3 to 7 a.m., making reasonable progress in a following sea. I noticed that during the last one and a half hours it was particularly difficult to maintain my target speed of between 2.5 and three knots and on the changeover I suggested to Phil that four hours might be too long to expect to row efficiently. Phil concurred, saying he had noticed a similar trend in his shift.

I slumped into the cabin pleased for the rest and within minutes was asleep. Phil woke me an hour later, saying he needed a hand as he didn't think he could make it alone to Tryphena Harbour on the southern end of Great Barrier. A south-westerly whipping through the Colville Channel was pushing us too far north. So together we rowed in a reasonably difficult crosswind until at 10.30 a.m. we arrived in the harbour. We paddled lightly up to a jetty, tied the boat off and began walking to the shops 2–3 km away around the bay.

The main reason we needed shops at this point was because Phil had a craving for dried apricots. No, just kidding. Our reasoning was far more practical. We needed Vaseline. Correction, we were desperate for Vaseline. We had considerable trouble with chafing between the cheeks of our buttocks. This chafing was caused by the row to the Barrier while seated in damp conditions. I guess we took roughly 11,000 strokes each to make the Barrier. Now the rash in between and on my buttocks was so bad that walking was difficult.

*

It had happened 18 years before. A mild itching had developed on either side of the "crown jewels" and quickly turned into quite a nasty rash. After a week or two the rash had grown down each side of my inner thigh, so much in fact that it protruded below my shorts, red hot and inflamed. A superb example of jock itch. Of course, Rob Hamill, Mr Naive 1979, had no idea what the rash was. My best mate Earl Austin, at least I thought he was my best mate, managed to convince me that I had a VD. This in spite of the fact that at 15 I was yet to experience a sexual encounter!

*

When the solitary car approached I stuck out my thumb hopefully. Much to our relief the car pulled over, a woman leaned across the front seat, opened the door and asked where we were headed. "To the shops," we announced, gleeful at the prospect of hitching a ride. How contradictory the situation seemed. We were happy to row for 19 hours to reach an island, yet the thought of walking a few kilometres was almost intolerable.

*

Kaye Milne, *Aotea Times*, July 1997

As a normally prudent, sensible female I rarely pick up male hitchhikers when I'm driving on my own. However, the two that I passed while coming home from the wharf looked too exhausted to hurt a mouse, let alone a substantial human being like myself.

"Thanks," they croaked as they got into the car. "You're a lifesaver – we need to go to a shop – forgot Vaseline and toilet paper."

They introduced themselves as Rob and Phil and said they had spent the night rowing from Auckland. "Oh, yeah," thinks me, "I've heard that one before", so I didn't comment. They asked the inevitable questions such as How long have you lived here? Do you like it? What do you do?

When I replied that one of my jobs was helping John run the local rag, they got all fired up saying they were newsworthy – they were going to row the Atlantic. My scepticism went out the window and I offered to take them home to Shalom for lunch to meet John and then return them to the wharf.

Well, we got home but they were too bleary-eyed to make sense so we gave them a cuppa and sandwich and pointed them in the direction of the spare bedroom. A couple of hours later they emerged, so we sat them down to be interviewed.

Lunch, sleep, interview and dinner passed. We took them back to the wharf about 8 p.m., complete with toilet paper and Vaseline!

10. Learning Fast

The trouble with experience as a guide is that the final exam often comes first and then the lesson.
Anonymous

WATERED, FED AND ARMED with precious lubricants we were returned to our vessel. We gave thanks, said our farewells and rowed off into the sunset, heading for Auckland.

We had learnt two important lessons. First, the concept of four-hour shifts at night needed rethinking. Our efficiency and therefore distance gained tailed off over the last one and a half hours. Second, we needed to combat dehydration. On this trip we had both suffered massive headaches and disorientation from dehydration.

It is important to understand that we were feeling our way here, testing our bodies against a theoretical ideal. That ideal was simply to row the whole way across the Atlantic non-stop — when Phil rowed, I would rest and vice versa, for as long as it took to get us there. What we didn't know yet was whether this was physically possible. Or what the ideal rowing shifts would be. Or very much else for that matter. Eventually we would decide to go for broke. The Atlantic non-stop express approach!

*

The following weekend, June 21, we planned to row out to the active volcano of White Island off Whakatane in the Bay of Plenty. I had arrived at my parents' place in Whakatane the night before and I placed the oars in the garage for safe keeping overnight. Unfortunately my father inadvertently drove over one of the oars with his car and so, on Saturday morning, I set out to borrow a pair of replacement oars from my old rowing club.

I visited my first rowing coach, Chick Hammond, and inquired as to the possibility of borrowing a set of oars from the Whakatane Rowing Club. He looked at me rather dubiously and mumbled something about history repeating itself. I had not the faintest idea what he was talking about until he reminded me of the previous two occasions when I had broken club oars. "Ahem, oh yes, that's right, I remember now." I grinned sheepishly, trying to cover my brilliant red flushing.

*

Chick Hammond, rowing coach, Whakatane.

The club had four sets of East German sculling blades – ex-German quadruple scull crew. Four sets. Eight blades, very stiff varnished timber and in excellent condition. Well, they were until Rob arrived on the scene.

One pair was parted after training on the river; Rob fell out of the double scull at the launching ramp and landed on an oar! One pair down, three to go.

About six weeks later, Rob has the aforementioned sculls sticking out of the window of his little red racing Torana and after sweeping into the concrete garage with a low roof and a very solid doorway, pair number two were down!

Ten years later he pops around for a chat and casually mentions he is one pair of blades short and can he have a loan of a set just for the row to White Island? Well, his record with these sculls is not good. Nevertheless, away he goes with set number three....

*

"Chick," I said in the most reassuring tone I could muster, "if you can see it in the kindness of your heart to lend me a pair of sticks I will personally see to it that they are returned in one piece."

"Yeah, right Robbie," he said totally unconvinced, "Flap! Flap! Flap! Look up there in the sky, it's a pig!"

I returned home with a set of Whakatane Rowing Club oars sticking out of the passenger's window of my car and parked up on the roadside, well clear of our garage.

Purely by chance a TVNZ television crew was on hand. Several weeks earlier the Colin McCahon painting, the Urewera Triptych, had been stolen and an informant had intimated it might be returned that day in Whakatane. The tip-off proved a hoax and so the television crew looked for another story and found the *Kiwi Challenge* parked at the Whakatane Heads.

Phil and I rowed out of the Whakatane River mouth, then headed north for White Island. A north-westerly wind grew stronger by the hour and threatened to blow us south of the island. If we missed White Island the contingency plan was to make for Te Kaha or Waihau Bay and make landfall on one of the many beaches if necessary. We crabbed across a 2–3 m choppy swell, the oars often searching for the water as our small craft rolled from side to side. Periodically a breaking white cap hit the port side bow, splashing cold shocks of winter water across me, bursting into my ears and stinging the soft flesh of my cheek.

The load on the oars increased in proportion to the elements opposing us. We changed to the shorter wooden oars that Chick had lent us. These proved extremely useful, eventually influencing the choice of oars that we took for use in the race.

*

Cloud filtered light from a full moon, just enough to see the outline of White Island, shrouded in steam which was quickly being whipped off eastwards. As the volcano loomed it became apparent that we might not make it around the northern point. If forced to go around the southern end there was a possibility of missing the island altogether, or even worse, being dashed upon jagged rocks.

We were a kilometre away from the island when Phil woke me. "I think the rudder has lifted off the gudgeons," he yelled, urgency in his voice. "You're gonna have to get the bloody thing back on as quickly as possible or we will wreck on the shore!"

The seriousness and tone of Phil's voice left me in no doubt as to how dire the situation was. I threw open the stern hatch, clambered out and peered over the transom. Sure enough, there was the rudder floating on the water surface, attached to the guide wires, occasionally bouncing off the stern as the boat pitched from side to side.

I wedged my legs against the internal walls of the cabin and leant out over the stern, stretching to grab the rudder. It was impossible to fit the rudder on the gudgeons while the control wires were attached, so I lifted it up onto the stern, undid the two small shackles and put them in my mouth. I let the wires hang free while I attempted to reposition the rudder. As I thrust the rudder into the water, the agitated sea forced it from one side of the gudgeons to the other.

Bloody difficult. I couldn't get the rudder on both gudgeons at the same time. I struggled for what seemed like an eternity, but probably was only a minute. I yelled and swore with frustration, cursing the bloody sea. Somehow the rudder suddenly went on.

The two shackles were now firmly wedged between my teeth, looking like extra fillings. These had to be manipulated through an eye on the end of each wire and attached to a fastening on the upper and rear edge of the rudder. My fingers were numb with cold and I couldn't feel the shackles properly. Here I was dangling over the stern of a row boat, bobbing around in a choppy sea, miserable, cold and wet and realising that if I didn't get this flaming thing operating in the next few minutes we would probably get wrecked on this God-forsaken volcano.

The first shackle was attached relatively easily. The next was difficult.

"How much longer, mate?" called Phil.

"Not long now," I yelled back, but my voice was lost in the wind.

If my fingers were numb before, I couldn't feel a thing now and I was working by sight alone. The U of the shackle went through the eye of the second wire without any problem. However, the slack was completely taken up when I tried to attach it to the fastening and the wire was taut. I adjusted my position in the hatch to lean out a little further so that I could get more leverage on the rudder. I had to stop it moving from side to side with the water pressure and pitch and roll of the boat. The extra purchase helped. With every bit of strength I could muster the rudder was held stationary while I fed the shackle bolt through the fastening and into the thread, all the while concerned that I might drop the pin overboard. A twist and it held.

We now rowed together, around the top of the island, but that was a little too close, thank you. We knew that the first job to do on our return would be to fit a pin that would hold the rudder in place and not allow it to lift off the gudgeons in a heavy swell. We finally arrived in the lee of White Island at 1 a.m. Despite the woeful conditions it had taken only 11 hours to make the 28 miles. That would be better than 60 miles a day. We wondered how much faster we could go in favourable conditions — 80 ... 90 ... 100?

At the top of the island we found a different world — flat calm with several fishing trawlers anchored. We also found an 18 m trawler and threw a line to it. In these conditions we gladly hooked on and had a chat to the crew about what we were doing.

*

We were up at 6 a.m. and rowed around the southern end into a howling westerly. Phil dropped out to ring my brother Peter on his cell phone; Peter had come down with his boat to help if we needed him. I was rowing as hard as I could, trying to keep position; the boat climbed up with each swell and crashed down over the back and into the next oncoming swell. The unthinkable suddenly happened. The oar broke. The Whakatane Rowing Club's prized East German sculling oar was wrecked! Bugger!

Peter towed us home and we loaded both boats onto their respective trailers. Peter then drove to Pauanui, Phil drove to Auckland and I drove to Chick Hammond's.

The next morning the *Whakatane Beacon* called into my parents' house for an interview. I did not want to say we had to be towed back from White Island but the intrepid reporter's direct line of questioning, "Were you towed home?" left me no room to manoeuvre. I told the reporter that my brother was on hand to tow us in and suggested that the incident did not reflect poorly on our preparations to cross the Atlantic. In a feeble attempt to defend ourselves I added that when we finished the race, victorious, we had no intention of turning round and rowing back to the start line!

Thank God the national dailies did not pick up this story. They don't give a hoot about areas away from the latte tables.

Peter Hamill, my long-suffering brother, has a different view of the same adventure, probably one a little closer to reality. Peter owns a service station and is so pragmatic and practical you wouldn't believe we were related! Having helped me financially when I mortgaged my flat in Hamilton, he became an official sponsor and had the name of Pauanui Service Station on the boat.

*

Peter Hamill, brother, Pauanui, July 1999

The whole White Island trip was a comedy of errors. It really was!

The main idea, as I understood it, was to go for an overnight row. Row all night to see what their shifts would be like, sleep in the cabin, get a feel of what it was like to be on the boat overnight and row further out to sea than they had been before. They asked me to come as they were concerned a westerly wind could blow them out to sea.

Both had commitments on the Monday, and they were on a tight time schedule. If the westerly got up, they wouldn't be able to get back in time. If this happened I could tow them back to Whakatane. Great! I was looking forward to going to Whakatane, seeing Mum and Dad, and getting out and doing a bit of fishing around the back of White Island.

Robert's organisation skills were a little … um … lax. The first thing, the night before Dad had backed over a couple of oars in the garage and broken one of them! Robert put them on the left-hand rear side of a car backing in! He borrowed a replacement set from the local club.

There was a TV film crew outside and Rob's partner Phil was late – nobody knew where he was. We told Rob a TV crew was there and he sat in the kitchen eating away. Then Phil phoned to say that he had broken down at Te Teko 16 miles away and I went to tow him in.

I couldn't believe it. Rob was just chowing down, trying to convince us that the food stores were the most important thing for the moment. Phil finally turned up, and really you wouldn't know they were doing this row in the morning. It just wasn't organised, nothing was ready the day before. Things were going into the boat at the last minute. Nothing seemed planned.

Eventually everybody got ready. We got down to the boat ramp, fiddled around, stopped other people getting in and out of the ramp. Getting ready to film seemed to take forever. Rob and Phil hopped in the boat and lo and behold, nobody had put the seats in the boat! They were at home sitting in the garage. What a comedy. At least Rob had had breakfast, there is no doubt about that.

At long last the boys got going. "I'll be out somewhere near White Island tomorrow, just give us a call if you need me." I reassured them.

Very good. Next morning I was keen to do some fishing. It is all of 8.30 in the morning and we get a call from Phil on the cell phone. "You better come and get us, and start towing now. We have broken an oar!"

I thought this was wonderful. I didn't even get a chance to do any fishing. I had to steam out there. It was rough as guts but I found them out the back of White Island and towed them home.

I just thought, "Hey, if they can't get out and back to White Island, how are they going to get across the Atlantic, how are they going to get everything on board the boat before the start day?'

Man, it was an eye-opener. I had a talk to Robert and said, "Boy, you are going to have a major written down checklist!"

Big brother style, you know. That episode was not like Robert. His mind was focused on other things and he forgot about the present. I wasn't impressed.

I don't think he was either. He kept everything very quiet. He didn't tell anybody they hadn't been rowing all night, didn't tell about the broken oar or being towed in first thing in the morning. No, that was all tucked away.

We, that is, the family, were starting to wonder just a little bit. Like the overnight rowing sequence, they just hunkered down in the lee of the island. So I was sort of thinking, "Hey, you guys are running out of experimental time." They were lucky that they got more time, in that someone funded the boat to be flown over to the UK, that was a Godsend to them, because otherwise they were right behind the eight ball.

*

Although I didn't tell anyone at the time, a problem emerged on the White Island trip that was quite serious. In the late afternoon of the first day, after completing my shift, I was preparing for a rest on the cabin bed when the buffeting, quick lifting and rolling motion of the little boat got to me. I launched myself out of the cabin and just managed to grab hold of the toilet bucket in the nick of time. Phil didn't comment on my seasickness; the mirth in his eyes was loud enough, thanks.

While lying down or rowing I felt fine. The problem appeared to be the transitions between shifts and I seemed to be particularly vulnerable in the cabin. Trying to sit up, hunched over because of the lack of headroom, attempting a change of clothing was not conducive to good belly relations.

This wasn't the first time it had happened. Most times when we were out training I had felt a little uncomfortable, a little queasy in my stomach, and once we had cleared the protected inner Hauraki Gulf I was nearly always ill. It was a surprise to me. Until then I hadn't considered being vulnerable to seasickness. I had suffered as a kid when fishing with my father, but I thought that I had long since grown out of it. Now it was looming large as a debilitating problem that had to be overcome somehow.

*

That night, June 22, Phil flew to Canada with a police mate — Steve Westlake — and I didn't see him again for five and a half weeks. They went to compete at the World Police Games before going on a rafting and kayaking trip in the Rockies. In the Police Games, Phil was 12th overall in his age group and took two medals in the rowing. Then they canoed the dangerous white waters of the Nahanni River, ran through the forest of Montana and climbed its snow-capped peaks for two weeks.

The "trip of a lifetime" had been organised long before Phil had been committed to the Atlantic Rowing Race. One of my stipulations when choosing Phil as my team-mate was that — if time was short — he would withdraw from the trip to Canada or at the very least would return home straight after the games. When the time came I had asked that he consider doing only the Police Games and miss the rafting trip, but he refused, citing the training possibilities of rafting as helpful to the campaign.

I didn't agree. I have always believed in sport-specific training: to train for the Tour de France, go cycling; to train for the "King of the Mountain", run hills; to train for the Atlantic Rowing Race, row at sea. And more importantly, row with your team mate. Cross-training is essential, but we were both doing plenty of cross-training anyway. It was the sport-specific sea rowing we were short on.

He was insistent that everything was fine and that we would make the starting line with time to spare. I didn't necessarily disagree with him, assuming that we were going to get the boat air freighted to the starting line. However, at that stage nothing concerning the freight was guaranteed. Besides, the boat itself was far from ready for the Atlantic and still needed work.

At the time I felt Phil was deserting me to go off and have a bit of fun overseas with his mates, while I was left behind still raising funds, finishing off the boat and training. Maybe I was being unfair. He had planned the trip a long way back and it meant a lot to him.

11. Sea Legs

Keep going; if you can't walk, creep.
Unknown

PHIL RETURNED FROM CANADA on August 6, leaving just over nine weeks before the starting gun. We recommenced training, going out to Kawau Island and back to Auckland, a round trip of 56 miles that took 26 hours in changeable conditions. We did the overnighter more or less without any major hitches, although it reminded me of just how tiring it was to row alternate shifts of 2–4 hours. We were persisting with the four-hour shifts at night to see if we could develop fitness to maintain efficiency.

This was the first time dehydration was not an ongoing problem. In previous sessions, we found that after 6–8 hours of rowing our bodies seemed to stop absorbing water. Sometimes I would have to stop three times to urinate during a two-hour session. This, on top of the fact that we were sweating profusely, meant our hydration levels were getting dangerously low, leading to extreme fatigue. By rule of thumb, fluid loss of only 2 per cent can reduce performance by up to 20 per cent.

We decided that supplementation was necessary. I had always been a cynic about supplements. Consequently, I had only used them sporadically over the years, but this experience taught me that some supplements really do work. We solved the problem by adding Horley's Replace to our drinks. This is an isotonic sports drink, formulated for rapid absorption by the body to prevent dehydration. It replaced the vital electrolytes (sodium and potassium) that we were losing and supplied extra carbohydrate to aid absorption and energy levels.

*

As a third-former, I decided to follow my sister's footsteps and have a crack at volleyball. In the first tournament our school entered I was selected to play in the "D" Team. It was the bottom team in the school. I couldn't believe it. The "D" team!

The shame. The agony. Had there been some kind of mistake? Had the coach not seen my talent? Life is so unfair! I played that tournament totally believing that I was better than the other boys in the team. For all I knew I might have been the worst player on the team. It didn't matter, I believed I should have been in the "A" team and that's exactly where I was headed.

The point is it didn't matter how good or bad I was at the discipline. What mattered was that I believed I was a good volleyball player and that with a little practice I could be a very good volleyball player. And practise I did.

Mum would go spare at me for practising and wearing a bald patch on her front lawn from countless hours of setting, jumping and spiking the ball over a rope strung between two trees. After a couple of years it paid off. I captained the senior school team and played for the successful New Zealand under-17 side that toured New Caledonia in 1981. I was the shortest spiker in the team. I wasn't the best, but I had the highest jump.

I was the only member of that third-form intake to go on and make national honours. Henry Ford said, "Whether you think that you can, or that you can't, you are usually right."

*

It was a late August, Friday, around 8.30 at night, when we launched the boat in the now familiar Okahu Bay. We were planning to row to Great Barrier again. An elderly couple stood on the pier watching our strange looking vessel as it drifted off the trailer. "Where are you headed?" the man asked.

"Not sure, really," said Phil casually, "We'll head for the Barrier and weather permitting we might go through Colville Channel and visit my father in Whitianga."

"I take my hat off to you guys. You're certainly keen," the man said, a bit taken aback, "especially on a Friday night. I'd expect you blokes would be out having a few drinks."

"The drinks will be on us when we win the race," Phil replied.

*

We planned to head north along the coastline towards Whangarei but the weather forecast predicted south-westerlies and we decided to take their assistance and hit out for Whitianga. We left Auckland and experimented with four-hour shifts, just to see how we coped. When I was roused at 2 a.m. I was amazed at how much the sea had changed. I started to swing on the oars and immediately the boat surged on the top of a swell. It was the best lift yet and I enjoyed the power of it all.

The wind and sea seemed to continue to increase over the next hour, gusting up to 35 knots. Occasionally, white water hit the stern quarter of *Kiwi Challenge*, sometimes kicking her slightly sideways and sending us down the side of the swell like a surfboard. At first I was a little apprehensive about the boat's ability to cope, but she coped masterfully. Midway into the shift my confidence in our little plywood boat had increased considerably. It seemed that *Kiwi Challenge* might be able to handle most seas. The problem appeared to be how the crew, rather than the boat, handled the open sea. And initial indications were that I was not handling it too well at all.

Again the motion was getting to me and the last hour and a half of my four-hour shift seemed to take forever. At 6 a.m. I woke Phil. The moment I climbed into the cabin, my dinner wanted to join Phil back out on deck. For the second time at sea I was ill, this time with great violence and equally boisterous sound effects. Mind you, I immediately felt better. I had a drink of water, climbed into my sleeping bag and fell asleep.

At 9 a.m. my body aroused me from a deep sleep. At first I felt good, but then I sat up. Belching several times I quickly put on my rowing clothes and by the time I poked my head out the hatch I was ready to let fly with an encore. At first there was not a lot of colour. Matter of fact all I could muster was a dry retch, then came a bit of clear fluid. Time for a quick breath, another dry retch then thick yellow bile gushed forth, leaving a frothy slime in the bottom of the bucket. Once again I felt okay.

*

The sea sickness wasn't the only thing that disturbed me on that trip. While crossing a strip of rough water off the coast we weren't making great progress and I suggested that we go in closer to shore where the waters were calmer. Phil refused to recognise the logic of my argument and insisted we battle onwards. This we did to little effect. Finally he relented and we came into calmer waters. He then informed me that the wind had suddenly dropped. It hadn't. It was a small incident, but it gave me a new insight into Phil's character. He could be very pig-headed when he chose to be. But then again, maybe he felt the same about me.

*

That night, anchored in a small Coromandel inlet, Potiki Bay, Phil gave some indication that he was very concerned about my seasickness. He had noted that most people got over the initial upset within three or four days but some never got over their sickness, and that second possibility was the basis for his worry about me. He made mention of how his brother Steven had sailed with their father back from Noumea earlier in the year. Apparently he had an extremely uncomfortable trip and was ill for eight days before making port in the Bay of Islands. Because I had never been on an extended sea trip, I did not know if I would settle down. Neither did Phil.

We discussed the possibility of my withdrawal from the race in favour of someone who could get over the initial seasickness. To step aside at the

11th hour was a thought I did not relish but all our preparations to date had been with a view of not just entering but winning. That goal, to win, had been established right from the outset. We were not going to Tenerife simply to make up the numbers. We wanted to win and this had constantly influenced all decisions related to the project over the last six months.

My head told me that this could be the best thing for the campaign and the sponsors if things didn't improve. The *Kiwi Challenge* campaign was larger than some bloke who happened to have a big dream. A replacement would be necessary. I knew Phil had someone in mind. He was Steve Westlake, with whom he had recently campaigned in Canada. Steve was something of a legend in police ranks, having won the Top Cop title in both Australia and New Zealand. I had never met him. Nor did I know then that Phil had already told him to be standing by to fly to Tenerife.

In the end, of course, what my head told me was of limited importance. What my heart thought was far more consequential — and it had something very different to say.

"There's no way some scumbag imposter is going to steal our thunder and take the glory of the victory which is ours, Rob. Bugger that for a joke, mate. This is our show!"

As they say, listen to your heart.

*

"60 Minutes" programme. Interviewer Mike Valintine

Mike: Does Phil have a weak link?

Rob: Women.

Lots of laughter then a pause.

Rob: Yeah, there are a couple of weaknesses. He can be quite stubborn. When he thinks he's right, that's it. He has to try and look at the rational side or the other person's view. I think that is the one issue we have to look at. It's the only weakness I can see in Phil in that he can be so set, he can get really set on things almost to the point where it can be detrimental.

Mike: You accept that, Phil?

Pause.

Phil *(grinning)*: No. I usually know when I'm right.

Lots of laughter all round.

Mike: That sounds like a worry to me.

More laughter.

Rob: I think we communicate pretty well though.

*

The next sea training was from Auckland to Tutukaka. Not surprisingly, the elderly couple had gone from the wharf. A reasonable south-westerly assisted our progress and by dawn we were approaching Little Barrier Island. In 12 hours we had covered more than 53 miles, our best effort yet.

We rowed to Little Barrier, then had a break to test the sea anchor. The system seemed to work really well.

Rowing again, we changed to the two hours on, one hour off routine we had experimented with the previous weekend and found this to be particularly fast. Every second hour we rowed together lifted the boat's speed significantly.

The problem for us was that if we were to use this system on a regular basis, it would severely cut into our personal physical recovery time. As it was, we were planning to row a minimum of 12 hours a day. To use the "two on, one off" system for a 24-hour stint meant we would each be on the oars for 16 hours. Based on our training to date this seemed too intimidating, especially if it was to be done on consecutive days. We decided to follow this roster at sea but only when we felt able and if tail conditions prevailed.

*

We had rowed since early morning and although I experienced some discomfort, I thought I was grappling with the situation satisfactorily. In the late afternoon my belly had started to rumble with discontent. Again seasickness was kicking in and was beginning to make me feel anxious. This was our last training row before LEP International were to air freight the boat to London. It was imperative we find out if I could gain my sea legs.

I came off my shift, ate and rested in the cabin. At 10.50 p.m. Phil's call aroused me from a deep slumber. Again, I felt fine until I sat up. Mild nausea moved through me as I organised myself in the cabin. As quickly as possible I was on the oars, trying to row the nausea away. I had decided that I had to get through this four-hour shift, battling into a headwind and choppy seas, and not be ill.

At first I thought I could cope as the nausea eased. Then it came back more severely than before, almost totally preoccupying my whole being, my mind, my rowing psyche, everything, then came the stomach cramps. Damn it!

Two hours went by as I fought the enemy within me that was threatening my position in my boat, in the race I had dreamed of for 12 months. Everything was on the line here. Throw up and I'm out! This was personal, this was the very me, this was my battle. I could not permit myself to vomit, for in my mind, I knew I would never forgive myself. If I vomited, I would have to withdraw myself. Period.

I placed my hand over my mouth as I belched and tried to make it as quiet as possible. I mustn't wake Phil, mustn't let him know how sick I felt. My stomach suddenly contracted, the vomit was pushed up into my mouth but I managed to swallow it. The whole lot, back down. Another hour passed. It happened again, again I swallowed. And yet again the battle between upper and lower body was enacted. Yet again I forced myself to swallow.

Each and every time this battle was on I had to stop rowing, then try and make up the ground I had just lost. I felt weak, pathetically weak and it was all I could do to stop from vomiting. Rowing was a minor consideration. Finally, time was up. I woke Phil and prayed he would not take long to change over.

*

"You haven't gone too far, mate," said a disappointed Phil, examining the log.

"Yeah, I'm feeling as weak as a pizzle at the moment. Can't explain it, really. Didn't put enough electrolyte in my drink perhaps," I suggested hopefully. Quicker than Flash Gordon I was in the cabin and on my back. Relief was almost instantaneous. Incredible, the speed of bodily change. One minute I was rowing on the briny feeling as crook as a politician, the next I was lying down feeling at least partially alive and happy. I had a dull sense of achievement, but obviously my feelings were tempered by the hollowness of such a specious victory. For the moment my stomach and I declared a truce.

Phil rowed for the next four hours and covered twice the distance I had done in the same length of time. We were well past the Hen and Chicken Islands now; Bream Head and the entrance to the Whangarei Harbour lay ahead. My stomach was put to the test again as the sun lifted off the horizon, but surprisingly I managed much better and actually ate breakfast.

In the final stages of the trip I felt a niggle in my left shoulder. It didn't seem serious and I ignored it. Why should I worry? In this sea training run I had controlled my seasickness, in a manner of speaking. I had won a small battle, even if hadn't won the war. By the criteria I had set myself, I was still in the *Kiwi Challenge* crew.

*

Someone had told me that yachties swore by a concoction — actually it was two pills taken together — that was only available from a pharmacy in Paihia. I decided to contact them and invite them to become a sponsor; providing free product of course. I faxed them a mass of information about the bid, thinking that they would be most impressed to receive so much good stuff.

My follow-up phone call received a most hostile response. It appears that I had jammed their phone line just when they wanted to use the EFTPOS machine. It had been their busiest time of the day — but not that day.

Eventually they mailed me some product.

*

Richard Newey, New Zealand representative rower, August 1999

It was 10.30 Sunday morning and my phone rang. I was hungover and grunted into the receiver.

"Rich? Phil Stubbs here, mate, how are you?"

"Yeah, good." Typical cliché bullshit answer. "Nice day, eh?"

"Don't know, I'm majorly hungover."

"Hard night, was it?"

"Yeah, what's up, what are you doing?" In other words, go away and let me get some sleep. "Nothing really." Now it was Phil's turn at the bullshit.

"Oh yeah."

"Do you want to come and pick us up?"

"Where are you?"

"Tutukaka."

"What!!??"

"Tutukaka."

"That's 200 Ks. Right now?"

"Yeah."

"Where are you right now?"

"Oh, about 8 miles out."

"So you want me to pick you and your boat up."

"Yeah."

"Can I tow it with my car?"

"Nah, just shoot over to town and pick up the truck and trailer at Okahu Bay, the keys are inside the tyre."

"Hey Phil, what would you have done it I wasn't home?"

"Oh, we would have found someone."

Casual bastard! So I drove to Tutukaka. On the way I heard on the radio that Princess Diana had had a major car accident. After four hours I arrived to find the boys playing pokies in the pub. While putting the boat on the trailer I told them about Diana. In the truck on the way back we heard the news that Diana had died. It blew me away. We had a short discussion about it and the repercussions. The boys were soon back on their topic. I noticed at the time that they had a very narrow sense of focus and anything else was just a side issue. In the truck we had talked about safety issues – they were using everyone as sounding boards to make sure there was nothing they had missed.

When I dropped them off I realised I wouldn't see them before their departure. I said good luck and I also said remember to play it safe, it's not worth drowning for. They both spun toward me and said almost together:

"We are going there to win." It struck me that their focus was almost angry determination.

So the sea dog and the chocolate muncher (I once saw Rob eat five king-sized Moro bars in one sitting) waved goodbye and drove off into history.

*

Phil rang me first thing the next morning and said a friend of his was prepared to take me up for a flight in an aerobatic plane with the specific intention of trying to make me sick. "When you throw up," Phil said, "you can land, take some medication, get up in the air again and see if anything works."

"That's a good idea, mate." Besides, I thought, it would be another of life's experiences to add to my list of "been theres, done thats".

I met Neil Hyland that afternoon and he directed my attention to a large motor mounted on a flimsy piece of balsa wood.

"Is that it?" I asked incredulously.

"Yep," said a cheerful, confident Neil. Phil reckoned that Neil was a pretty gutsy character.

"He'd have to be, looking at this thing," I hear myself mutter sceptically.

"Pardon me?"

"Oh, ah, ... you must really enjoy this flying thing."

"Yeah, sure," he looked at me sideways.

Phil claimed that Neil was a damned good pilot. Looking again at the tiny balsa wings held together with a string mesh was of little comfort; I desperately hoped that Phil was right about Neil's flying skills. Neil had been over the Aniwhenua Falls on the Rangitaiki River, a 10 m drop into a seething cauldron of river currents. And at that time Neil had been a novice paddler! I didn't need to hear the kayak story to work out this chap was indeed courageous.

We climbed into the cockpit, sat side by side, and he pulled the plastic canopy down around us. There was nothing but a motor and a couple of propeller blades in front of me. A half bubble of "protective" plastic encapsulated us.

"Great protection."

"What was that, Rob?"

"Nothing mate, just a comment on the canopy." My comments were drowned out in metallic coughing as the engine started.

We taxied, and waited to see if the engine would stop or continue running. It farted and spluttered, or so it seemed, but it didn't stop, so we took off and climbed. I tried to relax — we both knew what I was here for — when he hit the first of a series of stalls. Basic stuff for Neil, but my guts hit my Adam's apple and my brain relocated to somewhere near my knees.

I relaxed a little more. We slipped off the horizon and I didn't have a clue where the sky was and actually it didn't feel too bad at all! Hey, a loop and the world went upside down. Cool. A barrel roll and I didn't know which way was down or up; cut the engine and we were spiralling to the ground — now I knew exactly which way was down. The engine roared into life and then I got a lesson in "G" forces. Up we rocketed. This was wicked fun!

"Thanks mate, that was awesome! Sorry I couldn't get sick. I thought that was unreal. Great!" We shook hands. I didn't get sick, didn't even feel the sensation. Damn. But, man, what great, original fun!

12.

Count Down

The future belongs to those who believe in the beauty of their dreams.
Helen Keller

WE VERY NEARLY DIDN'T get to pack off the *Kiwi Challenge* at all. Just before we were due to do so, Phil and Neil Hyland — the pilot who had failed to make me throw up — took the craft out on the Gulf at night to check the water-maker, which we still weren't 100 per cent happy with. They launched off Buckland's Beach and headed straight out, clearly lit.

Somewhere in the dark they heard the roar of a powerful outboard and then, suddenly, saw a big runabout approaching at full tilt. It was headed straight at them. At that speed the boat would have easily cut the *Challenge* in half. They screamed and waved and — at the very last moment — were spotted and the engine was cut. The two craft touched, but disaster had been avoided.

Had they been seen a couple of seconds later, our Atlantic race would have ended then and there. It was a sobering thought, and didn't help my growing fears about the myriad of things that could go wrong at sea. As my father said to a TV interviewer at the airport when we left, "The sea is very unforgiving."

*

One thing that I had seldom discussed with Phil or anyone else for that matter was the question of fear. Phil wasn't interested in the subject, or at least so he claimed, but I was. Indeed, as the time for us to leave New Zealand came closer, I thought about it more and more. I was uncomfortably aware of the fact that a disconcertingly large proportion of rowing craft that had attempted ocean journeys — around 20 per cent — had simply never been heard from again. Or, as in the case of the *Puffin*, had been found upturned and empty.

More and more the thought of drowning at sea began to worry me. And especially the fact that I would not have had the opportunity to say goodbye to my family and friends before dying. This became such a big thing in the weeks before departure that I wrote a letter to my mother reminding her of the good times and the poignant times that we had shared, sealed it and handed it to a friend for safekeeping. She was to give it to Mum if I was lost at sea.

It didn't stop there. I kept noticing things that would otherwise have passed me by. For instance, I switched on the television to see the tough and uncompromising Captain Bains from *The Onedin Line* giving the "Abandon Ship" order as the waves crashed over him. Even a *National Geographic* documentary on sharks gave me a few bad nights' sleep. I told Carolyn — who was leaving New Zealand ahead of me — about these thoughts when I farewelled her at the airport.

On arriving home that evening I switched on the radio and heard the song "Why?" by Annie Lennox. I was struck by what the familiar lyrics actually said....

*

Annie Lennox, songwriter and singer
Why can't you see this boat is sinking?
Let's go down to the water's edge
We can cast away those doubts

*

The day before we left New Zealand I went into the Air New Zealand Travel Centre in Hamilton to pay for our flights to London. The manager, Hinemoa Sharmen-Salter, had agreed to sponsor us by giving us the tickets at industry rates, a huge saving but one that still required a substantial payment. In Hinemoa's absence I spoke to Rachelle Power. When Rachelle told me we did not owe anything for the tickets I assumed a mistake had been made.

"Are you sure?" I asked, "Hinemoa told me she would do the tickets at staff rates."

"Yes I'm certain Rob," replied Rachelle, "It says right here on the computer, 'FOC — Free of Charge'."

And with that she issued our tickets.

Awesome!

The next morning I received a call from Hinemoa: "Rob, you remember yesterday how you reckoned the tickets were at staff rates and Rachelle thought they were FOCs?"

"Yes I do," I replied.

"Well, you were right."

"Oh dear, I will drop a cheque into you within the hour," I offered.

"That won't be necessary Rob. I think it is such an amazing thing you are doing that Air New Zealand will cover it this time."

Totally awesome!

We flew out mid-September 1997, less than four weeks to the race start. Seasickness was still a formidable opponent. Some expert sea-sickers reckon there are two stages that you pass through: the first is when you think you are going to die: the second is when you fear that you won't. I haven't felt like that. I've felt bloody uncomfortable and I couldn't row very well when I was being sick. Phil suggested a last throw of the dice.

Erich Brosel, a German millionaire, wished to emigrate to Tasmania. Rather than just fly, he wanted to sail his own boat to Tassie — not your normal everyday migrant was Erich. But he needed crew. Dave and Sonya Stubbs, Phil's father and stepmother, Phil and muggins here were Erich's crew. The not-too-subtle plan was to cross the North Sea in autumn from Denmark to Scotland, a rough stretch of water at any time, so that I could try to gain my sea legs, or at least attempt to find a cure for my motion sickness.

So we four turned up in Denmark and boarded the magnificent ketch *Holga Danske* in Svendborg, Denmark. For several days we travelled between the Danish islands in the Baltic Sea, getting the feel of *Holga Danske* and her sails before coming to port in Middelfart. I kid you not! Middelfart is a quaint fishing village squeezed between the island of Fyn and Jutland, the mainland.

We then headed for the Kattegart, north to Langerak and through the inland waterways of the Limfjorden. The westerly wind was on the nose going through the Limfjorden, and the vessel motored by the impressive wind farms to port, 100 windmills at least, probably more. Each windmill generator had huge white blades slowly, silently scything air. It was an interesting compromise between visual pollution and environmentally friendly electricity. The spectacle certainly made me think of Don Quixote and I posted a short reminder in my brain. No tilting at windmills for us, focus on the task, and forget the peripheral.

*

After school, I was usually in the dinghy or on my surfboard trying to catch the perfect right-hander off the Whakatane Heads, which was famous amongst surfers in New Zealand. If I was nowhere to be found during school hours, the chances were you would find me, and a few mates, sitting out the back on our surfboards waiting for the mother of all waves.

If I wasn't in or on the water then I was climbing the steep hills behind our home. Often I would get home from school ravenous with hunger, stuff my mouth full of food then scramble to the top of the ridge. I never timed myself but imagined each time I was going faster and faster and the time to reach the summit was getting less and less.

*

We left Denmark from the small coastal port of Thyboron and headed straight for Scotland across the North Sea. Some of the locals suggested we wait a little longer for the sea to calm down, but we had had enough motoring through buoys and were keen to get on the open sea. I knew my stomach was in for a genuine test. I thought it was rather an unfair tactic when Erich prepared a lunch of rich German sausages and coffee. But we were under way.

Just outside the Thyboron bar we took a series of waves that sprayed over the whole yacht and they set the tone for the following 12 hours. Nevertheless the *Holga Danske* handled the rough, rolling seas with grace and aplomb, but it was a bumpy, turbulent ride. The bow rose through the oncoming swells and down into the following trough, rising rapidly time and again through the next swell crest. The sea was a cold, unfriendly grey-blue. The wind from the north was catching us on the starboard and she rolled well, very well. After half an hour I began to feel my German sausages!

Surprisingly, Erich made a quick movement to the port railing and expertly threw up! I went below deck where I felt most comfortable. Two hours later I was called up for a four-hour shift at the helm. Cool fun, but the mast's movement in relation to the sea was definitely affecting me. I felt my temperature rise quickly, and a period of burping heralded the inevitable before my stomach inverted itself and then it was I flashing to the port rail and hanging on. What a waste of lunch. Oh dear, there was more coming. After making close acquaintance with a particular stretch of railing for a few minutes or so, I felt better and went below. As I returned through the galley there was Erich, a small cup of water in one hand, a pill in the other. It was a German-made anti-nausea preparation known as Rodavan.

"Take this!" he commanded.

I wasn't going to argue with Erich. I drank and went out on deck. Erich followed.

"You must have something to throw away. Then you immediately take your medicine. Now you should be right." Erich reasoned.

An hour later I still felt okay — not wonderful, but okay. Two hours, the same. Four hours later I had a light tea and was able to sleep comfortably when I came off watch. Hey, this was feeling promising! I enjoyed looking at the huge North Sea oil rigs, some of them real slabs of villages on skinny legs sticking into the sea, others with flares with black smoke trailing rapidly towards the south. Slowly I began to enjoy my first offshore yachting experience. Thanks, Stubbsie. Thanks, Erich. It worked! The last apprehension relating to the challenge of the Atlantic seemed to have been solved. Again I looked forward with confidence.

On reaching Peterhead, Erich gave us each a legionnaire-style sun hat.

"You'll be needing these!"

Quite unexpectedly Phil chose the blue. Now, who would have expected a cop to choose blue? Mine was red. We would use them at the start of the race, both to celebrate finding my sea legs and because they were damned useful.

In England I went looking for some Rodavan but couldn't find any. I would have to rely on my Paihia Pharmacy medicine.

13.

Los Gigantes

Carpe diem, quam minimum credula postero.
Seize the day, and put the least possible trust in tomorrow.
Horace ODES I. xi

WE FLEW FROM GATWICK on the southern outskirts of London on one of those red-eye tourist flights that cram one more day into a package holiday by leaving around 10 at night and arrive, wherever, before breakfast. Mind you, Phil got little or no sleep during the flight due to the magnetism of a good-looking air hostess who seemed almost equally distracted by him. Every time I glanced up there was Phil's wide grin and the hostess' enormous eyes with huge lashes fluttering the night away. Mind you, my sleep patterns weren't much better. I slept fitfully, anxious about our boat, anxious to begin this race.

We touched down in Tenerife in the Canary Islands at about 5 a.m. on the morning of October 2, 1997, much to my relief and probably Phil's disappointment on bidding goodbye to the cabin crew. Tenerife is approximately 216 miles out into the mid-Atlantic, well off the coast of Morocco. It was warm and sultry, an hour before dawn. Daniel Byles, the youngest competitor in the race at 23, was at the airport in the gloom to meet us and drive us to the west coast village of Los Gigantes, where we were to be based initially.

To get there from the airport you can choose either a coastal route or an inland journey. The coastal route trails along a volcanic coastline a little similar to a dry summer cross between Paekakariki and Punakaiki on the west coast of New Zealand. The inland road climbs the flanks of El Tiede. This is an imposing 3700 m high volcanic mountain with roads that wind through tortured volcanic lava flows, layers of ash and rocks, not dissimilar to the northern valleys of the Desert Road of the North Island, and then back down a steep road to Los Gigantes. Dan choose the coastal route.

During the drive Dan cheerfully updated us on two other entries. *Key Challenger* and *Cellnet Atlantic Challenger* had been in Tenerife for more than two weeks already. They were big-budget campaigns where nothing had been spared. For example, one boat had a Landrover flown in to assist their preparation. Dan reckoned these two crews had put a lot of work into their preparation and looked sharp. My stomach knotted slightly as I felt the excitement rise up through the haze of my insomnia-induced state. I had felt this many, many times during this project but never as powerfully as now.

*

Apart from his youthfulness the other remarkable thing about Dan was that he was preparing to row the Atlantic with his mum! Jan Meek, a former mayor of a small English village, had been widowed several years previously and was looking for a challenge. When her son's original rowing partner pulled out he had suggested she take his place. Her first reaction was to ring her doctor and ask if she was fit enough. He had replied that she was — with some serious training. The 52-year-old, 1.63 m Jan had acted with aplomb while her women friends looked on in amazement.

Later, when one of the sponsors asked her what would happen if the race was cancelled, she had flashed him her winning smile and said, "We've got the boat. We've got the Atlantic, and we're going!" As you will have gathered, Jan was vivacious, bubbly, full of beans and a great help. She had offered us accommodation in Los Gigantes until we secured our own. Over the past months she had been a great contact in the UK, providing information, gossip and contact with other rowers in this adventure.

Dan and Jan's boat was named *Carpe Diem*, Latin for "seize the day". It certainly reflected their positive attitude. Shortly before we left, Jan showed us their boat. Apart from being very heavily loaded, their oars were hopeless. They were far too long and would never have made the journey. We told Jan this and she immediately rang her partner in England and ordered up some shorter ones. He said to her, "You've been at this for two years. Why didn't you think of this before?" She replied, "I'll tell you later."

*

Some athletes thrive on the feeling of anticipation before the start of an event and some hate it. For me it is a mixture of the two. I love the element of competition, of going into battle. That unknown quantity, the opposition, can cause huge emotional swings and roundabouts. If one visualises a negative result such as being beaten at the finish, the resultant anxiety causes considerable distress. If one imagines victory, especially against the odds, the emotion becomes euphoric.

Personally, I prefer the latter pre-race thoughts. However, in previous world championship and Olympic rowing regattas I found it was the waiting in the final moments that I hated most. As the days tick down to hours and finally minutes the pre-race tension can become unbearable. Relaxation techniques help: feel the tension flick out the tips of your fingers; deep breaths releasing anxiety with each exhalation; focusing on the positive result, feeling happy and confident.

The sheer audacity of the Atlantic race was the excitement. In talking to people in New Zealand I had frequently used the phrase, "3000 miles, 2 people, 1 boat". Now we two were at the starting point in Tenerife, the ocean was waiting, our boat would be here in two days, the tribulations of the past year had been overcome. The waiting was over. Our reason for entering was really very simple. Both Phil and I had a burning ambition to win this unique endurance race. Rowing in the race certainly was a desire, but the real fire, the real passion we both possessed, was to win!

*

Robert Whitaker, crew member, *The Golden Fleece*, November 1999
I remember when Phil had left his bike about 10 miles away in Tenerife, baking hot. I said to him, "Do you want a lift over there?" And he said, "No, no. It's all right, mate, I'll run." I said to Dan, "Bloody hell!" And I thought, "That guy is a nutter!" He said things in a determined way and initially when you first met him you thought, "Gosh, that was really brash." But in the end that wasn't brash at all, it was just him and the belief in what he was doing. He wasn't one to mess around.

*

Los Gigantes is an alluring place. The name means the "the giants" and refers to the huge precipitous cliffs butting into the Atlantic. One hundred metres high and dark ochre red and black, they plunge into the dark azure blue of the Atlantic. Inland the terrain rises quickly and higher again, there are rocky, dry, barren, volcanic slopes. You get the feeling these west coast towns are tolerated by nature only until the next volcanic outburst or vicious ocean storm. Tucked into a kink in the coast is the beachless resort town of Los Gigantes, a pleasant mix of Spanish old and tourist new.

Brilliant flowering red bougainvillea contrasts sharply with narrow streets fronted by whitewashed, solid, windowless concrete walls of the inward-facing Spanish houses. There are craggy-faced old men with 48-hour stubble and resplendent in classic 1920s-style white straw hats, 1950s jackets and worn, tough, go-anywhere black trousers and boots. Mamas dressed in featureless black with wide-brimmed floppy hats gracefully angled on their proud heads, walk painfully up the hill, canes in their hands, slowly and deliberately.

The Los Gigantes-Sol, the imposing 200-room four-star tourist hotel, was tailored to the steep mountain slope; each suite, with its private balcony, crept up the hill like double chins creep on a wealthy neck. From the hotel everything is sharply downhill. In a couple of days we had found an apartment near the marina downhill from the Los Gigantes-Sol.

The marina, where the boats would be moored and from where the race was to begin, was immediately north of our hotel. It was about the size of the Taupo boat harbour, three pontoon wharves wide with an impressive west-east artificial breakwater with huge concrete blocks that reflected a sophisticated engineering accomplishment. Close to the towering cliffs on the eastern side of the breakwater was the narrow marina entrance.

But first things first. We fell down the hill and set out to explore the village, meet the race organisers and hopefully some of our fellow rowers. We were looking for groups of two or three people but, as we were unable to identify any walking around, we called in on the race organisers.

Teresa Evans had been my main contact with The Challenge Business over the last 13 months. She was ever helpful, cheerful, efficient. I now learned that she was also youthful and pretty. She and her associate Alison Smith were in stark contrast to race supremo Sir Chay Blyth. Chay — while not being tall — was solid with a shock of white hair, and had a presence about him that said, "State your business and get on with it, laddie." He was open to suggestion, listened well, but didn't tolerate fools easily. I was still in awe of Chay.

14.

Harbour Lites

Men often compete with one another until the day they die; comradeship consists of rubbing shoulders jocularly with a competitor.
Edward Hoagland

THAT AFTERNOON, CLAD IN shorts, singlet and shoes, we began exploring the area surrounding Los Gigantes. At first we scrambled up a hill covered with loose rocks, small cactus plants and straw grass. Rocks slipped away underfoot as I followed Phil up the craggy slope. At the top of the small hill we turned left and headed for a more intimidating slope. At first the incline was gentle but soon turned steep — reminding me of my school days climbing in the hills behind home — and our running speed slowed.

We had run many hills in training back in New Zealand and then as now Phil struggled to carry his muscular 93-kg frame upwards. I passed him and continued up until I could run no longer, the rocks becoming larger and more jagged. We scrambled through the rocky ruins, running along intricate, weaving, crossing paths in a maze-like pattern.

Twenty minutes later we emerged on a ridge that overlooked the village and the enigma that was the Atlantic. Of course the Atlantic stretched to and over the horizon, and we just stood, chests heaving, dragging in air, examining our adversary. At that moment the ocean was calm, a low sun reflecting off its surface, looking eminently conquerable. I briefly wondered what confrontations we would have. But Phil was off again along the ridge so we ran a few kilometres more before turning and retracing our steps. We arrived home at dusk, puffed out but pleased to have cleared a few cobwebs.

The Challenge Business informed us that the unofficial centre for the English contingent was a local pub called the Harbour Lites, located directly opposite the marina. So that is where we headed for dinner. It was a typical English pub, hosted by an English couple, Steve and Gail. Already there were plenty of signs that the Brits had made it their home.

A map from the *Salamanca* crew, UK Army captains Martin Bellamy and Mark Mortimer, tickled my fancy. "First here" — an arrow indicating Tenerife, "First there" — another arrow pointing to Barbados. Good, positive thinking, *Salamanca*. Mind you, they had good reason to be confident. They had been granted a year's leave to prepare and take part in the race, and as part of their preparation they had spent several months training in the Mediterranean. Lucky devils.

*

Sponsors' T-shirts were clearly in evidence and there was a fair bit of partying going on. We joked that it was sleep deprivation practice that we were engaged in. Joking aside, it was not unlike the last-minute drinking of soldiers about to leave for the battle front. None of us knew what lay ahead.

We met club rowers from Exeter, Neil Hitt and Peter Hogden, (their boat was the *Hospicare*), Dorset firemen Steve Isaacs and Mark Stubbs (*TocH Phoenix*), a husband-and-wife team, David and Nadia Rice (*Hannah Snell*), Middlesex policemen Roger Gould and Charlie Street (*Sam Deacon*), Norwegians Arvid Bentsen and Stein Hoff (*Star Atlantic*) and a real character in Graham Walters (*The George Gearry*). The Brits had a lot in common as many had previously met at The Challenge Business functions in the United Kingdom. They were a sociable lot and supported one another well.

*

While out strolling before brunch the next morning I spotted the army lads from the *Salamanca* entry. They were noticeable by their absence from the pre-race gatherings and the rumour was that they were not talking or socialising with any of the opposition. I doubted this to be true. So when I saw them step out of their Landrover, I seized my moment and stepped forward to introduce myself.

Their response was polite and brief. Obviously, more important things awaited. They climbed back into their vehicle and drove off. Their attitude seemed typical of what mine had been in my early years as a rower. On race day I had thought a prerequisite to success was to scorn the opposition, to ignore them and treat them with complete disdain in the belief that somehow that would improve my performance. I would turn up at the regatta, fire snorting from each nostril, ready to eat the enemy before the first stroke was taken.

Over time I realised that such an attitude did very little to improve my results. I learned that it was important to control those factors that I could control and not be concerned with those that I could not. Interestingly, I was soon to discover that the *Salamanca* crew were pleasant, determined guys, just like the other crews. The most important factor I could control was me. I had discovered the fact that my performance was dependent solely on how well I had prepared long before race day and believed it was no different with the *Kiwi Challenge*.

Preparation was everything and no amount of eyeballing at this late stage was going to change that.

*

Roger Gould, *Sam Deacon*

As each crew arrived during the next couple of days, the bar games grew more and more "manly". Silly things like who can lift up the bar stool by the base of one leg? Who can do handstand press-ups? Who can do one-handed handstands? Duncan Nicol from *Mount Gay Rum Runner* and his girlfriend Nettie even took the time and trouble to organise a replica boat race on a tea tray. They filled it with water and placed a cork with a cocktail stick and sail afloat for each team. Each sail had a team's name on it. At one side of the tray they had put a sign, Tenerife. At the other side another, Barbados. Simple rules. Stand on the side of the tray saying Tenerife, and BLOW your boat to Barbados. The tension mounted as the crews gathered around the small table holding the tray. Nettie was the starter. She held her hand aloft. Everyone crouched down close to the tray to get a real good BLOW.

"On your marks! Ready! GO!!"

And she slapped her hand down into the water, soaking everyone in sight! We all put on our donkeys' ears and drank another beer!

*

Wow! Early evening beers at the Harbour Lites. The pub was almost always full of laughter. Roger Gould would be setting up Steven Isaacs, Duncan Nicol would be engineering a practical joke. It was a good thing that Duncan had a sense of humour and did not take offence easily.

It was Duncan's girlfriend, Nettie, who had staged the mock Atlantic race and given the crews their first dunking of the contest. Eight years before Duncan had been in love with a young English dragon-boater who had gone out to Malaysia to compete. While there she had met Sgt Philip Stubbs from the New Zealand Police who was determined to uphold the honour of his nation.

Her name was — and I imagine you have guessed it — Kate Cumper and she and Phil had become partners for four years. Now she was part of both their pasts and they had great fun jousting each other over her, but in more sober moments both spoke of her with great affection. I would have liked to have met Kate.

*

The barge from Falmouth carrying our precious boats arrived the following day. The port of San Juan was 5.4 miles south of Los Gigantes. Here port cranes dot the wharf's edge, both of them. The ferry to the nearby island of Gomera arrives and leaves, and boats fishing for tuna and other wet fish, octopus and squid are based here; but today all our interest centred on the cargo carried by the barge. Crews silently appraised one another's boats. They were unloaded using a double sling under them and their accompanying cradle, then they were lifted ashore.

The boats were parked 20 m from the wharf, sterns snug against the solid concrete wall marking the port boundary. We completed a quick inspection of our boat, and once again it was fine.

The Golden Fleece of Rob Whitaker and Daniel Innes had a slight ding on the starboard side, but they weren't too worried and were busy preparing their damaged hull for fibreglassing. Theirs was the only boat to suffer any damage, although Victoria Murden and Louise Graff — the only all-women crew — were anxious rowers for a few moments. Their boat, *American Pearl*, had come directly from the United States to the larger port of Santa Cruz and then by road to San Juan. It was crated for protection but when the driver came to unload the crate it was too heavy for the mobile crane.

In an attempt to solve the problem by opening the crate so that a sling could be attached to the boat, a resourceful Canarian labourer came up with a chain saw. Before Victoria could say "Oh my God!" the crate was sliced, but perhaps more by good luck than good management the *Pearl* was unharmed.

*

Ranulph Fiennes, *Mind over Matter*

An expedition's aim is best achieved by individuals who can look after themselves, need little or no directing or nursing, and are tough in body and mind.

*

One of the things that I noticed in Tenerife was that while some of the rowers worked as equals — sharing the decision making — as Phil and I would do, others actually had a skipper who would take the lead role. Peter Haining, the only other competitor with an international rowing background, was clearly going to make the decisions on *Walter Scott & Partners*. It seemed to me at the time that this was unnecessary. An ocean liner needed a captain, but a two-man rowing boat didn't. It went against my sense of Kiwi equality.

Mind you, I must have thought that I was in charge of the pre-race organisation at least. For instance, I had decided that we would both definitely take worm tablets before we set sail. That was a must. I didn't think I had worms but I wasn't taking any chances. All energy-sucking parasites were banned from boarding the *Challenge*.

*

Rebecca Hayter, *Boating NZ* editor, January 2000

Before the race, I asked both of you who would be skipper and you both gave the same answer: "Well, we're even but if it comes down to it, I'll be skipper!"

*

As Phil and I arrived at the starting venue, we were far more focused than we had been in the early stages. We were particularly concerned by what I will call "the unknowns". These broadly centred around three factors: the boat, the rowers and the sea. The boats were all of the same kitset design, many being built by the crews themselves, but they were tiny craft only 7 m long. Second, crews would have to co-exist on these tiny craft for 50–90 days and this was expected to be a trial in itself.

But the greatest unknown was the Atlantic Ocean. Only one person in the race, Frenchman Joseph Le Guen, had rowed the Atlantic. The rest, including both of us, were ocean-rowing novices. For over 400 years mariners had gathered a considerable body of knowledge as to what to expect from this area of the Atlantic. But there was nothing on how these boats could be expected to react to the ocean and no way of knowing how we as individuals would react to the mix of ocean, rowing and each other.

The question of how I would interact with Phil at sea was obviously one that I had pondered long and hard. Joseph Le Guen — massive, bald and heavily moustached — had no doubt done the same, but — unlike myself who had chosen a clean-cut policeman to row with — he had settled on a double murderer! Pascal Blond had recently been released from a French jail after serving 14 years for killing two men in bar room brawls; one with his fists and the other with a knife.

Anyone for a drink?

15.

The Craft

Boats at a distance have every man's wish on board.
Zora Neale Hurston

THANKFULLY OUR BOAT HAD arrived in excellent condition and that was a huge relief for me. At first I was amazed at the gulf in quality between boats. Some had superb paint jobs, colourful, stylish, high quality finish, and sophisticated equipment; such as one with a miniaturised hydraulic steering system. Collectively they certainly looked like the Rolls-Royces of ocean rowing boats. In part the superb finish came from a wrapping of kevlar and fibreglass around the hull, both to strengthen and protect the boats.

At first glance this was all very intimidating. Our boat was so basic. At the other end of the spectrum, a few boats were rough and poorly finished, had patchy paint applied by hand, over built riggers and bulky seats. Notwithstanding this, after a little reflection and re-examination of the boats there, the intimidation faded and the excitement rose inside me. Though some were wonderfully made it was apparent that the core philosophy of some crews was misplaced. After all, an adventure boat is very different from a racing boat.

A few boats had all manner of set-ups and toys: stereo systems, a silver foil-insulated cabin with air conditioning units and miniature refrigerated drink bottle units in the stern well. But for many the rowing set-up looked odd somehow; the rowing ratios for ocean rowing didn't seem correct.

The two main factors appeared to be overly long oars and fulcrum points, the "rowing gates", set too far out from the hull. This could make cross-sea rowing very difficult. By cross-seas I mean when the seas are coming at the boat from differing angles at the same time, and the water on either side of the boat is at different heights and moving in different directions. We expected cross-sea conditions like this most days, therefore shorter oars and rowing gates closer to you would make for better, easier rowing.

A couple of the immaculately finished boats had stainless steel bowsprit protectors moulded to the shape of the bow and a solid core of timber inside going back 30 cm. It could probably cut a container open, or break ice floes. The crew, though, were anything but kamikaze pilots. So I ambled up to one of the support crew and casually said, "G'day, mate. Do you think the stainless steel bow might be a bit of overkill?"

"Well, tell me this Kiwi, what is stopping the bow of your boat from splitting open right now?"

"Okay, no trouble, just asking."

I backed off. If we hit a container we would be in trouble, otherwise I hadn't foreseen such a problem with the seas. I felt his reaction was defensive and so I moved on.

The rest of the day I cruised about chatting to the rowers about their boats. The atmosphere was friendly, even buoyant, our competitors welcoming. There were loads of characters. Take, for example, Graham Walters, a carpenter from Leicester. Graham had collected his kitset only two months ago. Here he was complete with saw and hammer in hand still building his boat, *The George Gearry*. The first coat of paint was still tacky and while that was drying he was working out the best set-up for the rowing positions.

Graham had yet to fit any of the major items of equipment, including solar panels, compass and electrical system. I tried to offer whatever assistance I could. The enormity of the task facing this likeable man with the broad accent made me feel quite feeble and inadequate. However, I did manage to convince him that fitting a water desalinator would be a good idea. He was considering carrying all of his water across the Atlantic with him, the same way previous ocean rowing crossings had been achieved. This, I politely suggested, was not the way to provision with water this time. Though it was perilous to rely on this kind of equipment, one had to do so if you were going to have any chance of winning.

*

Keith Mason-Moore, crew member, *The George Gearry*, November 1999
The boat shell met the deadline for Tenerife, followed shortly after by Graham and three close friends who had been working on the flat-pack since it had arrived in Leicester. I was still making arrangements for the add-on bits and pieces, such as oars, rowlocks, life-jackets, food, medical kit, charts and just about everything else that we needed for the journey.

I arrived at Heathrow six days before the start date and over 250 kg overweight (which the airline charged me for), but I was on the way. I was about to see the results of Graham and his boat-building team's endeavours from the previous two weeks: some progress had been made but still a miracle was needed. The rowing stations and sliding seats had yet to be fitted to the deck, the rowlocks attached to the gunwales, the rudder to the stern – the list was endless. Onlookers could not believe that we were a part of the same race!

Chay's team of scrutinisers over-viewed our progress in disbelief. Often I arrived on site to witness fellow rowers giving a hand in an attempt to get us ever closer to the water. None could believe it would happen.

*

Another interesting character was Robert Whitaker. He was a club rower, coach and teacher. We hit it off straight away. Mind you, his rich sense of humour and non-stop, lighthearted banter made it difficult for anyone not to like him. He even showed me his secret weapon: his dog's stainless steel feeding bowls had been recessed into the gunwale walls and converted to house stereo speakers. These speakers were located either side of the rower.

Robert mentioned that he had three objectives that made up what he called the "golden triangle". First, he wanted to survive. Second, he wanted to finish. And third, having taken care of the first two objectives, he would have a crack at winning. To me that attitude seemed overly conservative. The first two objectives seemed to typify the attitude of the fleet. It was fair enough to think that way. Of course one wanted to finish safely but that priority seemed to override the fact that this was a race.

The most profound impression of the fleet was that not a single craft — other than our own — seemed to have been built with a view to keeping weight to a minimum. I wondered if the same philosophy applied to other aspects of their preparation, such as food, and to the few remaining boats I had yet to see.

That evening at the hotel I was excited. Phil listened as I blurted this bunch of information on what the other boats were like and in my haste I guess I was a little incoherent. After about four minutes I paused for a breath.

"So what d'ya think, Phil?"

A long pause as Phil gathered his thoughts.

"Mate, we're gonna win this race."

I couldn't help but smile.

"Damned right we're gonna win this bloody race."

*

It was now October 4, eight days until the start. On the hard at San Juan, Tenerife, Phil wandered around the boats with me. He agreed with my earlier assessment, but also he was concerned about the rudders. A number of them were very long and had differing shapes outside what we both thought the race class rules prescribed. The rudder length was important because as a boat is lifted by the following waves the boat's stern comes out of the water and in the case of our boat, so did the rudder. This meant that for a brief period the boat had little directional guidance.

Phil vowed to make a longer spare rudder so we could match the control exerted by the rudders on display. One of his greatest strengths was the manner in which he unstintingly carried out the tough and tedious tasks that I would instinctively shy away from. I never once heard him complain.

Another thing was obvious. A few boats had keels, and one in particular had two fins, much like the secondary fins on a surfboard. Several boats had solid structures on top of their boats to support radar reflectors and aerials for radio communication. The general consensus was that these structures were unnecessarily large for their purpose.

The deepened keels also caught my interest because of the possible effect on minimising the sideways drift of the boat in side weather conditions. I thought the keel might aid the tracking of the boat. I discussed this with one or two other crews who were making preparations to add 7.5–10 cm of keel. Phil and I discussed the issue at great length and in the end I came around to Phil's way of thinking that such additions were unnecessary. In this case it was better to focus on the rudder only and he immediately set about sourcing materials to build it.

*

Normally there was great frivolity in the Harbour Lites. But tonight the mood was flat. The Brits had noted the fins on the new boat *Atlantik Challenge*, Joseph Le Guen and Pascal Blond's French entry. There were as many opinions on whether or not the fins would help the boat as there were hands on handles of beer. Some were scheming to match the French and attach fins while wiser heads were counselling a meeting with Sir Chay Blyth and an examination of the rules.

The Challenge Business set up a meeting for the crews. Sir Chay was obviously aware of the feeling in the competitor community. At this meeting, all sorts of accusations flew regarding the legality of the underwater appendages, especially the keels and fins. Then came questions about the above-water appendages, namely the masts.

Someone even suggested that the real reason for all of the structures was to aid the potential for cheating. This did not go down well with Chay Blyth who immediately stopped any further discussion by saying that if it were a sailing race then it would have been organised as such. He resented anyone suggesting the likelihood of cheating and said that the mind-set of suspicion alone was not a good way to go into such an event. People, he said, were entering a rowing race and a rowing race it would be.

He later delivered two very clear but contentious rulings. First, all boats would stay as they had arrived in Tenerife; that meant the *Atlantik Challenge*'s fins stayed. Second, he explicitly said this also clearly meant that no new appendages could be added to boats. Nobody was to have fins or tiny keels put on their boat. Chay also thought many rowers were overly concerned about the race, as opposed to the adventure. That surprised me. I think he had misjudged the emphasis and priorities in some competitors' motivation.

Phil was one of those that felt an injustice had been done. He rose to speak, no dramatics, just a quiet Kiwi accent. "Chay, I think this ruling is unfair. The fins could easily be ground off, then all the boats would have the same hulls. I am annoyed with your ruling and am of the opinion that frankly you couldn't organise a piss-up in a brewery!"

This outburst seemed to echo for a long time.

Chay took it in his stride, and both rulings stood.

*

For our part Phil had already decided that rudders were the issue for us. He had begun work on a spare rudder for our boat and we felt, as this addition was under way before the meeting, Chay's ruling didn't apply in this particular case. If it was acceptable for some rudders to be 30 cm longer than ours, we would carry a 30 cm longer replacement rudder for use when we struck following seas in the trade wind belt. So, we were able to participate in discussions with a little bit of detachment and later as the beer flowed at the Harbour Lites we thought the tensions had subsided, the jesting and laughter returned and the Brits were back to their true form.

Other Brits offered a different kind of camaraderie. Dr Carl Clinton who would partner John Searson on *Commodore Shipping* offered to give people suturing lessons (you know, stitching fleshy wounds). John and Carl were big guys from Jersey in the Channel Islands and were prime competitors. John is a meteorologist. Both had sea experience and had rowed in the Guernsey-to-Jersey races.

We missed that session but Phil assured me he was expert in the art of stitching! Should he himself need stitches he would talk me through the procedure, no worries at all.

*

Steve Isaacs, *TocH Phoenix*

Dr Carl Clinton from *Commodore Shipping* offered to give people suturing lessons in Los Gigantes a week before the race started. We didn't take up the offer because we had already had our [lesson] under the despairing eye of our team doctor before leaving the UK.

We had spent a day making a complete pig's ear of a pig's foot as we attempted to at least gain a basic proficiency in the surgeon's art.

We tried desperately to pull together the loose pieces of pig flesh and hold them together with neat little stitches tied off with delicate little knots, untouched by unclean human hands just as we were being taught.

Unfortunately our ham-fisted attempts resulted in no more than a table full of broken needles, a proliferation of granny knots and a lot of reassuring conversations eliminating the likelihood that anything requiring stitches could ever happen to us.

By the time we'd finished you wouldn't have let either of us darn your socks, let alone come near your head with a needle and thread, but we were okay because we knew if we were careful there was no earthly reason why we would ever need to practise our new skills or expose the lack of them. Poor deluded souls that we were.

I was also adamant that, even if for some unforeseen reason the unthinkable should happen, I would take full responsibility and do any patchworking I required myself.

This was not because I had any real faith in my own ability to perform a neat cross-stitch but simply that I'd seen the damage Mark could do with a pointed object. He was an ex-marine after all, trained to kill with his bare hands. Give him a weapon and carnage was sure to follow.

All in all, that day was one of the lightest moments of our preparations. We were in tears by the end of the day. If we'd known then how soon in the race we would need to put into practice what we'd had such fun trying to learn, I don't think we would have been laughing quite as much!

*

To break away from the race hype, Eduardo (Eddie to us) Brynnel — another flight attendant from our flight out — arrived to take us all out to dinner. He wanted to take us away from the rowing milieu and down the coast further south to Los Christanos.

"You must be alert to the winds between Tenerife, Gomera, and El Hierro. (Gomera and El Hierro were the two neighbouring islands pointing the way to the open Atlantic). The winds here along the south coast of Tenerife are magnificent for board-sailing, but would be bad for you."

"Yes, but we are going south-west away from this coast," said Phil.

'Si, but the mountain will still push the winds between the islands and the seas will be rough. I would stay away from all three islands, you could get caught in the current or a wind change, and then … ", the Spanish shrug of fatalism.

"Phil," I interrupted Eddie at half-shrug, "do you remember that conversation I had with Peter Blake? He mentioned then to be wary of the acceleration zone around the Canaries. This is what Eddie is talking about."

"… about a boat for the start?"

"Sorry, what was that, Eddie?"

A quick smile.

"Would you like me to organise a boat to take your friends to the start line?"

"We sure would, Eddie. Great idea, thanks."

Later he would also fix us up not only with a watch that told the time but also with a compass, barometer, thermometer and altimeter. The latter would — we joked — come in useful for indicating the size of the wave we were to surf, based on our altitude. Eddie was now well and truly one of our shore-based team.

16. Mutiny

Do you remember the tale of the girl who saves the ship under mutiny by sitting on the powder barrel with her lighted torch ... all the time knowing it is empty?
Isak Dinesen SEVEN GOTHIC TALES

THE NEXT MORNING PHIL was busy at work putting the finishing touches to the spare rudder. Unfortunately there wasn't any hardwood available so he made do with marine ply. The rudder was taking a few days to complete.

While Phil was on the production line, I went off to the airport to collect Bror Muller, a long-time rowing buddy with a great sense of humour who had come to help with last-minute onshore jobs. Bror was famous for his love of a good time. He and I visited the boats at San Juan where I showed him the "revised" silhouettes of our competitors while expressing my concern about the shifting goalposts of the boat building rules. We then visited *Kiwi Challenge* and spent most of the day repacking the holds.

The prime reason was to rearrange vacuum sealed daily food rations. Before leaving New Zealand Phil had gone over our route and calculated four key way points that constituted the most direct route to Barbados, provided that the expected wind and sea conditions were true. The distance of this route was calculated, then divided by the average daily distance that we had achieved in training. Finally he added in a factor for adverse weather conditions which we could expect.

This had given him what he thought would be the number of days we would take to complete the crossing. Phil's figure was 50 days. This we kept to ourselves. We had food for 75 days and had decided that we would keep this amount on board, at least until we got under way and then could reconsider our position in the light of the distance we were making under actual race conditions. The repacking was to ensure that any dumping we did at sea would maintain the balance and trim of both our diet and the boat.

*

That night we were in party mode again. The bars in Los Gigantes were packed with people and humming. Loads of British and German holidaymakers were there catching the end of summer and we simply merged with them and had a great time sampling the beers of Europe. We might have sampled a few twice over for, although it was easy to fall into town from our apartment, it was a necessity to fall into a taxi to get us home again in the wee hours of the morning.

I had this idea that the journey would lead to a life-long friendship with Phil. That we would be totally committed to each other by the end of the race, like the closest of brothers — where one would drop everything at any time to come to the other's aid should he be called upon. I told both him and Bror about this one night. Phil ridiculed the idea. Bror agreed, saying, "Na, fuck off, Rob. You guys are going there to win this race, not to kiss each other."

We really relaxed in Tenerife. It was as if a weight had come off our shoulders in finally making the starting line. As a consequence we were effectively training for the inevitable sleep deprivation that we were soon to encounter for real on the ocean. The difference being that here in Tenerife we were having a flaming good time in the process.

*

Late the next morning we needed some fresh air and exercise. So Phil and I drove up the flanks of Mount El Tiede and went for a two and a half hour run up towards the caldera rim and back. It was a gruelling, tiring slog but most enjoyable, many many miles away from people. Just Phil and myself, rocks, little alpine plants and shrubs. There wasn't a lot of oxygen up there and we were really blowing hard, but the run, similar to a high-country run in Central Otago in late summer, again cleared my head (and bloodstream) and definitely lifted my spirits.

*

Once we had readied our boats at San Juan they were to move up the coast to the Los Gigantes marina. The problem was that there weren't enough berths available and we couldn't afford to pay the asking price for any that were.

The solution to our problem came in the form of Ferry van Veldhoven, who ran the local car dealership. Ferry quietly accepted us at face value and let us use his berth. All he asked in return was to put a small sign on our boat. And to try and help to look for his lost brother who he thought might be in New Zealand. He eventually found him in Auckland, no thanks to us!

One evening Bror and I were having a meal at a sidewalk café when Ferry happened to walk by. He came over and quietly chatted, and asked how our preparations were going and if there was anything he could help with. He then quietly and inconspicuously placed more than sufficient cash on the table to pay for our meals. "The meal is on me boys, enjoy your evening." Unobtrusively he turned and walked off down the street.

*

We were now free to move our boat from the hard at San Juan to the new marina at Los Gigantes, a row of nearly 4 nautical miles. Phil and I rowed together comfortably, concentrating on our rhythm, timing and technique; this was a little difficult with such stupendous scenery. Those west coast cliffs of Tenerife really are awesome when viewed from sea level in a little row boat travelling at just a few knots. At the time of day that we rowed they were a little in shadow, a layered dark looming over our left shoulders. From my position they just seemed to go on up and then further up, then way up there was a clear blue sky.

Adjacent to the cliffs you look directly over the side through incredibly clear, turquoise deep water. Lift your eyes and the ocean is an opaque blue at any other angle. The air temperature was in the high twenties with a two-metre swell and a fairly stiff head wind. I was enjoying the row, but couldn't stop thinking, "This is all a little surreal." It was captivating, the light amazing, the contrasts vivid, yet we were only a few days away from this race which we knew would be extremely demanding, tiring and testing of our limits. The contradictions pushed in on my mind.

"Bloody hell."

"What's that, Rob? You talking to yourself again?"

"No, no. Just thinking about the race next week."

"Forget it, the race will come soon enough, mate."

*

On leaving San Juan harbour we spied a lone figure watching from the breakwater. I didn't know at the time that it was Jock Wishart, partner of Duncan Nicol and a hardened adventurer. Later at the Harbour Lites Jock confided to a group over a beer that he had observed the way we were rowing, the way the boat was reacting, and stated that the *Kiwi Challenge* was looking pretty sharp and was going to be indeed that, a challenge to the fleet. I was in that group. Jock looked straight into my eyes, but I didn't respond. I drank my beer in silence, not particularly wanting others to concentrate on our prospects.

Not so Peter Haining, my old foe from world and Olympic rowing championships. Peter is a great guy, a genuine hard nut, a fierce competitor, and a self-confessed opportunist. We obviously rated him as a very serious opponent indeed. He with his crew, David Riches, and the other boats came up the coast a few days later in favourable, flat, calm conditions.

*

Keith Wheatley, The *Sunday Star-Times*, October 12, 1997

On the dockside in Tenerife, amid last-minute preparations, Haining was enthused by a small victory.

"David and I now hold the record for the course from the Old Port to the New Harbour," he said. "It took 1 hour 34 minutes, which was 26 minutes better than the Kiwi crew. We kicked ass."

*

David Mossman from *Key Challenger* was still angry about keels and appendages and Chay's subsequent rulings. And he was not alone. So he organised an informal meeting to discuss the issue. A group of approximately 40 people gathered at the *Key Challenger* base.

On arriving there I couldn't help but notice some of the supplies that lay in piles around the room. Every item seemed to be in large multiples. For example, a pile of AA Batteries lay on the kitchen table. They were commercially pre-packed into lots of 12 batteries and there must have been 20 packs stacked on top of one another. Here apparently was another crew not in the least concerned about weight. A quiet murmur went around the room. Bloodshot eyes made me think that headaches were the reason for the subdued tones rather than the tension of the moment.

Mossman opened the meeting by saying that only the competitors whose boats *Key Challenger* felt were fair had been invited to the meeting. His sponsors were disappointed with Chay's handling of the competitors' rule interpretations. It was suggested that we all wait on the starting line for an hour after the start gun before heading out into the Atlantic. This protest would hopefully gain worldwide media attention and put pressure on Chay to amend the rules of what constituted a valid entry. *Key Challenger*'s sponsors were prepared to put up prize money as an incentive to those crews who waited.

Phil finally put his 10 cents' worth into the pot. "It's my opinion that you would be completely wasting your time. Chay couldn't care less if we stalled at the start. Any extra media attention would be all the better as far as Chay is concerned. In this case, any exposure for Chay is good exposure." Phil's statement had most crews nodding in agreement. "And besides," he continued, "it would only give our opposition a head start!"

There was frustration but the revolt folded and we all disappeared to complete those last few jobs. Bror and I went and got the *Kiwi Challenge* out of the water and lightly sanded the antifouling coating on the hull. That done, we were ready to race.

*

The rules of the race still concerned Phil. Our boat was very light. You will recall that six months before, when we were building the boat, we had a long-running debate about the permitted weight, with major differences of interpretation. A paragraph in the class rules stated that the boat would be weighed "in a dry condition". Steve Marten, Phil and I had assumed this meant that the 150 litres (150 kg in weight) of water ballast was *not* included in the basic 410 kg minimum weight specification.

When I had rung Teresa Evans she told me that this was incorrect. In fact, the 150 litres *was* to be included when the boat was weighed. Add that 150 kg to the 200 kg *Kiwi Challenge* shell and we only needed to add 60 kg of equipment to meet the 410 kg minimum requirement. As we had added well over 60 kg in equipment weight to the boat I was comfortable that we met the class rules. The problem, I now realised, was that I had gained verbal confirmation only and hadn't sought written confirmation.

Now, here in Los Gigantes, Phil was again unsure that I had it right. Talk around the crews was that 410 kg was the minimum, then the 150 kg of water was to be added. Now who was attempting to psyche out who? Were some crews deliberately having Phil on? Again I went to The Challenge Business headquarters.

"Teresa, we have a minor dispute out on the marina. The 150 litres of fresh water or water ballast. Is this water included in the minimum weight of 410 kg per boat?"

Teresa looked at me as much as to say, "Haven't we been through this?" Nevertheless she examined the rules again.

"Rob, it is quite clear that the 410 kg minimum weight includes the water, 150 litres of which must be carried as ballast at all times."

Again I had made a seemingly small mistake; I hadn't taken Phil with me. He was unconvinced that this ruling was correct, but dropped his argument and we got on with preparing the boat, for tomorrow was race day. Little did I realise that we hadn't really laid this issue to rest and that it would come back to haunt us on the water.

*

Carolyn arrived two days before the race began. I was delighted to see her but we were unable to spend much time together alone. On the last evening before the race numerous small groups of boat crews and supporters gathered in Los Gigantes. Small dining groups of close friends, no raucous parties. When leaving Gatwick two weeks previously I had purchased a bottle of fine French wine and so that night Carolyn and I had a private dinner. Great wine, food, and company. In spite of the wonderful evening, I had a sleepless night. I was anxious, restless; Carolyn was too and I guess 59 others were equally so.

17.

The Start

When men come to like a sea life,
they are not fit to live on land.
Samuel Johnson

AT LONG, LONG LAST it was October 12, 1997. The day of reckoning dawned spectacularly clear and calm but with a gentle breeze. I was down at the wharf at 7 a.m. and was double-checking the freshwater tanks. Phil was still worried about whether the boat was up to weight, so much so that when the scrutineers came around he threw a heap of additional water containers aboard while the boat's waterline was measured.

Later he was being interviewed by French television on the pontoon beside me. "The winning boat will arrive in Barbados in approximately 40 days," I heard him say. Water spilled everywhere. So now it was 40 days. I wasn't really worried that Phil had come clean with his revised prediction. What the hell, who cares?

An elderly woman quietly appeared on the pontoon. A New Zealander, who had lived in England for many years, she had heard a Kiwi boat was in the race and wished to make a contribution. "Have a drink on me in Barbados," she said, handing me a cheque for 100 pounds sterling. I really appreciated the gesture as much as her generosity. That cheque went into the side curtain rack in the cabin, along with my passport and credit card.

A number of small, irritating, last minute jobs were done and then we were saying our goodbyes. We shook hands with well-wishers, including Eddie Brynnel and Bror. Then Carolyn. This was the hardest. We hugged and kissed, both of us crying, unsure if this would be the last time we would see each other.

I let go and stepped into *Kiwi Challenge* where Phil waited patiently. Eddie escorted Bror and Carolyn to the chase boat. We cast off, leaving the mooring rope behind. That was extra weight even I didn't want. Ferry's employee collected the rope, tied it around a bollard and waved goodbye. By now a swarm of butterflies was making a home in my stomach.

At 9.45 a.m. we gently eased the *Kiwi Challenge* away from Ferry's berth in the marina, both of us standing like Venetian boatmen using an oar as a paddle. We turned her into the freeway between the rows of berths.

Once under way, Phil sat down, adjusted his seat, set his oars in the gates, locked the gates and quietly rowed gently through the marina while I acted as a helmsman until we reached the end of the pontoon rows, where we then swung around towards the entrance.

The breakwater was packed with people; half of Los Gigantes must have been there. We could easily hear bursts of clapping, cheering, shouted comments and laughter as each crew rowed inside the marina parallel to the breakwater, then turned and slipped through the marina entrance and into the wind-protected ocean starting arena immediately beyond. Almost affectionately we moved *Kiwi Challenge* through the deep, narrow entrance on the marina's eastern or mountain side — those huge brooding cliffs glowering over us — and slowly rowed out onto the ocean.

We eased past John Searson and Carl Clinton in *Commodore Shipping*.

"Are you going north or south of Gomera, John?"

"I don't know yet."

There was a storm several hundred miles to the north-west of the Canaries and talk on the marina the previous day had been how to get an advantage from the winds in this storm. At that moment we were going to stay with our plan of going south of Gomera, taking heed of Sir Peter Blake's and Eddie Brynnel's warnings.

We were third to last out into the starting area, where 27 boats were already waiting. Phil and I talked very little. However, my nerves were taut, I could feel my muscles tingling in expectation but loose, wanting to get into action. My mind was racing. "This is what I have worked for. This is living. This is great." I loved that atmosphere.

It only took three minutes to row to the starting area. Looking up to my left, the starboard side, those massive volcanic cliffs of Tenerife dropped 100 or so metres vertically into the sea, and then down. They brooded over the starting area. I was drawn to them. When we started the race these dramatic cliffs would be directly over the stern. The ocean was protected and calm. There was only a zephyr in the starting area but already it was getting hot and sticky. I was starting to sweat and my legionnaire hat had a flap down the back that stuck onto my neck. Perhaps I was more nervous than hot. Phil and I slowly brought the boat around to face west, and the Atlantic.

Damn. We forgot to take the worm tablets.

*

Sarah Edworthy, *The Daily Telegraph*, April 2, 1997

Nadia will bring a lot of determination and singlemindedness with her. Whereas a guy might say, "I'll take the day off", Nadia will say, "Get out there and get rowing." We are not a very powerful team physically but it is not that sort of race. It's more about determination and seamanship and navigation. These boats aren't going to go any faster whether they're pulled by us or 6 ft

4 in. rowers. The difference will come in the ability to manage the boat and we should be better than most at that.

Sarah interviewing solo trans-Atlantic yachtsman David Rice. Husband-and-wife team, Nadia and David Rice, crew Hannah Snell.

*

Over to the left, over our bow, was *3 Com*, one of two mother ships and the starting vessel. She was one of the BT Challenge boats. The starting line was a direct line between her and the westernmost marker on the marina breakwater. Behind this starting line, nestling back into the Gigantes cliffs, was the marshalling area. The rowing fleet appeared to be grouped in two flocks. One was close to the start boat, the second was at the other end of the starting line not too far clear of the breakwater, with a few scattered in between.

We headed towards the middle of the starting area and hung back a little. Our start plan was to hang back, keep well out of everyone's way and wait for the hooter to bleat. Phil and I wanted to row steadily to see what impression we could make on the fleet. This was going to be the only time in the whole race that we might be able to gauge our capabilities in relation to others. We had the feeling we were definitely lighter than most, if not all the boats, but we didn't know this for a fact.

I wanted to see what we were like, what our boat was like before everybody scattered. I was ready to fly. But Phil, the experienced yachtie, insisted on no errors at the start. Above all, he wanted to avoid copping a 12-hour time penalty for a blatantly premature start. He was right, of course.

Searson and Clinton definitely looked as if they were going to go around the north coast of Gomera as they were heading towards the starting vessel.

"Phil, Searson and Clinton are going around the north coast. Do you think we should reconsider our route?"

"No, mate. I've thought about that. They would have to be able to gain a lot of assistance to make up for the extra mileage they will have to row. Na, let's stick to our plan, surely the shortest route is best."

"Yeah, righto."

The French pairing of Joseph Le Guen and Pascal Blond were also in the centre of the starting area with us. They were probably oblivious to the meeting turmoil of just three days ago, but there certainly was knowledge and power aplenty in that crew.

Cellnet Atlantic Challenger was over my left shoulder, moving towards the starting boat also. "Phil, Simon Chalk is heading up to the north too."

"Oh, forget them Rob, we have our own race to row!" Phil's confident voice rang with a hint of irritation, so I dropped the subject. I was nervy and wanted to get going. It was just that George Rock, a big, strong, likeable man, and Simon Chalk, short, chunky and a competent

Global Challenge sailor, were such a well-prepared crew, they must have had their reasons.

The two firemen from Dorset, Mark Stubbs (no relation) and Steve Isaacs, rowed just off to starboard. They were like us; they had a minimum budget and debts. They were adventurers, fit, friendly and tough, pretty short on experience in rowing but they'd get to Barbados more on guts than skill.

God, I could see this huge cross of St Andrew, the Scottish flag. That could only be Peter Haining. Now that was being patriotic. I was impressed and wondered if he was going to carry the thing all the way to Barbados, use it as a bed sheet or cast it overboard for a support boat to retrieve.

*

Although I saw and recognised other crews, none of them were a genuine worry to us. They never had been. We were our own major concern. We had planned our adventure, organised ourselves and our boat, trained and prepared mentally for our race. We were ready, not ideally, but hey, this was October 12 and we were here. We both felt that to win we must carry out our plan. Phil researched the weather and ocean currents and had come up with a best route scenario. We would focus on rowing our race. Our genuine opponents were a myriad of factors: nature, equipment, supplies and our differing personalities, any of which could prevent us from executing our race plan. The unknown and unexpected — they were our real adversaries. The Atlantic was our challenge.

*

The number of spectator craft surprised me. There was a mélange of boats milling around. Fifteen-metre powerboats with beautiful people on their bridges, a number of hired water taxis loaded to the gunwales with spectators, small, squat powerboats packed with onlookers and a graceful contrast provided by a couple of elegant ketches that glided a little further out from the mayhem. There was a lot of banter going on between rowing boats and spectator and supporter boats mixing inside the marshalling area, laughter, encouragement, goodbyes, predominantly in English, but with French, German, Norwegian and Spanish adding to the excitement.

"See you in Barbados for a rum!" floated over to us. The rower's excessive volume gave a clue to his anxiety. For many this was a picnic day. Our support crew arrived on a small boat. They weren't many but I couldn't help smiling. They were so bubbly and full of Kiwi and Canarian bull, waving, jumping up and down; they were in party mood. Carolyn sat quietly at the stern. A lump formed in my throat. They moved on across the ocean as we concentrated. We were ready and began to move forward. The great adventure was about to start.

*

Bror Muller, rower and friend

When all of the boats were in the water for the start, it was immediately obvious that *Kiwi Challenge* was lighter than the boats around it. It bobbed in the water like a cork compared with the slow, laborious wallow of many of the other entries. This was enormously satisfying to see. The weight gamble seemed like it might pay dividends.

*

The one-minute flag was raised. The water was very calm. We checked our watches.

"Twenty seconds," I said.

"Check."

Oars readied, we were well back from the start line.

"Ten, nine, eight, seven.... "

SCCROOOONK! The start air horn sounded.

Oars entered the water.

"Shit! How on Earth did we misjudge that!"

SCCROOOONK. The air horn sounded again.

"Is that a false start? What the fuck's going on?" It was Phil again.

I didn't have a clue! I don't think I have ever missed a start before, yet here we were six seconds out in our timing. And I had no idea why the hooter went a second time. We were rowing and could see that no one had stopped. It was unsettling. We were not really affected but our athlete's pride was injured and we overreacted. After 20–30 overzealous strokes we settled.

"Okay Phil, let's just go for rhythm!"

I lengthened out the stroke and lowered the rating and Phil followed. I could feel the boat pick up speed. All the support boats and spectator boats buzzed excitedly around. They created an agitated chop that made it uncomfortable in a 7 m rowing boat bobbing around like the proverbial cork. The centre of the fleet seemed a prudent choice and a good place to be, as most of the frenetic action was on either side of us. We began to reel in a race boat, which was good evidence that we were travelling well. The swell increased noticeably as we left the lee of the marina breakwater and cliffs — I was glad to leave those mesmerising cliffs — the bow rose higher and fell more, but the extra movement didn't slow us.

The further we rowed, the bluer the water became, getting progressively firmer, darker, richer in colour. We comfortably rowed past another boat, then another. I didn't feel physical discomfort; we were rowing within ourselves and we knew we could keep this up for a few hours. I was acutely aware that in our over-aroused state it would be easy to row too vigorously and risk injury. We had originally thought that some crews would row away from us in the early stages, then they would eventually slow down and maybe exhaust themselves. However, everyone was aware of their abilities.

*

We rowed steadily, making 3 to 3.5 knots and seemed to be moving through the fleet. The swell increased even more and now we were getting a light head wind. The fleet was beginning to spread out. We were still on the middle course, heading south-west. Thirty minutes into the race, I could again see the cross of St Andrew; Peter Haining and David Riches were over my left shoulder, off the starboard bow, about 100 m in front of us.

"Haining," I grunted to Phil.

"Gotcha," was the grunted reply.

We both unconsciously lifted our rating a bit, put a little more leg into rowing. Now we were racing. I think Peter must have been getting his flags down as next time I flicked a glance, there were no flags and they were much closer, but now they had a rating higher than ours. Lifting my eyes, over the starboard stern I could see *3 Com*, the mother ship, coming up. We stuck with our rhythm. I could see Chay Blyth, his solid shock of white hair, standing near the bow, watching intently. His strong Scots accent powered over the ocean.

"Come on Kiwis, you're only second!"

I could visualise the twinkle in his eye.

"Not for long," I replied, loud enough for only Phil to hear. We still stuck to our rhythm, keeping up our rating and rowing alongside Haining and Riches for 10 minutes. Gradually we overtook them. We were moving faster and with a slower stroke rate. They were superb rowers, so the difference must have been in weight. I think we were lighter. I could see Peter dart a rapid look over his right shoulder; they were working harder than us. Good. They made a course change and over the next hour we lost sight of them. As we rowed away from Haining I started to feel genuinely confident. I felt good, the boat felt good, we were moving faster than those we could see.

We concentrated on rowing; there was no conversation between us. Then quietly, firmly, assertively, from behind me a voice: "We're gonna win this race!"

Positive Phil. I agreed.

"Damned right we're gonna win this bloody race."

I was still excited, still pumped up and remarkably everything seemed to be going to plan.

The joy of rowing and the desire to win raged within.

*

The Tauranga Picnic Regatta was my first rowing race. I was 19, a member of the Whakatane Rowing Club's novice eight. An absolutely great bunch of guys, great fun being with them, training with them, drinking beer with them (as I remember, lots of beer). I would have died for them. But little did I think I would have to do it in our very first race.

We were all first-year rowers, testosterone-overloaded, technically raw young men, the exasperation of coach Chick Hammond's coaching career. The race course was off Memorial Park at the bottom of 11th Avenue in the Waimapu Estuary, part of Tauranga Harbour. The water's edge, the park's considerable grassed area, well protected by the city from the westerly winds, was packed with skiffs, oars, and a huge range of rowers, most athletic, some nervous (me). I remember little of the pre-race activity, but the race I will never forget.

Our opponents were mainly school kids who had rowed before. They were smaller than us but well prepared, technically proficient and, by our standards, experienced. We began reasonably well, and by the 500-m mark were third, but beginning to slip a little. By the halfway mark we had dropped to two lengths behind. Someone in the crew called for greater effort, someone else called to dig deep: the next moment we were all talking, then "c'mon" in unison.

I launched into the next stroke with all my power, and three strokes later I experienced this horrible pain. I hadn't realised what this rowing game was all about, what intense pain.

"God, how can I get through this?" Alarm bells rang in my mind. I forgot the bells and concentrated on pulling above my weight. I had previously played explosive sports, volleyball and rugby, where there was always an opportunity for a blow and quick rest, and I had never experienced such concentrated exertion and endurance demands on low oxygen. But now we had 500 m to go and I was really hurting. We were back into third and catching the first two.

Everything was hurting. I thought my lungs had ceased working 100 m before, my legs burned, my back ached, my arms screamed, my head pounded, my vision was blurred and my arse was sore. Slowly we inched up on the leader and just passed them on the last stroke.

I collapsed, no yahoo, no rebel yell. Then I realised I was still alive, everything attached to me was still working, I managed a feeble croak of triumph and raised a limp fist. I had pushed all sorts of barriers and triumphed.

Back on the grass we recovered, we lay in a group, joked, laughed and talked the race through 100 times.

"Man, the 10 strokes we put in at the last 500 made all the difference, we pulled up half a boat length on those guys."

To my life, yes, those 10 strokes sure made the difference. There were new physical limits set, therefore new barriers to be tested. But for now our joy of winning was complete. The sport person's designer drug, the unbridled and unadulterated joy of winning. I was hooked.

*

Forty minutes into the race our support boat came up behind us. On board they were all excited, but Bror Muller was very excited. He was laughing, yelling, yahooing and giving the thumbs up.

"You're kicking ass! Go Kiwi go! You are the men! You guys are the best!" drifted across the ocean.

Again Bror yelled, "You've got more freeboard than the rest of the fleet. I'm CERTAIN you are lighter than the others. Go Kiwi go! You have blitzed everyone at the start, you are looking great!"

"Awesome!" I yelled back.

Bror's excitement mirrored our own. I was absolutely delighted. Carolyn was quiet. She sat at the stern of the support boat observing us. I called to her, she smiled and called back. Carolyn had been our biggest sponsor in terms of time she had given; folding newsletters and addressing and stamping envelopes by the thousand. Definitely my major sounding board, keeping me on track, quick to point out if I had gone off on a tangent (a regular occurrence). I was going to miss her. I already did.

*

In my pocket I had a book of quotes by Jim Rohn which she had given me that morning. It was less than the size of my passport, but I hadn't yet told Phil I was carrying it. We had agreed that there would be no books. The dedication read, "Rob, hope this helps get you through. Love and kisses, Carolyn. PS See you in 2–3 months."

*

The support boat stayed with us for half an hour. They were all smiles and cheerful good humour. The positive feeling transferred from them to us. With final exhortations, meaning plenty of yahoos, waves, and encouraging faces, they turned, waving vigorously, and headed back to Los Gigantes and the post-start party. Bror loves parties. They were lucky, but Phil and I had our own party; we are very pleased with our effort so far. Pleased, almost smug.

Gomera Island loomed off our starboard bow, comfortably to the north of us. We kept our rating and headed south-west, out to sea, away from Gomera, into the Atlantic proper. I was feeling good. But this feeling good at sea was for me an entirely new experience. Phil, rowing behind me, was feeling strong in the water and very confident. We had begun well but we knew we had a long way to go.

18.

Racing

What lies behind us and what lies before us are small matters compared to what lies within us.
Ralph Waldo Emerson

ABOUT 10 MINUTES AFTER the start I had noticed some of the boats were indeed going around the north of Gomera. Quite a few actually. Interestingly, there appeared to be four diverging routes that the fleet was following. A few boats were heading for the north west coastal route along the northern coast of Gomera, while some were heading almost due west closer to the south coast of Gomera. A minority was heading in the same direction as we were, on a direct course for Barbados, and the fourth group was heading in a more southerly direction.

This early divergence did surprise us. Our course was Phil's call, but I was in eventual agreement. Barbados is south-west. We couldn't see the sense of going around the north coast of Gomera. Nor could we visualise the gains to be expected by heading further south. Both were seeking extra assistance from ocean currents and thus put more miles on their log with the aim of picking up following winds earlier. However, a consequence of choosing another course was that they would have to travel much further to reach Barbados.

Phil's father, David Stubbs, a former land surveyor, had argued that any deviation less than 10 degrees from the rhumb line, the direct route, would only add unnecessary kilometres to our route. The tactical advantage of choosing a different course for a rowboat would have to be guaranteed. "If it can't be guaranteed, don't do it," was Dave's argument. In discussions with yachties about the mid-Atlantic, the universal reaction was, "With the Atlantic, or any ocean, there are no guarantees." Phil and I talked about our route the day before we left Los Gigantes and, although alternative routes were obviously a hot conversational piece at the Harbour Lites, Phil was unmoved by the rhetoric of others. We were following the most direct route possible, end of discussion.

Phil also had some fairly strong views on the manner in which we should exert and conserve our energies. In the first third of the race we would look after the individual. In the middle stage we would worry about the team. And in the latter stages we would say to hell with the human concerns, we would just go for it. This would be pretty much what we did, although not in exactly the manner Phil had imagined.

*

Four hours into the race we were comfortable, neither of us talking but pausing to refill our drink bottles. Although we had dropped the intensity of our strokes we still kept the same rating. We were like two metronomes, ticking along at an economical and efficient rate. As the sun rose higher the water in our drink bottles went down, both the temperature and the wind rose, and so did the sea. It was getting very hot on deck. The warm wind was coming directly on the starboard side, slowing us down to three knots.

We rowed together for five hours, until 3 p.m. In those five hours we had sweated profusely, and consumed four litres of water each. We had found out the hard way in training that continuous fluid replacement was essential. We also discovered that straight water didn't absorb into our bodies as quickly as we lost water and minerals. Dehydration meant decreased performance followed by massive headaches. Naturally we wished to avoid any of these.

Phil pulled his oars in one at a time, as you would in a dinghy. He stepped out of his shoes, stood up, had a satisfied stretch.

"What do you reckon, Rob? Should we turn the water-maker on, mate?" A very satisfied tone to his voice. Again this encouraged me as he too was obviously pleased with our beginning.

"Yeah, why not?" I replied, "We've had a fair bit to drink already, I suppose."

He stepped past me, and the *Kiwi Challenge* listed to his movement and weight. He stuck his head inside the cabin door, one foot in the well, his torso half in and half out of the cabin and reached down for the water-maker switch. I sat rowing, waiting to hear the whirring of the motor as it filtered the water. Phil pulled himself back and stood up straight again, an astonished look on his face.

"Nothing's happening!" An anxious voice.

I heard him crystal clear, yet responded, "Eh?!"

"Nothing happened! The water-maker's not working. I can't get it to go."

"Are you sure?" I couldn't believe it.

"Yes, I am sure."

The heat was intense. For a couple of seconds my brain suspended all operations. My guts felt as though there was a jagged ice crystal embedded deep down, slowly rotating. The past 15 months whirled before my eyes. "Let me have a look." I was an electrician in a previous life. We swapped places. Phil quietly, thoughtfully, picked up the oars, keeping the boat as steady as he could.

I reached down to the switchboard myself and turned the switch on, off, on, nothing. I checked the cabin light, that was okay; we had power. I tried the water-maker again but to no avail. I opened up the hatch where the water-maker was located and had a play around with the cables when it suddenly burst into life. A melancholic sound, rather like a Morrie 1000 starter motor grinding over, rang like music. I jiggled the cable. The Morrie stopped. I pushed the cable in and the water-maker started again. Obviously there was an electrical short circuit as something wasn't quite making a regular connection. This was definitely fixable.

We had an intense discussion on what to do next. We considered three options: jiggle it each time we wanted it to start, second, fix it at sea, or the third option, fix it in sheltered water. Staring each other and probable disaster in the face unless we fixed this problem permanently, we opt for the third choice. Fix it, in sheltered water.

*

We actually had two problems. We had the wrong-sized spanners for the water-maker. We carried metric tools instead of imperial. All the other components in the boat were metric! We were also slap in the middle of the acceleration zone, the Cook Strait of the Canaries through the western Canary Islands where the wind funnels between each island at a great rate of knots. Tenerife's mountain, Pico del Telde's 3700 m, was sure pushing winds our way at that moment. We decided we had to get into the lee of the next island, El Hierro, to effect repairs in calmer sea conditions.

So it was back to the oars with a very different mindset; the euphoria of the start gone, the reality of a race like this ramming home much earlier than I had imagined. I carried on with my shift while Phil rested. I rowed, my mind darting from one thought to another, all related to getting this project started, never thinking for long about anything before darting off onto the next. One sequence kept on returning and each time my self-recrimination became stronger, my anger and frustration with myself growing each time I mulled over the sequence.

*

Two days before, the boat had been berthed at the Los Gigantes marina where I had been busy repacking food in the boat. I was going through my checklist of last-minute jobs to do when for no known reason I checked the water-maker. I turned it on. It didn't start immediately; there was a second's delay. I thought, "That's odd. The water-maker motor should start immediately." I switched it off and on several times and it started immediately each time. I called Phil over and together we switched it on and off a couple more times and again it started without any delay.

I suggested that it was probably nothing and that maybe I had got it wrong. Phil agreed. His agreement and the fact that I was halfway through my checklist meant that I never revisited that slight delay. I had rationalised, "Damn, that should start immediately, but it started so it will be okay." It was as if I didn't want to know about the illogical delay. If only I had heeded that warning. In normal circumstances I would have taken notice and checked it further. Under pressure I had ignored a clear warning signal and now we were paying for it. The expletives were flowing, but an inexcusable mistake had been made. Time had moved on and we were reaping the consequences.

*

And so we moved on to Phil's shift at dusk. I tucked myself into my bed, by which I meant collapsing on my sleeping bag which rested on the thin air cushion and foam floor of the cabin. This was the first time I had had a lie down and a break since the start of the race. It was strange to think that at this instant I was initiating a regime that would become a regular thing for the next 50 days or so at sea, the regime of a one and a half to two-hour break.

Lying down was a dual relief. The first, obvious reason was that it was good to have a break and rest the muscles that had been swinging oars for six hours. Second, the non-functioning water-maker was creating huge anxiety and my stomach was doing somersaults as well as cartwheels and crosses on the gym rings. Nausea had washed over me time and time again while I was rowing. I rested fitfully.

*

One hundred minutes later I was summoned by Phil's call — it was time to get on the oars again. As I sat up in the cabin nausea returned with a vengeance. My second crunch time and we were only within the first few hours of the race-start. Straight away I sensed that the movement of the boat was rather abrupt as we crabbed across the seas.

Kiwi Challenge was pitching sharply back and forth and more sideways roll movement now complicated the pitching. The consequences of nausea flooded back to me. I vividly remembered the training row from Auckland to Tutukaka. Then, fraught with nausea, my efficiency had dropped off dramatically and, battling into an offshore wind, we were pushed out to sea away from the coast. I knew I must get over the nausea as quickly as possible.

*

I slid out from beneath the sleeping bag and pulled on my rowing shorts. As it was a little cool I slipped on a polypropylene long-sleeved shirt plus the slightly damp T-shirt I had used for the previous six-hour row. On opening the hatch door the darkness hit me; it was anthracite black out there. The sea had risen significantly and the wind had intensified from the north. I had to be careful emerging from the cabin, careful to get secure handholds as I tentatively put one foot out of the cabin into the open well of the boat. I proceeded to mix my drinks, spilling powder all over my feet. Then I gave the two drink bottles a good shake.

"Righto, I'm ready. Change over."

Phil stopped rowing and shipped the oars. Just as I was strapping my feet in the rowing shoes I heard a wave break about 50 m astern of us. "Hmm.... That was a little close."

"It's got a little bit rougher, mate," warned Phil.

"Yeah. I'd noticed."

"It's actually getting quite dangerous."

"Okay, mate I'll keep a look out." Not that I could see much.

I began rowing, concerned both with my seasickness and the sea. The swells were coming at me like kamikazes from the north and were quite difficult to handle; the timing of my strokes needed to be spot on. So with one eye over my left shoulder and with the rudder sharply angled driving us into the beam-on seas, I rowed out my two-hour shift. Predictably enough I felt miserable, I felt seasick, but I had not vomited.

*

We changed shifts and changed again. I was having a most uncomfortable time. I could rest, but not sleep. My mind just would not relax. I cursed the decision during construction not to incorporate a sleeping tie-down. Another reason I felt miserable was my reaction to my first meal cooked from freeze-dry food. Freeze-dry is fine, but the first time it goes through me in a flash. Anyone with a sense of humour trying to market freeze-dry food could use this slogan: If you've had a bad day and the bottom has fallen out of your world, eat freeze-dry and feel the world fall out of your bottom.

The water-maker crisis had sent thunderbolts through my subconscious. I was worried sick. Phil called me out for my 2 a.m. shift. We were quartering the sea. I was tired and feeling sorry for myself. The nausea became almost unbearable as I rowed. And I couldn't forgive myself for not having spotted the problem with the water-maker before we left port. There I was, no more than three minutes into the stint, feeling dead, weary and ...

KAWHOOSH!

A wave hit me. Shit! I was still disorientated and had not yet fully adjusted to the lack of light when the wave crashed across the deck from the starboard side. It seemingly came from nowhere, but it was big, ugly and all over me. The boat heeled over 80 degrees, foam and water breaking over the top railing, black water leapt and surged up from the scuppers below on my right. I tried to grab the aluminium seat rails and was momentarily held horizontal to the ocean. The boat was being carried along beam-on by the wave. I fell down the near vertical deck and got caught under the gunwales.

The 20 or so violent metres we were carried felt like a couple of kilometres in my mind map. We slid up onto the wave's crest and the *Kiwi Challenge* rolled upright. I was sitting in the ocean, an ocean that was rapidly draining from the deck through the scuppers as the boat was surfacing. I was wildly awake, grabbing the gunwales either side as the boat rolled too sharply to starboard, then to port, shaking out excess ocean water and the surprise clout it had received.

Then both the boat and I sat. The moment of genuine terror had passed. I did a quick body check. Everything was intact, no broken bones. Whew! I scrambled for my rowing seat and reached for the oars, only to discover that with the equipment not everything had remained intact.

*

The port side oar had gone under the boat and *Kiwi Challenge* must have rolled over onto it, trapping it under the water as the boat crushed over it on its brief ride with the wave. The black carbon fibre oar had virtually splintered in two, rendering it useless. So at that moment I had only one oar. The shock of the incident had me bewildered but aware. I hadn't been wearing a safety harness. I sat there for a second or so with my skin prickling and water washing around my feet as it scurried out the scuppers and realised how lucky I was to still be *in* the boat!

An inkling of fear germinated over the following second and I realised that my life was still seriously in danger. The next wave could arrive at any second. I spun around, quickly opened up the bow compartment storage area and hauled out the life-jacket and safety harness attachment. I threw the life-jacket over my head and tied it off around my waist, clipped the harness first onto the attachment and then onto the safety line. The safety line was strung the length of the boat alongside the rails that the seat rolled on.

To row the remainder of this shift without wearing this equipment would have been tempting fate. As fast as I could, I removed the broken oar from the gate and replaced it with a new one from the spares lashed to the gunwale. Then I set off rowing again to gain some control over the situation.

"What the hell happened?" Phil yelled. "Are you okay?"

"Yeah. I got caught by a bit of a rogue wave. Did it wake you?"

"Sure did, Rob."

"We rolled on the oar. It's stuffed, but I think we are in control again."

"Okay, mate."

*

Given what had just happened it was amazing that the remainder of the shift was more or less uneventful. The sea was difficult and confused and so was I. Finally, thank God, I threw up. It was almost an anticlimax. After vomiting I took my specially concocted Paihia Pharmacy seasickness medication. Then I rowed on, waiting apprehensively to see if this technique of being sick then immediately taking medicine was going to work and settle my stomach. It did, and from that point on I had no further problem with seasickness.

Later in the shift I noticed a soft light occasionally coming into view, shining as it was being lifted on the swells, then disappearing in the troughs for a while before we and the light carrier both came on the crests of the swells at the same time. The light was further out to sea, heading on a south-westerly course, while we were on a north-nor'west course. I wasn't sure because of the distance between us, but there were probably two boats. Given the speed they were making they were probably race boats, or perhaps a fishing boat further out and a rowing boat closer in.

Whatever was out there was slowly but very definitely putting distance between us. I speculated silently that at least one competitor was rowing through us and that took the zip out of me. And here we were going the wrong way!

*

It was a great relief to wake Phil for the changeover of shifts. I stepped inside the cabin and lay on my sleeping bag, flat on my back. My body was tired but my mind was still operating at a million miles an hour. Nevertheless the relative security of the cabin was great and, of course, rest was very welcome even if sleep eluded me. Phil, by contrast, could sleep anywhere, anytime.

At six in the morning, just as I was coming out of the cabin to allow Phil to take his rest, I spotted what looked like a fishing boat headed in the general direction of Hierro. To Phil it appeared to be heading further downwind than what we had thought was the best course to Hierro. Thinking that the locals must know best, I decided to alter our course to parallel that of the fishing boat. As we got closer to Hierro we had to start crabbing further across the sea again, more or less going directly into the east-nor'easterly wind to avoid being pushed past the island altogether.

*

I woke Phil at 8 a.m. and we rowed together to make sure we made landfall. Finally we made the island, at around 10 that morning. To our delight we discovered a tiny little harbour which we rowed into and found several small local motor fishing boats moored. God knows where the damned fishing boat we followed had gone. Much later we would find we were in the fishing port of San Sebastian, but right now the immediate task was to find the right tools to break open the water-maker so that we could gain access to the electrical connection.

Our Swiss Army knife came to the rescue. The knife contained a small pair of pliers and with these I managed to get the top bolts of the water-maker casing undone and then examined the electrical circuits. One of the contacts to the brushes in the electric motor was making only intermittent contact. A clothes peg in reverse would be the best way to describe the contact; it is sprung so that it opens out, whereas the clothes peg is sprung so that it will close. A little opening out or widening of the contact was all that was required. Just a small adjustment and then I put the motor back together.

The whole operation took a considerable amount of time, solely because it was so fiddly with a number of parts, springs and pieces which needed to be held together carefully in reassembling. And although we were in the tiny harbour, *Kiwi Challenge* was rolling constantly.

All told we were in the harbour rolling and sweating over the water-maker motor for approximately two and a half hours. We had no way of accurately guessing, but we estimated the time spent in the harbour plus the wasted time rowing across the weather instead of with it, meant we lost about six hours. In race terms, six hours of lost rowing at three or more knots translated into us being 20 or so miles behind those boats that rowed through us. This aside, the repaired water-maker lifted our spirits considerably. The Morrie was on song again.

*

We rowed out through the narrow entrance of San Sebastian harbour in considerably higher spirits than at our arrival a few hours previously. Again we launched into our rowing regime, although we were exhausted from the night's all-action activity and the nervous energy expended in repairs. It felt good knowing that the water-maker should now give little trouble. It had bloody well better perform.

Until the previous night I had never rowed with a safety harness. I found it both irritating and constrictive. It rubbed on my shoulders and back and inflamed an old back injury. The harness was also inhibiting my ability to row freely and it felt uncomfortable as hell, so off it came. Phil felt the same way. Eventually we decided to surrender a margin of safety to gain both greater comfort and more mileage. This was foolhardy perhaps, but we were determined not to compromise our chances of winning. It was an all-or-nothing approach.

*

What a tumultuous 24 hours. From excitement at the start, the ecstasy of rowing away from the fleet, the utterly organ-stopping reaction to the water-maker not starting. The trauma of nearly rolling, breaking an oar, of then almost being pushed by the wind and ocean past Hierro Island and finally the luck of finding the fishing harbour and the success in fixing the water-maker. I was physically exhausted, emotionally dead, and yet my mind was having a ball. I couldn't sleep, even though I desperately wanted to.

19.

Open Water

The snotgreen sea. The scrotumtightening sea.
James Joyce, ULYSSES

DAY TWO. WE LEFT the little harbour around 12.30 pm. Setting out on our south-west course we were at last able to use the prevailing winds to assist our rowing. We made good progress. The wind was 15–20 knots coming right from behind, dead astern. The following seas also aided our progress with swells and the odd breaking white cap. We were rowing with spirits regained but realising that we had surrendered our lead. Others must have taken advantage of the favourable seas, and made many miles while I was either being scared to hell, vomiting, or fixing the water-maker.

Later in the afternoon while resting in the cabin I heard Phil call, "G'day! How are you going?"

I sat up abruptly.

"What's that?" I inquired.

"The mother ship, *3 Com*."

I hoisted the rear hatch and climbed out of the cabin to join in. No show without Rob. There was the yacht sailing up to us from out of the Atlantic. With his back to the yacht Phil hadn't seen it until it was nearly upon us.

"You okay?" an anonymous voice boomed across from the yacht.

"Never been better," lied Phil, "had a little trouble with the water-maker."

A double score to Phil.

"You are lying fourth at the moment."

"Really?" I couldn't believe it.

"Yep! We've just visited a couple of boats in front of you and the last Argos reading we received confirmed that."

All the boats carried the Argos beacon transmitting a pulse every two minutes. This would enable the organisers to track the progress of all boats throughout the race and locate them in the case of an emergency. It was also a back-up emergency beacon. Normally an emergency would be signalled by one of the crew throwing the toggle switch on the EPIRB transmitter which all boats also carried.

"Who is in front of us?" I yelled.

"Muffle, mumble and *Commodore Shipping*. We have to go. Peter Haining's had a bit of trouble. We will catch you later."

With that they turned about and were gone. I grabbed the little VHF radio, but they seemed distracted, their minds on Peter Haining's plight and we were none the wiser, either about Haining and Riches or anybody else. What a bummer.

*

I couldn't help smiling though. Fourth!

I had contemplated a worst case scenario that we could well be last by now. Fourth was a great boost. Almost unbelievable. The roller-coaster emotion inside me leapt upwards on another climb. It wasn't really a mumble from *3 Com*, I just didn't know the names of the boats well enough to catch them. I knew the rowers, not the boats. But I did know *Commodore Shipping*, and we were not surprised. The rest was over for the moment, the adrenalin was flowing freely again. I went out on deck and cooked the freeze-dry meal for my lunch, washed the pot and put in Phil's meal to absorb water. Yeah, we were well and truly back in the race.

At dusk we changed shifts and I was rowing comfortably but could begin to feel a twinge in my left shoulder. "It will come right," I thought and continued to row on through a calming sea. Off the starboard bow I sighted some navigation lights and on the next change I pointed them out to Phil.

"What do you think?"

"It's a boat, all right," said Phil, "Wonder if it's Searson. He's rowing third."

But as with Peter Haining and the boats during the previous night we slowly lost contact.

*

***The Times*, London, October 16, 1997**

Peter Haining and David Riches left the start line in their boat *Walter Scott & Partners*, flying a Scottish flag and with high hopes of victory. Within hours of the start, the pair had abandoned ship and were safely back in Tenerife airport. The problem was one of the oldest enemies in the seafarers' log – seasickness.

They were rowing south of the island of Gomera when Riches started to be violently sick. Haining kept rowing, but as they drew closer to rocks he dropped the sea anchor and began to worry that Riches was suffering from something more serious, food poisoning.

*

That night, as I slipped into the cabin and into the sleeping blanket, I realised my left shoulder was not coming right. It was still niggling and it felt as if it could be tendonitis. It felt fine just dangling at my side or resting on the cabin floor, but as soon as I moved the arm, the tendon around the joint objected. I knew it was a reoccurrence of the problem I had first felt and ignored at Tutukaka. Sleep was virtually impossible.

I wondered if the cause might be the height of the oar handles, making me pull my arms higher than I had been used to in skiff rowing.

The pain in my shoulder was only partially to blame for my not getting any sleep. Phil had eaten too many bean sprouts and they must have irritated his throat. He was coughing the entire shift, attempting to clear his throat with a raspy, barking cough and the sound came right through the cabin hatch like a tanker's klaxon. Even wearing ear plugs didn't help. Cough and shoulder, it was becoming a great life on the ocean!

My shoulder was still sore during the next shift so I eased off the rowing pressure. I "stirred tea", as rowers say, just keeping under way to keep the boat on course and the sea on the stern. We changed shifts and repeated the cough and shoulder routine!

*

Steve Isaacs, *TocH Phoenix*

Our wind generator was perched on the bow of the boat, the regulation height above the deck, and in order to further conform to the rather vague race rules we had had to cut down each of the solid plastic vanes that powered it, leaving an exposed edge on each one that with hindsight could have done with smoothing off.

As I bent forward to try and inspect the connection its true malice was revealed. It buried two of its razor-sharp teeth deep into the top of my head, gouging out two deep parallel strips of flesh.

Mark had to stitch my head to close the wounds or our race could be over. The gouges were too wide for steri-strips or plasters, and the position of the wound made it impossible for me to even consider performing the repair myself. What followed was a sketch any comedy writer would have been proud to produce.

Less than four days into the trip and the one thing we had both said wouldn't happen had already occurred. The last thing on earth Mark wanted to do was to go poking around with a needle and thread in the dark and the last thing on earth I wanted Mark to do was to go poking around with a needle and thread anywhere near me.

The first couple of prods were the worst by a long stretch, I had to get used to the pain level and Mark had to remember how to tie a reef knot. Now, was it left over right or right over left? Who cares? Just tie it off!

Fortunately after nearly three hours' work and more than a few dropped stitches (literally) Mark closed the gashes and declared that he was finished and quite pleased with his handiwork into the bargain. I was left looking like a Tellytubby with antennae poking out of my head but the job had been done.

As soon as the gory bit was finished I went straight onto a course of antibiotics to fight off any infection and Mark went back to the oars. It was to be nearly two months later, when we landed in Barbados, before I got to see Mark's workmanship and I've got to say I was very impressed.

He can darn my socks any day!

*

At the conclusion of my next shift I was exhausted, in pain and concerned. I woke my team mate for his shift. "Look Phil, I have been really stupid. I should have told you this earlier. I know from my experience that I should have stopped, but I've got a bit of an injury. It feels like tendonitis is flaring up in my left shoulder."

He was pretty phlegmatic about it. After a considered pause he replied, "Oh well, looks like we will have to make some adjustments."

"I suggest I have a short break. I'll jam Brufen into me and see if I can get it functioning properly again. I might use some arnica as well."

"Okay, you take a four-hour break, I'll do a double shift."

First, I had a good go at massaging my shoulder. I stood in the stern well with my left arm straight, pointing away from me, resting over the stern decking, parallel to the solar panel. Then with my right hand I used my second finger to dig into the flesh in the centre of the shoulder until I could feel the inflamed tendon. The tendon was painful and easy to find. I then moved my fingers back and forward, back and forward, back and forward over the tendon, cross-frictioning it. I did this for a considerable time, moving up and down the tendon, working the scar tissue, getting the blood circulating around the affected area; painful but hopefully limiting the extent of the injury.

I had been told to do this by kayakers back in New Zealand. Cross-frictioning the shoulder actually made the injury flare up even further, but I was hoping that this was a short-term problem, not the long-term outcome. Then, massaging completed, I dolefully climbed into the cabin, feeling unbelievably tired and for the first time since the race started I fell asleep.

*

I slept from eight till noon. Ever so welcome, but my first real sleep in two days had only served to make me feel even worse. I felt simply wretched. My eyes were sunken and there were huge dark bags under them about the size of 50 cent coins.

"You're looking good, Rob."

Phil's sarcasm reminded me of the movie *Trading Places*.

"Feeling good, Phil," was my flippant Eddie Murphy-style response. My left shoulder remained painful.

Phil rowed from eight in the morning to two in the afternoon, a six-

Brett O'Callaghan

The lonely existence of the single sculler. Each stroke is – as Brad Lewis said – "all muscle, strength and eye-popping effort," combined with subtle technical application, the result being a fluid and graceful movement.

Kerry Williams

Phil Stubbs (centre) getting cheeky during a race with the Titahi Bay surfboat crew. Guess what happened next.

Hamill Collection

Phil Stubbs sizes up the cabin entrance during construction of Kiwi Challenge.

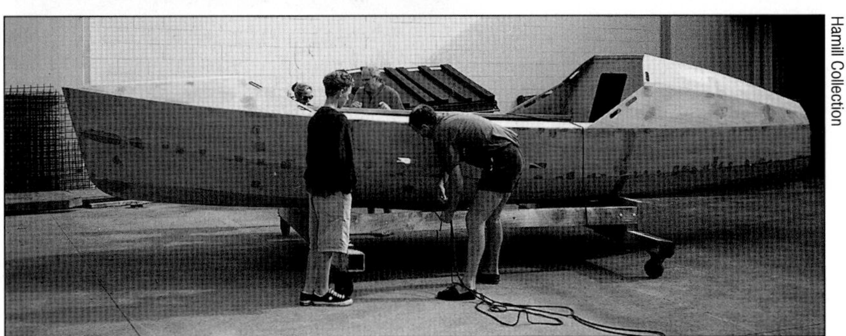

Hamill Collection

The kitset boat constructed — now for the painting and sanding. Graham Dalton (right) and Steve Marten (second from right) were an integral part of the TEAM (Together Everyone Achieves More).

Kerry Williams

My mother, Esther Hamill, quietly names the boat Kiwi Challenge. The TVNZ microphone had difficulty picking up what she said.

New Zealand Herald

Phil Stubbs in uniform looking as if he has stepped straight out of a police recruitment poster.

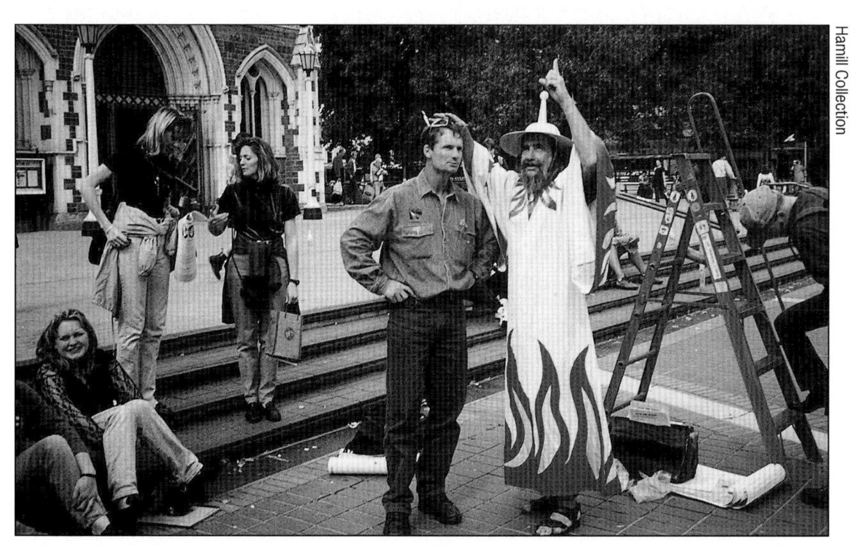

Hamill Collection

While in Christchurch trying to raise funds, The Wizard casts a good luck spell upon me for the voyage. Obviously the spell was not designed to help financially as not a single dollar was raised during my stay there.

Hamill Collection

ABOVE: Phil Stubbs appears to row into the smoking crater of White Island. Note that the Whakatane Rowing Club oar I had broken lies to the left of Phil.

Hamill Collection

RIGHT: 75 day-packs of food supplied the megacalories needed to power the two-stroke engine of Phil Stubbs and myself.

Hamill Collection

Chips off the old blocks. Our respective fathers Miles Hamill (left) and David Stubbs (right) greet us after a training session. We had just rowed from Auckland through the Colville Channel and down to Whitianga.

A training row in Tenerife, with the cliffs of the volcanic island looming behind us.

Tim Huelin

ABOVE: Americans Victoria Murden and Louise Graff, the only all-woman entry, make final preparations before the race start.

Tim Huelin

RIGHT: Tenerife, the morning of the race start; my girlfriend Carolyn McNabb and Phil Stubbs are making preparations while I tentatively step aboard our tippy craft.

Tim Huelin

The race start at 10 a.m. on October 12, 1997: 30 boats departing to row the Atlantic Ocean.

Hamill Collection

Peter Haining and David Riches, with flags flying, lead the charge from the start. Haining, my nemesis from international rowing regattas, became part of my motivation to swing on the oars a little harder for a little longer each day.

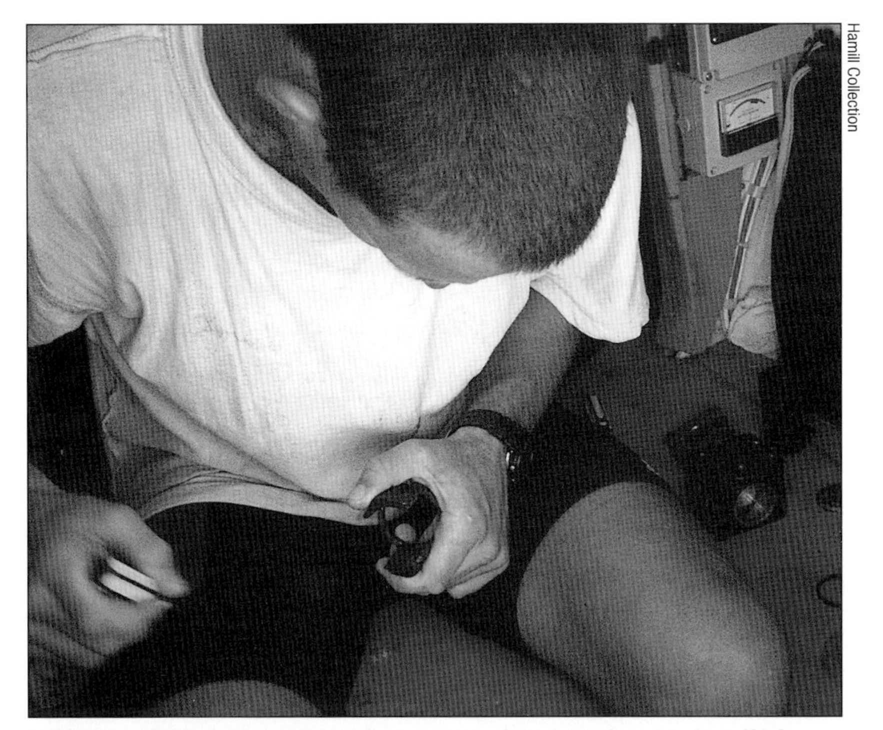

Hamill Collection

Phil Stubbs pulls the broken water-maker apart to replace the seals and o-rings. If left unfixed, we would be out of the race.

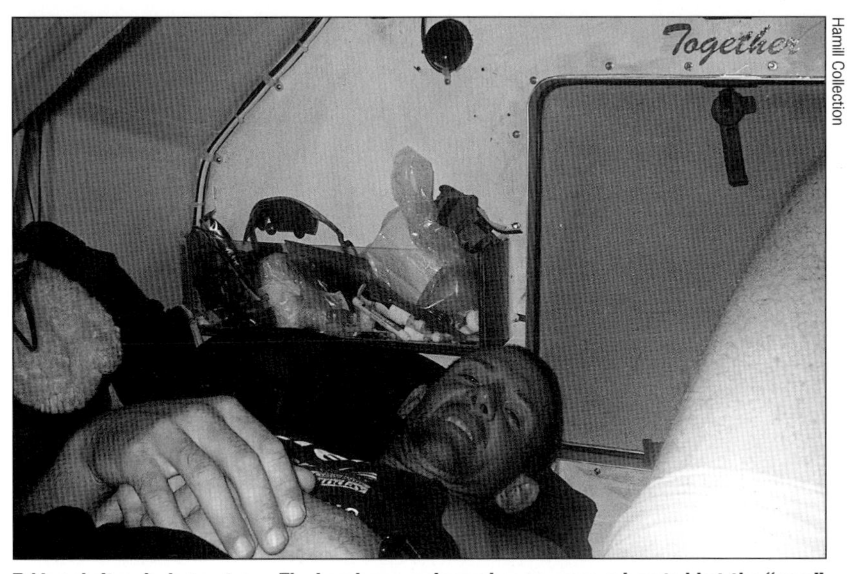

Hamill Collection

Taking shelter during a storm. The break was welcomed as we were exhausted but the "cosy" cabin made sleep difficult. Note the sign-written word "Together" above the hatch; it helped me focus on our goal even when there was tension between us.

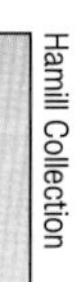

I found a feed of Dorado was a welcome relief from our freeze-dry staple diet. The fishing was good fun. Phil had other ideas....

Hamill Collection

The spare rudder only lasted a few hours.

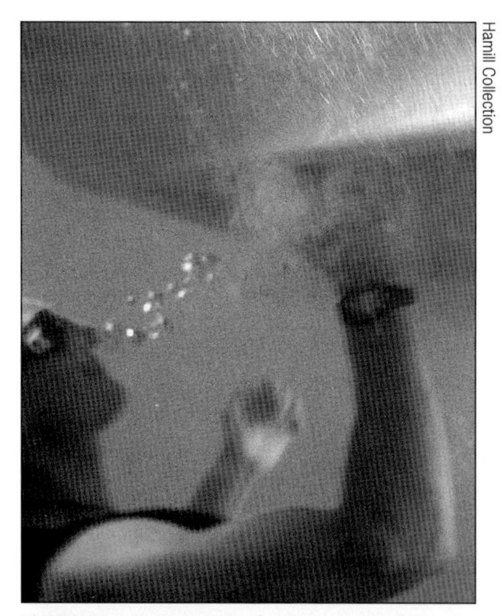

Hamill Collection

Phil Stubbs removing algae and barnacles from the underside of the hull.

Hamill Collection

Having a crack at naked rowing. Lucky I had a strategically-placed Sunsmart drink bottle!

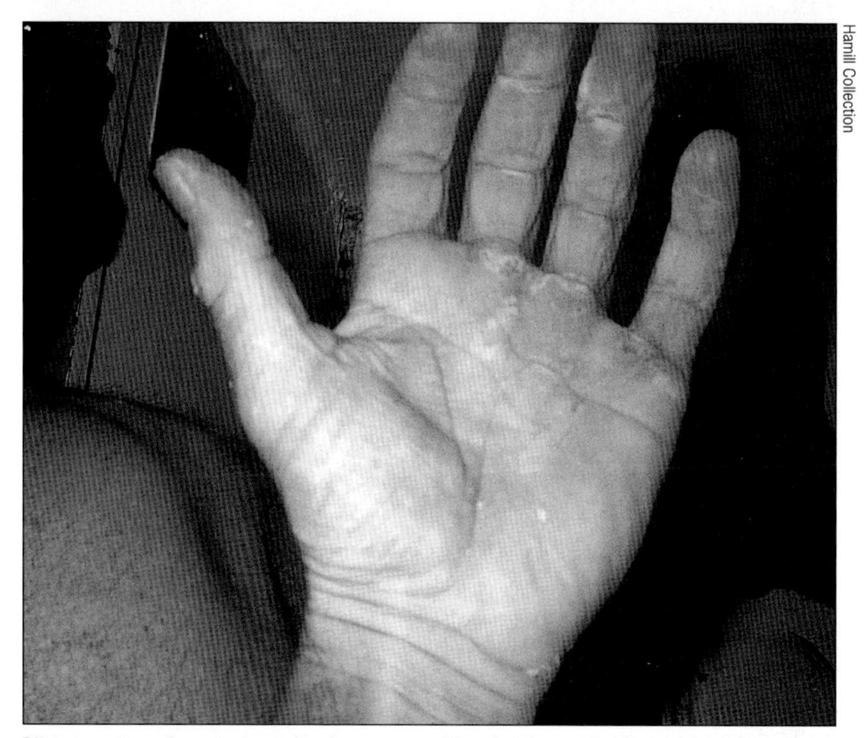

Hamill Collection

Blisters, cuts and sores on our hands were a problem but it was the finger joints that you couldn't see that caused the most problems.

Jon Nash/PPL

Kiwi Challenge partially submerged. At times, the sea tossed us about like a rag doll.

Hamill Collection

Our first real contact with a vessel for 40 days.

Land ahoy! Arriving in the Port St Charles marina to a firm handshake.

Firemen Mark Stubbs (left) and Steve Isaacs on TocH Phoenix arrive in Port St Charles, Barbados.

Chris Brandis

Yes! The Times' newspaper version.

Jon Nash/PPL

Yes! The Daily Telegraph's newspaper version.

Jon Nash/PPL

Myself, Sir Chay Blyth and Phil Stubbs in Barbados drinking fine New Zealand wine.

Tim Huelin

Jersey oarsman John Searson rowing the Atlantic solo.

Exeter rowers Neil Hitt and David Hogden in Hospicare finished within minutes of the TocH Phoenix crew.

Tim Huelin

Policemen Roger Gould and Charlie Street – some of the race's many characters as they approach Barbados.

Another character, Graham Walters, happy to be back on terra firma.

Tim Huelin

Tim Huelin

The British army lads, Mark Mortimer and Martin Bellamy, arrive in Port St Charles, Barbados, on Christmas Day.

Richard Brookes

Phil Stubbs enjoying one of his many and varied hobbies. Here he is piloting a small plane with Karekare Beach in the background.

hour shift, then took a well-earned break. I felt guilty and tried to repay his generosity by doing a four-hour shift so that he could also get a decent rest. I rowed lightly, "stirring tea" again and trying not to irritate the shoulder. The sea had calmed down appreciably and the wind had now dropped to a pleasant tail breeze of 10 knots or so. It was warm, not hot, and very good rowing conditions. Yet here I was barely adding to the boat's momentum.

Phil was back on the oars at 6 p.m. My left shoulder had worsened and was now painful all the time. It needed more rest. On my next shift I sat despondent in the seat, just watching the tiller and compass. At the very least I was making sure we were aiming in the right direction. What exacerbated my despondency was that these were ideal conditions to try and make up on the fleet in front of us and here I was sitting, forlorn, frustrated, and thoroughly brassed off. Rather than become a mental mess as well as a virtual passenger, I disentangled my Walkman, plugged in and turned up the volume. Jimi Hendrix blasted a few tangled cobwebs out into the sea. I didn't row for three shifts.

I talked to Phil and we agreed that I take a complete break for 12 hours. Meanwhile Phil continued his normal sequence of shifts. I could do nothing during my two hours and I was feeling increasingly dispirited. Had I taken on too much? Had I really taken on more than I could handle? What a daylight nightmare. There were no more beautiful big butterflies in my stomach; rather, the pit was a very large, black, cold void.

*

Teresa Evans, The Challenge Business

American Pearl. Tori Murden and Louise Graff were rescued by the Canarian Maritime Rescue Services on October 14. Both were suffering from food poisoning, Tori in particular had a severe bout of poisoning. Both were taken straight to hospital in Tenerife.

Key Challenger. David Mossman and David Immelman activated their Argos beacon on October 15. David [Mossman] had also been suffering from food poisoning and was ill before he left. They even delayed their start until 10 p.m. on the start day. David was taken on board *3 Com* and later returned to land. David Immelman rowed on alone.

*

It was becoming obvious that my negative thoughts were not helping the situation at all. If this injury was to heal I needed to think positive thoughts, imagine the healing powers of my blood multiplying, pouring into the inflamed area and removing toxins and scar tissue. I imagined the arnica coursing through my veins; the homoeopathic remedy for inflammation combined with Brufen working wonders on my shoulder.

I thought that visualising the internal healing going on might have helped but at the same time realised other more practical solutions were going to be needed; an alternative to being a sitting sad sack was obviously required. If I simply sat we would not win the race, that was certain. I had to find a solution, I had to think laterally.

I thought back to other New Zealand adventurers. I remembered the story of Sir Edmund Hillary getting to within a short distance of Mt Everest's summit. There a sheer wall of ice and rock met him. At first there appeared to be no way up. Then Hillary noticed a crack between the rock and the ice that he managed to wedge himself into; his back on one side and feet on the other. Slowly he inched and hauled his way up the fissure now known as the Hillary Step. His climbing partner Sherpa Tenzing followed and shortly afterwards, history was made. I had to think like Hillary: an alternative had to be found.

*

It was now the morning of the fourth day. Phil had just completed another two-hour rowing shift. Tentatively, I picked up the port side oar, put it in the gate, locked it in and began rowing. Sitting on the moving seat I used my legs and back as normal but only swung on one oar with my right arm. It was okay, it worked. I could move the boat. I kicked the rudder over to port, the same side as the oar, and began rowing with it only. A one-armed pirate. At first I was diffident as it felt very unusual, but it was working, so I put in more effort and began to make headway at around one knot.

With a little more adjustment of both rudder and technique I began to make one and a half knots and still keep the course. I almost began to enjoy myself again. That night rowing conditions were conducive and I rowed with one arm. But we were making progress and I was beginning to contribute again. A little pride was returning.

20.

Nightmares

Our eyes are placed in front because it is more important to look ahead than to look back.
Anonymous

I WAS STILL VERY worried, but didn't feel so low. Was this the alternative, the Hillary Step that I was looking for? In the longer term I doubted it, in the short term perhaps it was an intermediate strategy. In this fashion I rowed for the next 24 hours and Phil rowed in a normal fashion, making very good progress. I managed to sleep, but now I began to have nightmares.

They were horrible nightmares of skulls, of bones, of talking to people and then they would turn to me with sallow skin, cadaverous sunken eyes, open their mouths and say nothing. Not a repeating nightmare, but skulls at different places, situations and various stages of bleaching. I would wake up with a start, calm myself down and drop off to sleep only to dream afresh. Perhaps my mind had not yet adjusted to the extreme excitement of the first 24 hours nor the sapping regime of two-hour shifts.

In spite of all this drama I knew that I was still excited about being in the race. It was probably what kept me going, just being there, competing, out on the ocean. I was figuratively pinching myself as I couldn't believe it, and I couldn't sleep, either!

We were waking up to day number five, and I was waking up to an uncomfortable reality.

My right shoulder was now becoming uncomfortable also. I could feel twinges similar to those when the left shoulder started playing up. To me it was unbelievable that the right shoulder was packing a sad too. The injury to the left shoulder clearly was going to take a little time to heal. At the end of each shift I'd consistently stretched my body. And in addition, for the past 36 hours I had given my left shoulder a thorough going over, working the whole area, massaging the afflicted tendon in cross-stitches, every four hours after I'd finished a shift and then again in the cabin.

That night, on hearing the news about my right shoulder, Phil mentioned that he wanted to keep the boat moving at all costs. He suggested that he row two hours, I row one, then both objectives could be achieved; we keep the boat moving and I could rest my shoulders. I tried to keep my shifts to one and a half hours, to give Phil more sleep as one hour seemed too short.

*

The next morning my injury and the lack of sleep got to me. We were just a few days into the race and I was already a mess. The wrinkled bags under my eyes hung like cows' udders; the hand of gravity weighing far too heavily for my liking. At our 5 a.m. changeover, I suggested to Phil that my shoulder was still not coming right and I needed to give it another rest.

Phil smouldered, his eyes cold, hard, his body language aggressive.

"If that is to be your attitude, then we have lost the race!" He brushed past me, entered the cabin and shut the hatch. In the east the dawn of October 17 began to arrive.

*

We were in a mild consistent sea with a tail wind of 5–10 knots for the third day running. I got up, made my milkshake and then my Replace isotonic drink, returned with the two plastic drink bottles to the seat and sat. I focused my thoughts a little. Phil's hard-arsed attitude was understandable, but it had shaken me. Perhaps I had been overly concerned about myself, my shoulder and my wretchedness through lack of sleep. Maybe he was right. I was sorry for myself.

I got up off my seat, went to the well by the cabin hatch and stretched for five minutes, working both shoulders gently. Then I climbed back to the seat thinking only of this boat, this body, this moment. I sat. My focus shifted downwards. I wriggled my bum. The seat didn't feel right. I glanced at the seat trolley in front of me then splayed my legs and looked very carefully, then checked the other seat in front.

My seat was in Phil's rowing position and my seat is fractionally narrower than Phil's as well as being fractionally higher because of slope of the deck when the boat is trimmed. I had been sitting on Phil's seat and he had been sitting on mine. Shit!

We had been rowing in the wrong seats since Hierro four days ago. I swapped the seats. Unhurriedly I put my feet in the rowing shoes, loosely tied them, collected the starboard side oar, placed it in the gate and locked it. The port side was already gated, locked and ready. Gingerly I flexed my shoulders. No, I definitely was not imagining my tendonitis, it sure was there but I put on both rowing gloves. I picked the oars up and slid forward on *my* seat, bent my knees further than usual and deliberately set both oars.

Into the water they dipped and through the stroke I straightened and drove through with my legs, straightened my back but kept my arms straight and lifted the blades out of the water. And repeated the stroke. I'd decided to try to row without bending my arms, just bending my legs and back. Hopefully I would be able to isolate any movement in the shoulders and make minor adjustment as the hands went up slightly to place the oars in the water and down slightly to take the oars out again.

The technique was about 80 per cent effective. It gave my shoulders the rest they badly required. Over the whole two hours I concentrated on this straight-arm ocean-rowing technique.

*

The early morning sun was directly in my eyes, a blazing glare off the sea, but for the first time on this quest the glare and sun assisted with concentration. The sea, thank God, was predictable and with eyes shut most of the time I thought my way through rowing without using my arms to finish a stroke. Gradually the technique improved and the power generated by my legs and back brought the speed up to two knots. I was delighted and my roller coaster began to come out of the dip and started back up the slope again. I believed I had found a viable long-term alternative. I had my Hillary Step.

At the completion of this shift, when Phil emerged just before 6 a.m., we had a little discussion about seats. Phil had been having a difficult time with chafing; the silicone barrier cream was plainly an assistance yet he felt as if he was on the bones of his arse. Now the reason was crystal clear to us both. The wrong seats had directly added to both our woes of the past five days.

The rest of the day was great apart from the little things that irritate. Like when I was getting ready for my mid-morning shift I couldn't find my hat. Phil, who appeared to be annoyed, passed the comment, "Come on Rob, don't be an idiot."

I knew he was tired, but I still felt he was being negative as all I had done was to temporarily misplace my sunhat. I didn't need that remark. Maybe I should have told him I was brassed off, but I held my silence, confining my comments to my diary. He never made a comment like this again. Later, when I started to get a little paranoid, I wondered if he had read what I had written.

*

Ranulph Fiennes, *Mind Over Matter*

As always when we walked or jogged together there was an unspoken element of competition. I had never quite made up my mind whether this was a key component of whatever success we might have had as a team or whether it was a lethal chemical awaiting a chance tinder spark to ignite.

*

While on my morning shift I listened to my little Walkman with renewed pleasure. Jimi Hendrix, the sound track to *Pulp Fiction*, the mixed tape with Van Morrison and Crowded House. I had made the Van Morrison/

Crowded House tape whilst staying in London with my cousin Robert Rossiter and his wife. I was given *Pulp Fiction* while visiting Gary McAdams in Nottingham. Gary, a fellow rower from Whakatane and now a Great Britain representative, had also given me the Jimi Hendrix tape before I left the UK for Tenerife three weeks ago. It was new music to me. I loved it and wondered what else I had missed out on in life. Hendrix was great on the ocean, just the four of us, Jimi, *Kiwi Challenge*, the Atlantic and me.

This was better. I was beginning to enjoy the odyssey a little more. I attached the Walkman to the rear of my shorts and quietly hummed as I stiff-armed the Atlantic. At least I thought I quietly hummed as I didn't want to disturb Phil because if it wasn't a hum it would be a great flat sound. (Have you heard anybody quietly sing with headphones on?) Van Morrison's "Piper at the Gates of Dawn" was next and I loved that.

I thought of Rob Whitaker, from the good ship *The Golden Fleece*. Rob, of dog-bowl speakers fame, was a very pleasant, co-operative person, a young teacher and a rowing coach, who was to row the race. Five days before the race started, he pulled me aside and had a word with me. As he talked, he became more downcast and tears slid down his cheek. He had tendonitis in both his shoulders, which had been playing up for several months. He had a number of tests on them but at that time he literally couldn't lift his arms above shoulder height.

He was out; he would have to withdraw from the race. Luckily *The Golden Fleece* had a back-up person, but that hadn't consoled Rob. He was distraught and so disappointed. He had taken a deep breath, straightened up, said thanks and slipped off, to go and assist with preparations for this boat. As I thought of Rob Whitaker, I wondered how the *Fleece* was going, and thought of my good luck to still be rowing. I wondered about the shoulder tendonitis. Was their rig too high? Had he aggravated the tendon through rowing the *Fleece*? Bad luck for that Rob, but good luck for this Rob.

*

Macaroni cheese was for lunch. After freeze-dried food it tasted great. I actually like macaroni cheese. When I cooked I left it a little runny as cleaning the pot afterwards would be difficult if I had allowed it to stick. Thick sticks, thin is great! Yes, I ended the shift heaps more positive and felt afresh that this was a great adventure. I was feeling confident that when I became fully fit once more, we would be able to make up lost ground on those in front of us.

In the few days we had been racing we had discovered that our day packs had slightly more food in them than we could physically consume. So our 75 day packs probably carried 85–90 days' worth of food. We talked about the progress we had made, the amount of food we had, and how long the journey was likely to take us at this rate of progress. Phil called for a gentleman's wager and reckoned 43 days would be our time and I picked 52. Either way we felt we had too much food.

We took a calculated risk and dumped most of the contents of 20 day packs overboard. We kept the bags and wrappers but dumped most of the rations, excluding some of the Mother Earth fruit bars we carried in the packs — they were a bit of a favourite. This lightened us by about 20 kg and although it is stating the obvious, it was 20 kg less that we had to drag through the water. I suspect that we were the only crew to take such drastic action so early in the race.

*

Mid-afternoon we hit a calm patch with a flat sea, and of course no wind. The ocean was a clear, sharp crystalline blue through which you could see for a great depth. Phil went for a swim to inspect the hull for growth and baby barnacles. Fortunately there was only minimal growth, suggesting the anti-fouling coating was doing its job. I remained in the boat for 10 minutes, trying to pluck up the courage to dive in. I would get up on the gunwales and look at the ocean before stepping back onto the deck. I chickened out, so instead I had a thorough wash in the bucket, our one and only multi-purpose bucket. I have this irrational fear of sharks.

"Fear, a wasted emotion," was one of Phil's common phrases. I would hear it again.

There were no signs of any fish, let alone sharks, yet I couldn't bring myself to jump into the ocean. You see, there were 4000 m between the bottom of the boat and the next bit of land, the ocean floor. Four kilometres! Four kilometres down — there must be something between that ocean floor and us. Maybe that something was harmless, there probably were layers and layers of harmless things. On the other hand.... Na. I opted to stay on board.

The end of day came as it had started. I cooked my tea, ate it and headed for a rest before my 8 p.m. shift. Pain and movement in my stomach was not my nemesis, seasickness — it was an old-fashioned lurgy coming on. As a consequence I began my shift early, sitting on the bucket in the bow with diarrhoea roaring, all rumble, bubble, pains and trouble then fizz and froth when the honey soy chicken came on through. I thought it must have been a headless chicken the way it ran.

Nevertheless it put me off honey soy chicken for the remainder of the race, and I'd just completed the food dump! Damn.

21.

Storm

The sea is mother-death and she is a mighty female,
the one who wins, the one who sucks us all up.
Anne Sexton THE POET'S STORY

LATE THAT AFTERNOON THE weather altered very quickly. Thirty minutes later the calm had given way to a light head wind which was right bang on the nose coming straight out of the south-west. The postcard blue sea changed to a coarse darker hue and a light chop enveloped the surface. By nightfall the wind had lifted further. Later on I stiff-arm rowed the 10 o'clock to midnight shift when the wind was getting up to a significant strength, say around 10 knots. At midnight, after I called Phil out, we decided to row together to see how much progress we could make. For an hour we plugged away but the log was slowing to the point where we were down to only half a knot.

The seas were getting up to a couple of metres while the wind was up to 15 knots. The combination of sea and wind was a problem now that we were beginning to be pushed backwards. The sea anchor came out of its insignificant orange bag, rather like a large duffle bag. It was attached to a small orange buoy which floated off downwind, spreading the anchor. When the anchor deployed it acted like a 3 m diameter parachute. A large shackle weighted at the bottom kept it vertical in the water, at a depth determined by the flotation buoy attachment ropes. It had a hole in the apex allowing some water through, which also helped to keep the anchor open.

The sea anchor counters the effect of the sea and wind. Because the sea anchor was deployed from the bow and was lashed to a cleat on the strengthened front bow cabin bulkhead, the bow swung around so that it faced the sea, neatly slicing the larger swells. This minimised the drag of the sea on the boat. Effectively the sea anchor functioned rather like a monster jellyfish, undulating, expanding and contracting (a little) as it slowly moved through the water, preventing our tiny boat from being blown all the way back to the Canary Islands.

The effect on the boat was immediate. It bucked, strained and creaked at the leash, movements that were very different from the free soul in the sea we had been rowing. The seas weren't too bad but the blustery wind was too strong to row into, even as a pair. With the sea anchor out and apparently working effectively, we retired to the cabin.

*

Lying in the cabin, the boat being buffeted and bounced around the ocean, I wondered if any other crew had a partner as tough as Phil. Other more practical questions beckoned. Did the others have this storm, had the leading boats escaped out the front of this storm; if we were the front boat then others would be caught in it, but were we? What of those going south in the attempt to gain the north-east trade winds first? Had they eluded the storm? Eventually I was rocked to sleep.

Sleeping two in the cubby cabin was no treat. This was the first time Phil and I slept together in this cabin with all our paraphernalia packed in. In retrospect it would have been funny, viewed by a cockroach on the roof of the cabin. (Incidentally we didn't find any roaches or other non-working crew.) We had both endeavoured to get some sleep lying under our sleeping bags, with our heads towards the hatch and feet towards the tapered stern.

After about an hour, I woke and found Phil's feet touching mine. I moved them and went back to sleep. A wave crashing on the bow and sloshing about the deck woke us both and as I turned I noticed that our feet touched, but Phil moved his away. I went to sleep again. When I awoke next our feet were once again touching. The cramped space caused me to nudge Phil's feet enough so that he woke and moved them, ever so slightly, to his side.

I subconsciously thought, "If I touch his feet, he will move them, then I will have that tiny bit of extra room." We both recognised that we kept each other awake during the night and that neither of us liked our feet touching the other's. The following night we decided to top and tail. I was willing to sleep next to Phil's delightful toes in the interests of a peaceful sleep. He was equally happy, so top and tail it was. How bizarre, I thought. Here were two grown men too macho to feel comfortable letting their feet touch. As if anyone really gives a stuff!

*

The cabin was small, and with two crammed in, it seemed tiny. We were frequently banging into each other, waking each other up. Having just got used to the free range movements of the *Kiwi Challenge*, the jerky unnatural movements of a tethered boat meant there was a set of quick movements to become accustomed to. Finally there was the aspect of two sweaty males, each devoid of deodorant, sharing a double coffin. The air was a little rich, which did not make for pleasant dreams.

Pleasant dreams. I thought I was having dreams of terror. Phil was having dreams the nature of which I suspect policemen the world over experience. Dreams of work. About four in the morning Phil started thrashing around, grappling with the ceiling joist, grinding his teeth and muttering incoherently. I had to give him a hefty thump on the shoulder to wake him up, before he inadvertently belted me.

"Uh?"

"Sorry, dude. You were dreaming and I thought I'd better wake you up before you smashed the cabin apart."

"Oh, sorry. I was just chasing some low-life scum down the street. I had just apprehended him and he was resisting arrest. I was in the process of calming him down when you woke me."

He turned and dropped immediately back into the force, breathing deeply.

*

As I lay there I realised that Phil must be absolutely exhausted. Three days ago, when my shoulder pain was at its height, he had rowed a 16-hour day; since then he had rowed a minimum of 12 hours a day. I had no doubt the effort he put in during his turn at the oars was above what we had planned as a consistent output. It must have been — the log showed that we had moved 54 nautical miles, on day three, the day I had either "stirred tea" or rested.

All I had been able to accomplish that day was to keep the boat on course. The first day that I tried rowing without bending my arms we covered 65 miles. Plainly, the bulk of the rowing had been done by Phil. Moving an 850 kg boat 45 miles a day — that is pretty strong stuff. We had agreed that we would conserve our energies in the early stages, but here we were — just six days into the journey and he was being called upon to deliver a superhuman performance, session after session, to try and maintain our daily targets.

I was disgusted with myself, but looking back on it now I can see that — from his point of view — Phil was doing exactly what he had always said we should do; protect the individual in the early stages. The only problem was that he was putting an inhuman strain on himself. I thought I was coming right slowly, but he definitely needed a break.

Time on the sea anchor would benefit us both. Phil could then give his body a breather and allow some wounds on his backside time to heal. Also I could use some time for my shoulders. The Brufen and cross-stitch massaging of the tendons appeared to assist; just a little more time and I would be a genuine partner in this effort. On the other hand, I wanted to get going and if I mentioned it there would be no stopping Phil. Regardless of his personal condition he would push on.

*

What do two men talk about, imprisoned in a tiny cabin for three days while an Atlantic gale howls outside? Well, they address the deep philosophical questions of life, of course. Why does it rain more at night? Why does the Earth's mass increase by 2 tonnes a day? Is the Bactrian camel the only mammalian quadruped with the ability to invert its nostrils totally inside out? Not to mention the matter of which was the world's most incredible pregnancy.

While we were at sea two things gave me a great sense of security. One was being in the cabin. It seemed to me that, providing I was in there, nothing could really go wrong. Ultimately I would be safe. The other was completely illogical. I was greatly reassured by the fact that there were another 29 craft like ours out there somewhere. Why I felt this way I don't know — none of them could have helped rescue us had we got into trouble — but I did.

*

It was a great breakfast the next morning. There was no rush and I could eat sitting down. The bad news was that the wind was still blowing from the south-west and we were still firmly on the anchor. Whilst we were out on deck checking that everything was tied down, and fretting about the situation, Phil thought he saw two opposition boats. Then he thought it may have been *3 Com*, the mother ship. Then he wasn't sure. I sure can relate to that feeling as there were a few swell caps getting blown away with white water moving off the top of the crests and it played havoc with our perception of distance and whether it was white water or a white boat or something else. The condition of the sea remained the same: not rough, just short swells of 1½–2 m.

*

The next morning, after staring at the sea for a while, we decided to have another crack at the conditions. In came the sea anchor and out went the oars. Together we rowed as a pair for two hours but it was hard work and we were going nowhere. For the moment we had to admit defeat. Reluctantly out went the sea anchor once more and in came the oars. I stretched, scratched, scanned the horizon for competitors, ships, a break in the weather — anything — while all along the south-west wind roared on through.

Into the cabin I went, pushed the stern hatch right up and sat out over the stern, contemplating. I liked this position. It's the equivalent of being captain on the bridge of a large vessel. Well, dream on, Rob. Something moved near the stern. Fish! I moved faster than I had for a week. Being no idiot, I knew where the fishing line was. Out on the deck in a jiffy. I made up the lures, tied on the hook and threw the line in the briny. Something tugged and took both the lure and hook. Bugger.

I had no sinker (there is a weight restriction on this craft) but this time I took a little more care tying the lure and the hook. Over the leeward starboard side again. I waited and waited, and waited, then — bloody hell — it took my lure again. This time the blighters were not going to take my lure. I only had six. Another hook was tied and over the side the line went again.

Strike! I got it. Better than Lotto. Out of the water it came. I lifted the fish high and performed my first fish-at-sea dance. The dorado wriggled, flipped and slipped the hook. It thudded onto the deck just as the boat lurched on the sea anchor. My dorado slithered towards a port scupper and to my absolute horror returned to the ocean. I shut up in one big hurry.

Crestfallen I checked the line, lure and hooks, cast all to the starboard ocean and waited. And waited and waited again. Phil passed some obligatory remark about a fish in the hand is worth two in the sea, but patience, Phil.

Another strike. More yahoos, much more care, a subdued fish-catching dance and carefully, quickly into the bucket. I unhooked the fish and then I saw it was another dorado. Off I went to cast again and this time another strike came quickly. Now you have to admit this was really living. Into the bucket it went to join its fellow fish. I cast again; patience was required this time but by now I was delighted to have fresh fish.

*

Bror Muller, rower and friend.

Do you remember our fight with Phil over taking a fishing line? Too heavy! I guess he was then pissed off to find you had it on the trip. I don't remember how the fishing gear actually came to be in your stuff but I certainly recall thinking that once Phil thought he was right you couldn't change his mind and I thought he was wrong about this issue so I would hide it in your possessions anyway. You could blame me when you found it at sea.

*

This time an amused Phil had gone to the stern hatch and had the video camera rolling. He was chortling away and offering encouragement. The problem was that this time I couldn't get a bite even though I could see fish everywhere. Finally I pulled up the line, hooked the dead fish on the end of it and threw it overboard. Then, with Phil as cameraman, I pulled it back up and thrashed the deck with it, pretending to be dealing it a death blow. Later this footage would shown on worldwide television. To the best of my knowledge no viewer ever noticed that the fish was already dead!

In one hour I caught five dorados. Then there was the skilled job of filleting the fish before I threw the remains over the side to satisfy all those teeth below. There was blood everywhere and I enjoyed cleaning the boat and washing everything down.

"Well Rob, if nothing else, you and the fish provided bloody good entertainment. Bringing the fishing line wasn't such a bad idea after all."

"Right on, dude, you are on the button there. Now if they only taste as good as the entertainment, we're in heaven."

We fired up the cooker and carefully fried the fillets one by one on the pot lid. It was great to have fresh fish. Rubbery sort of flesh, but above all it was juicy and fresh and coupled with imaginary fries and lemon it was superb. Even without the imagineries the fish still tasted great. We sat quietly eating our meal and enjoyed the moment while the wind blew and beat upon our boat. We were content.

*

Later that night we discussed our position in the race. We reckoned it to be no worse than fifth. In Tenerife we had had many exploratory talks with other crews and now Phil and I agreed that most of them carried less efficient drogues and maybe only two or three carried a sea anchor. Drogues were really meant for a following sea — they slowed you down very little in rough weather. They would be deployed from the stern, and the stern taking the sea was rather like a broad, flat board with a sign saying, "Push me".

The sea would accept the invitation and push the boat. The drogue would then slow that boat's movement through the water, but not to the extent of a sea anchor. The contrast between a drogue and a bow-deployed sea anchor would be apparent. If the storm ... well, it wasn't really a storm. In David Stubbs' yachting phraseology, this was adverse weather. Well, if this adverse weather continued for another day we convinced ourselves we should have picked up a couple of places as others slipped further back.

Riding on anchor all that night made for a very long night indeed. With the sea still rising it meant we were now entertaining incoming waves over the bow on a regular basis. I could feel the waves hit the bow and hear the foaming hiss as they came crashing along the deck, finally thudding into the cabin hatch. Before retiring, Phil went out on deck to check the watermaker had topped up all four fresh water containers which were part of our ballast in the centre hold. Just a precaution to have our maximum weight low down (150 kg), should the sea become nasty.

Huddled in the cabin, we listened to the BBC World Service. There was nothing concerning our race at all and nothing about the weather we were experiencing. I was disappointed that we had not heard any news of the race on short-wave radio since we began. This was most frustrating. At this moment I couldn't help but wish we had taken more sophisticated communication equipment, if only to know where we sat in relation to the rest of the fleet.

*

It was October 19. We were listening to the news as we ate breakfast. Then, quite unexpectedly, the presenter announced in that plummy BBC English,

"In Christchurch, New Zealand ... ", our ears pricked up, "inmates have taken over a prison and are presently holding their guards hostage."

Only a brief item, but as it finished Sgt Stubbs piped up from the other side of the cabin, somewhere in the vicinity of my ankles: "See what happens when I leave the country!"

We left the radio on and lay in the cabin stewing on our own thoughts. I stared at the doodles I had done on my side of the hull. One of them was a quote from my first rowing coach, Chick Hammond, which had become the motto of the Whakatane Rowing Club....

*

Whakatane Rowing Club motto
Bleed for speed,
Because pain is temporary,
Pride is forever.

22.

Sitting It Out

The biggest sin is sitting on your arse.
Florynce Kennedy

I COULD HEAR THE waves as they slip-slapped against the hull, the swells gurgling down the sides of the boat, the tormented creak of the rope off the bow, the bluster of the wind. Not being a seaman I had read and talked a little about the ocean to those that had been offshore. That was before we had left New Zealand. Now those conversations had authenticity. I remembered discussions about storms and lay there wondering if we were about to be tested. I thought a lot about drowning in those early days at sea.

*

Anonymous seaman

You don't know what pitch-polling is, son? No matter how big the swell, a non-breaking wave won't be a problem. It won't sink you. A single breaking wave, though, would flip you end over end if it was higher than your boat was long.

Typically, what would happen is you would climb the wave at an angle of 45 degrees, and not having enough grunt fail to gain the top, you'd slide down the face. Your stern would bury itself into the trough and the crest of the wave would catch your bow and flip you over. You would only need an 8 m wave.

Now, take foundering. That's where a succession of waves simply drives the boat under "founders", as we say. The dictionary defines founder as something like "to cave in, sink, fail, utterly collapse". On your boat the stern roof hatch would probably implode, the front and cabin hatches fail and the boat would down-flood.

You would be prevented from escaping by the sheer force of the water pouring into the cabin – it would be similar to walking into the blast from a fire hose. In that sense, pitch-polling is better than foundering because an overturned boat traps air in the hold and can stay afloat for a period of time.

Rolling. Rolling is when the height of the wave is higher than the width of the boat, and if you are not square on to the wave.

*

Another day, October 20, and still we sat tethered. The wind was exactly the opposite of what should be happening. It had swung round to the sou'-south-west. We theorised about the El Niño effect over breakfast. We were riding the storm okay and we hadn't accepted any waves aboard since early last night. But it was pretty boring. All we could do was sit and wait.

Phil read the Admiralty book on this area of the Atlantic again, searching for something he may have missed. I did my washing in the bucket; it was a major wash-out this time, both my T-shirts and one pair of rowing shorts. Whenever we got going again I would be sartorially well-equipped with a clean wardrobe.

My hair was uncomfortably hot so I decided a "number one" was called for.

Out came the medical kit and I hunted in it for the scissors. I then went forward to the bow, far away from anyone else, well, at least 1.5 m away, and cut my hair. Starting from the front I grabbed a lock and cut it as close to my skull as possible. I shouldn't have been surprised, but it was like cutting fibreglass. But eventually it was all gone. I sloshed the decks down and committed my hair to the deep. There wasn't much else I could do now, we just had to wait. The sea looked ugly from down here, a greywacke blue, lumpy sea, coming at us from the south-west, the wind still 15–20 knots. I returned to the cabin.

"Hey Rob, did you hear about the two archaeologists tramping in the mountains of Iran?" said Phil looking up from his Admiralty charts.

"No, what happened?" I absentmindedly responded.

"They came across two frozen bodies at the foot of a glacier. On close inspection one said to the other, 'My God, it's Adam and Eve!' How did they know that?"

"I don't know. How?" Still rather distracted.

"Come on Rob, it's pretty simple. Think about it, mate."

We repeated the entire conversation. I didn't have a clue as to why, and Phil was pressing me to be analytical and solve the riddle. It was just not my scene.

"Oh well, I'll ask you later," said Phil returning to the sole book we had brought for the journey.

Actually, he proposed a lot of these brain-teasers while we were at sea. Mostly I didn't get the answers. Usually he would tell me them eventually, but not with this one. I would keep trying to solve it, but I never got it right. He would urge me to try again.

"One day you'll get it, Rob."

*

A little solace rather than mind-teasers was what I sought. Out of the stern hatch I wriggled and sat up on the bridge to survey the Atlantic. The wind had swung a little further and was now coming from the west and the seas had dropped to one and a half metres. My Walkman was tucked into my shorts with my U2 tape inside so before I gave the volume a tweak I fitted the ear plugs in my ears and then I was away. Here I sat up in the hatch stripped to the waist, the result of both a warm wind and the washing of my entire day-wear wardrobe.

The jerky rhythm of the boat rising through the swells and settling down into the trough was being enacted before me, the unique guitar playing of The Edge resounding through my skull while here I sat almost detached from reality, enjoying the total entertainment offering.

A waning moon in fleeting flashes of soft light squeezed through gaps in the fast-moving cloud cover and gave the seascape a quilted appearance. The sea doesn't get tedious to look at. Its multifarious wave sequences converge and cross in patterns that have never happened before and will never happen again. It is all very satisfying and soothing and I could look at it for hours. But at the back of my mind, through the U2 sound, a little nervous twitch between synapses triggered the words "urgency" and "desire". I took another long look at the criss-crossing patterns, that lumpy greywacke sea and slipped inside.

"I think the wind is changing a bit, swinging to the west. What about giving it a go?"

'Yup, let's." Phil responded.

*

The Atlantic Rowing Race, October 19, 1997

Dr Carl Clinton was evacuated from his boat, *Commodore Shipping*, due to severe back pains, leaving his partner, John Searson, to go it alone. Carl was airlifted to hospital by the Canarian Air Rescue Service as it was felt that transferring him to a passing ship would not have been feasible due to his suspected slipped disc. Apparently, in the rough seas they were experiencing, Carl missed a stroke and fell, hitting John Searson's foot plate.

John Searson was adamant he wished to continue the journey as solo rower.

*

We got under away at 8.45 p.m., with the wind back down to sou'-south-west. Together we rowed directly into it, making one knot, but at least we were moving. I dropped out at 10 p.m., rested and changed with Phil at midnight. We rowed together again from 2 a.m. but at 3 a.m. we decided to throw out the anchor again. We had dropped down to less than half a knot and it was not worth the effort.

Again we rested, slept frustrated and woke caged and snappy with each other. This was the third day of "adverse weather". I couldn't help but think, "Christopher Columbus took this route and he had a benign journey out to the New World. So what the Christopher is going wrong here? Why is the weather so bloody perverse, when is it going to change, will it improve or will the winds whip the seas up more?" I had never enjoyed enforced inactivity. We had no books or reading material — other than a single Admiralty publication and my quotations. Short-wave wasn't interested in the race, the rest of the world seemed peripheral and all we wanted was to row this bloody boat away from here.

I turned and pressed my face into the hull and listened to that world outside again. The sea anchor was out. I lay on my back. The wind was still blowing at 20 knots out of the south-west. The blustery, relentless, shoving wind blasted up against the *Kiwi Challenge*, the rushing sound overriding the urgent slap, slap, thud, squish, slop, slap of the confused 2 m sea outside. We could rest and doze but sleep wasn't easy. The boat's movements continued to be tortured; tethered to the sea anchor, it wanted to escape downwind, but being unable to, leapt, twisted and dropped into troughs in the manner of a playful pup. I rested well but slept fitfully.

*

October 21 was day nine. We were both up at daybreak and talked about the weather as we ate breakfast. We were sure the wind was dropping and shifting a little to the west again; the clouds appeared to be lighter and more measured in pacing themselves across our sky and the barometer was rising. By 8.30 we had decided to have another crack at moving the boat westward. We stowed everything, Phil brought the sea anchor aboard and I was under way at 8.45.

Using my inelegant stiff-arm stroke, I put plenty of leg into the work, and began to make one knot, and by the end of my shift was moving through the dying swells at one and a half knots. Slow, true, but hey, we were Barbados-bound. Our first major marine sighting, a pod of dolphins, briefly accompanied us. I closed my eyes as the sun came out for the first time in four days; it was sharp, slanting, cutting into my eyes and a right bloody nuisance, but perversely I was delighted to have its dazzling company. Phil, while resting in the cabin, apparently heard another two pods of dolphins go by, but I missed them both as I concentrated on the sea and enjoyed the sun.

*

The Challenge Business, www.challengebus.co.uk, October 20, 1997

CB 24 made contact with married couple David and Nadia Rice on board *Hannah Snell*. They were both well but were experiencing problems with their water-maker, which they have had to convert to manual operation.

*

We changed shifts at 10 a.m. and it really felt great to have the cabin to myself. I rested with the rear hatch right up, enjoying the free movement of *Kiwi Challenge* and the fresh air in the cabin. Even the boat seemed to be reacting better, as if to say, "This is better, guys." Yes, this was better than being on the sea anchor. Phil called out, "Good having the cabin to yourself again, eh?"

"Sure is, mate!"

The sun was in my eyes. I wore both my floppy shirt and the legionnaire hat as protection. Although the sea was still coming at me with 2 m swells the white tops had disappeared and we could handle swells. I clipped the Walkman on the back of my rowing shorts and played my Van Morrison tape. "Piper at the Gates of Dawn" has a fantastic flute interlude that never failed to lift my spirits. "*... and listen to the silence of the wind in the willows and the piper at the gates of dawn ... and row the boat as the light grows steadily stronger.*" Van Morrison and Rob Hamill, inspiring stuff, us two, only I was the silent one.

During my 4–6 p.m. shift I could feel my shoulders being worked over by the tendonitis so I experimented with the shorter 3 m blades. They felt a little better: a lighter load, but I could lock the blade firmly in the water and as such felt I was making the same progress through the water. I used them for some days, feeling happier with myself because of the change of the effect on my shoulders.

*

Jeni Pearce had estimated that we would need a minimum of 5000 calories a day to survive the 75 days rowing originally scheduled. To race and to lower the crossing time we needed more calories, many more. Neither of us had the laboratory resources nor time to calculate either Phil's or my individual requirements, so the meal packs were common, a day's rations for two. They included high-protein and mineral-supplemented milkshakes.

When you mixed a milkshake at the beginning of a shift, they were warm, unappetising and gluggy. However, after eight days I was now able to consume more, and not think of them as rancid. They were just fuel intake, like eating your greens as a kid when everybody else was having their dessert. One flavour didn't make the grade — mocha. I questioned Jeni's pedigree before feeding mocha to those teeth lurking in the depths below! Each time I struck a mocha in my lunch I shared the contents with the sea life.

*

Insert from Rob Hamill's diary for that day

Said to Phil while he was pissing out the stern hatch, "Confucius say 'Knob must extend past hatch to avoid golden shower on pillow.'"

*

Overnight the wind and the seas had died right away, the moon was on the wane and low in the north-east I could see a bright light. Concentrating hard, I could make out the mast underneath and the hull below that. I was fairly sure it was *3 Com*. I was elated. We could at last find out what was happening in the race and, most important, where the hell we were positioned. I was about to yell to Phil, but first I blinked once. Damn! It was just a particularly bright star. I had been hallucinating, seeing what I wanted to see.

It wasn't the last time something like that happened to me. I saw flashing fins, sea serpents and all manner of weird imaginings before the voyage was over, but always at night. I'm told this is common at sea. A mate of mine tells me he sees possums on the deck of his yacht in mid-ocean. They never come out in the daytime, but then possums are like that.

*

I took a couple of Revive sprays under my tongue to try to bring me to my senses. We were using homoeopathic remedies to help our recovery and cope with sleep deprivation. We sourced three homoeopathic remedy combinations called Sleep Monster, Revive and Endurance. The first two were designed to help with the effects of minimal sleep, the latter to help recovery of muscles after each session. They definitely worked as long as we took them regularly as prescribed.

*

I rowed on, getting a little assistance from the breeze, which at the moment was a three-knot west-nor'-westerly. A whale blew in the distance. I saw not a thing, I had no idea where it was and I rowed on. These conditions were not bad and once again I wondered where on earth the other boats were. We could well be catching some of them if we kept on in this vein. I worried about whether those that had taken the southerly option had missed the storm by being further south, and whether they would be closer to Barbados.

I also wondered about the rowing season at home, which would be just getting under way, when a shooting star silently, beautifully and effortlessly slid across our sky. I strained on the oars a little as I rowed on, making two and a half knots and believing if I rowed at his pace I could keep the dawn at bay just a little longer. I had to go for a pee three times on this 4–6 a.m. shift so I must have neglected to put the electrolytes in my water, not a sensible thing to forget. At 6 a.m. I called Phil and mixed myself a milkshake and an isotonic drink as I couldn't afford to lose those salts into the sea. Rather tired, I rested in the cabin.

*

October 23, day 11, was an incredible day. It dawned with high whispery clouds and a gentle 4- to 5-knot west-nor'-west breeze that was a bit of a help and a bit of a hindrance. The seas were fine but all over the place like a mocha milkshake. I called Phil for his 10 a.m. shift and he ritually checked our position while sitting in the cabin.

He suddenly turned, smiling, "I'll check in a minute, mate, but I think that we have a new daily distance record, 67 miles!"

Phil was still wasting me in distance covered over a shift, but my distances were improving all the time. I was delighted with this distance, especially seeing we had had little assistance in the last 24 hours.

It may have only been 10 in the morning but already the day was warm, clear and beautiful. Phil worked on the slip, slop, hat and sunnies routine and armed with his plastic drink bottles he got into his rowing possie. Once settled he joined in with me and we rowed together for 10 minutes or so before I dropped out. We could expect six to eight hours of temperatures in excess of 30°C. As the weather improved, the temperature climbed.

At noon I made sure that I had my drinks mixed well as I had been most annoyed with myself yesterday, and set out to see if we could better the new record. The sun beat down unsympathetically while the glare from the sea was acute. I began to sweat. The air was crisp, but the boat was moving comfortably enough. Phil had mentioned that we should have these conditions 2 per cent of the time, so I hoped this was to be our one day of doldrums. Fat chance of that.

*

My next shift was highlighted by a feeding frenzy with dorados gorging themselves on hapless sprats. It was absolutely fascinating to row through the carnage as the water would suddenly churn with tens of dark dorados all over the area then all would be quiet before there was another seething eruption elsewhere in the vicinity. From the surface I could only imagine the life-and-death circling, herding and darting escape manoeuvres being enacted just below the surface. It certainly added interest to the Karapiro calm and the heat was ignored as the shift flew by. I knew who was going fishing come 6 p.m.

We had drunk about eight litres each this hot day. Consequently, the water-maker was on most of the day. Prior to the early evening 6 p.m. changeover Phil went and routinely checked the outlet to make sure we weren't overfilling the plastic water bottles. The four bottles we had connected were only a quarter full!

The outlet was dribbling salt water. Well, brackish water. Morrie was working so it must have been the water-maker filter system. We didn't say much but thought heaps. Phil suggested he pull it apart tomorrow when the light would be better. We changed over, Phil took the oars and I went fishing. I could feel that same ice cold stalagmite in my lower stomach again.

Phil was calm and thoughtful. He had dismantled the filter system back in New Zealand, so he knew how to do it. But repeating the operation at sea wasn't going to be so easy. This time it was for real. The consequences of failure didn't bear thinking about.

23.

Cool, Clear Water

The less said between individuals under extreme stress the better.
Ranulph Fiennes MIND OVER MATTER

I CAUGHT A DORADO while letting the line out, put it straight in the bucket up front, slit its throat and drained its blood. The next came in five minutes, the third 15 minutes later, but there was no elation; I simply fished for food. Silently I filleted the fish. With the remains I made my obligatory offering to the jaws below. I slipped past Phil, dropped the fillets in the cooking pot swaying on the gimbals and made preparations to lie down for a rest in the cabin.

"Would you mind rowing for a while, Rob?" Phil asked quietly. "I would like to take a look at the desalinator now just in case it gets rough tomorrow. I reckon the mast and cabin lights should give me enough light to work with."

"Yeah, sure. Good idea."

I moved back to the bow seat and with muted emotion took up my oars and rowed again.

"Could you pass us the spare O rings and tools, Rob?"

"Sure."

I stopped rowing and extracted the toolkit from the extreme forward port hold; one of the four small, watertight mini deck holds adjacent to the bow cabin in the front of the boat. Out came the complete kit. I screwed the hatch down and silently passed the equipment over.

"Cheers."

Phil wedged himself in the well, stuck his head into the starboard storage hatch and began undoing the bolts holding the desalination unit to the inner wall. He then undid the bolts securing the cylindrical filter and gently worked the gears out of the 50-watt motor to which the filter had been attached. He left the motor in the hatch still attached to its electrical connection — looking like the blackened and bodiless head of C3PO from *Star Wars* — then manoeuvred the filter into the cabin.

It was now dark, but there was adequate light coming from the cabin and the masthead light. Phil fossicked around in the cabin and got the

Power Survivor manual out of his side curtain rack. Silently he read for 20 minutes, then seemingly endlessly and minutely examined the exploded diagram for what was probably only a further 10 minutes. I watched him intensely as I absentmindedly rowed. The significance of the situation was written across his face. The strain was evident, a deep frown etched into his forehead, furrows dug deep between his eyebrows.

I rowed. What were our options? First, I had to rely on Phil's mechanical skills. He was once a diesel mechanic, but that was a bloody long time ago. Failing a successful repair, we would have to activate our EPIRB. This would bring the mother ship with one of two options. The first would be to take on board extra water and row on, excluded from the race. The other option would be to exit the race, torch the *Kiwi Challenge* and sail off to Barbados on the mother ship. Phil would have preferred to burn the boat.

There was really no choice, we would row on. We owed it to our sponsors, supporters and ourselves to row on, whatever the adversity. The objective remained — cross that line first, whether in the race or disqualified by equipment failure. Working quietly and slowly, Phil pulled the whole unit apart, scrutinising each part as he detached it from the unit then looked back at the manual. He then cleaned that part and placed it, each part sequentially across the cabin floor.

Out on the ocean the dorado had long since stopped hunting and were now following the boat, our mast light acting like the pied piper. The scene was ironically magical. As I moved the boat gently through the water these silver shapes moved carelessly with me. I pulled in the oars, stood up and observed as dozens of dorado now circled *Kiwi Challenge* like sharks eyeing their prey. I continued, awed by the beauty of the moment contrasting so powerfully with the emotion of our predicament.

The swell had long since gone. The night sky was subdued, the stars seemingly dim, interspersed with clouds floating leisurely, noiselessly, giving the illusion of nature not interfering with the concentration of humans. I found that unconsciously I was trying to row the boat as smoothly as possible, keeping a steady rhythmical pace.

*

Phil worked on oblivious of my attention, the unit in ordered pieces to the side of him, our only spares, the O rings for the pressure vessel, beside his left knee. He sighed, straightened his back, then returned, hunched over the diagram for a minute or two. With assiduous care he began to reassemble the unit, using the spare O rings to replace the existing rings.

"If you can get that thing going, Phil, I'll nominate you as *Kiwi Challenge* Man of the Week," I said, in a weak attempt at humour. He gave an acknowledging half-laugh. I realised that he would prefer to work in silence. This was something he had to do alone. I concentrated on my own thoughts. I imagined Carolyn and Bror hearing that we had pulled out of the race and tears pooled in my eyes like raw egg white. No, that couldn't happen. It just couldn't.

I watched in silence as Phil reassembled the filter. He then brought it out onto the deck, lowered it into the well, reconnected it to the motor, and bolted it back into position. Three hours had passed since he had begun his repairs. He leaned back into the cabin to throw the switch. I was rigid. Our race could end right here.

Morrie fired back to life. Now, would the little bastard work?

We had to wait a couple of minutes as the pressure built and the system could function. All our attention was on the outlet pipe. At first there was a drop, then a dribble, a spasmodic trickle evolved into a steady trickle. Phil tasted it, his expressionless face suggested it was okay. The trickle continued, my stomach began to thaw and my mind calmed. Phil cupped a handful of water to his mouth.

"It's fresh!" He smiled, stood and punched the sky.

Yes! We looked at each other laughed, hooted and high-fived.

"Shit, I felt that pressure. I knew I had to fix that damned water-maker or we were dead meat," Phil said. "I actually felt quite emotional," he admitted.

*

It was past 10 at night. I had rowed five of the last six hours. I then cooked up the fresh fish fillets.

"No fish for me," said Phil as he rowed, his voice suddenly stern again.

"Eh! Why not?"

"That bloody fishing is a diversion from what we are supposed to be concentrating on. Anyway, we have more than enough food with us, so why catch any more food? It's bloody stupid."

"Come on Phil, this is fresh protein, it will have many nutrients we aren't getting naturally in our present diet. Besides, fishing occasionally is a welcome distraction, mate; it's fun, entertaining and helps break the monotony."

I ate my fish.

"Sure you don't want me to save you any fish, Phil?"

"No thanks!" was the curt reply.

Unbelievable, I thought. All those good feelings we experienced such a short while ago had now turned into unnecessary negatives. I would have liked to have talked the event through; told him what a bloody great job he had done. Given him the *Kiwi Challenge* Man of the Week Award. We'd had a victory. We should have been on a real high. Memories like that last a long time.

*

The bad vibes remained for the rest of the evening. I hit the cabin floor at 10.30, knackered. This had seemed the longest day of the journey so far.

At least the problems of the last 24 hours had been solved. I collapsed, out to the world. After the extensive evening shift I knew the midnight to 2 a.m. shift would be particularly tough. The wind had got up a bit and — surprise, surprise — it was the dreaded sou'wester. My knees and left elbow along with my shoulders now complained and I found it hard to stay awake and concentrate. Phil called it quits at 3.30 a.m. and threw out the sea anchor as we made zero westward movement. Thank God. I was exhausted and in pain. We collapsed and slept on and off until nine the next morning.

*

Day 12, October 24. At 9.30 we decided to have a crack at the headwind together. We rowed for two hours and made a mile or so. Stuff it, the energy drain wasn't worth the mileage gain so we anchored. Out came the Admiralty pilot charts again and Phil hunkered down trying to find out why we were being punished. Escapism was for me. I opened the rear hatch, clipped on the Walkman and sat up, bum on the stern facing the bow, the wind and the sea and listened to U2.

Luciano Pavarotti came to join me on the bridge and what a stage I had, bigger than any earthbound stadium. In windy, wet weather, U2 and Pavarotti performed exclusively for me. They were brilliant, both of them lifting my spirits once again. The song "Miss Sarajevo" echoed in my headset. I asked for and received an encore ... "*Is there a time ...*" Power, passion, precision, the sounds of a tremendous melody. "Pavarotti at the hatch", a scintillating performance; once again I requested another encore and it was willingly provided and as uplifting as the original.

The concert over, I had dinner at my favourite rocking restaurant, moussaka from the chefs at Alliance, followed by a chocolate bar from Cadbury's kitchen. We decided on another stab at the Atlantic before dark. The anchor in, oars out routine again and Phil hit the 5.45–8 p.m. shift. During that shift he decided to alter our course 20 degrees north and abandon the struggle to get further south.

"If the winds are going to be on our nose all the time, and given that we need to make progress somehow, we will do better if we take the winds more on the angle," he explained.

"What happened to the idea of moving further south, Phil?"

"In these conditions, it's pointless."

"But isn't moving further south supposedly going to get us out of these conditions?"

"Look mate, I don't want to talk about it, just row this course."

I wasn't happy about that consultative process. But I rowed 20 degrees further north as requested.

*

During the next day the winds shifted right around to the north, so we altered back to our original course. The weather that followed was morale-boosting and we needed it. The sea smoothed out and 3- to 4-m rolling swells moved in like big steamrollers one after the other. Each swell was separated by at least 100 m with a valley that we would disappear into before emerging on the next peak. They were not steep, quite safe in fact, so we pulled on our oars harder, using the waves' momentum to help us surge, at times up to six knots, before dropping over the back into the next valley. This was more like the conditions we had heard predicted.

During the night we decided to row together in such favourable conditions and try to catch those boats we felt might be out front. At 10 p.m. Phil took over on the oars and I rested for only one hour till 11 p.m., then joined him through to midnight before he took a one-hour rest. We continued this two-on, one-off system for 12 hours. Every second hour we were rowing together and the extra speed gained made it worthwhile. We knew we were on for a record but had to wait until 10 a.m. to find out by how much. It was always the high — or sometimes the low — point of our day. We hooted when Phil announced we had made 82 miles.

*

When I hit the cabin mattress, I lay there for half an hour, awake, my mind buzzing, my body aching, letting the boat's movements side to side take me too. I let my body move from side to side like the proverbial rag doll. I didn't roll, but let my centre of gravity go and squished this way and that. Limp as a jellyfish on a beach. That relaxed me, the sounds of the sea on the hull were soothing too. I could feel the boat pick up a wave and the gurgle as the water speed increased and the little bubbles burbled by the hull.

*

I had noticed a constant pain in my head. I was sure it was a headache, but not a pounding, mind-numbing thing. This version was a dead pain, resulting in a dumbing-down effect. Not pleasant at all. I surmised that it must have something to do with a lack of sleep because when I had woken from longer sleeps while we had the sea anchor out, the pain was less; the brain functioning a little better. Given what was occurring with the rest of my body I could sense that this style of headache was going to be with me for most of the journey.

Phil and I managed to argue once again even though we had just had a record 24-hour run. I suggested that we not fill the water tanks to the brim to avoid back pressure on the water-maker. I thought this may have contributed to the water-maker failure. Phil didn't think so. Not filling the water containers to the top was an easy precaution to take, but he didn't want to know about it. Alternatively he suggested that the turning on and off and the starting and stopping of the water-maker was where the problem lay. Well, there wasn't much we could do about turning a switch on and off.

I wondered if we shouldn't have brought better communications gear. Our whole world revolved around what was happening on our boat. We were getting quite petty. Had we known what was going on with the others, where we were placed, we could have thought about that instead. Argued about it even. At least we would be bitching about something that mattered.

*

On the afternoon shift I saw an amazing flight by a flying fish. By now I had seen thousands of schools in flight, hurtling across waves and into the valleys like hordes of locusts, but this one stood out. I know amazing is one of "my" adjectives, but what would you call a small fish that leaps out of the water trailing droplets of water, skims the ocean's surface by up to half a metre, spreads its horizontal fins and seemingly gains lift over the oncoming swell? Over the crest it would glide down into the following trough and then climb the next incoming swell before folding its fins and slipping neatly into the swell. Amazing! This flight was close to 150 m. Beautiful. All I did was take two strokes and travel a few metres in the opposite direction; not so beautiful.

During this night I was rowing mindlessly. I was still recovering from the "longest day". It was the old moon. The new moon was due in two or three days so it was comparatively dark. I was watching the sea, but at the same time was watching nothing. I was stuffed, but not too stuffed to row and I was feeling my shoulders, all very egocentric. The sea was not a problem; 1- to 2-m swells coming roughly from the north. I looked over my left shoulder and my mind and heart exploded.

It was over my right shoulder! It was a bat. My head whipped to the right. No.

There, half a metre from my face was a bird about to alight on my shoulder. Apart from me nearly being the first Kiwi to take off into space, the bird's eyes opened and it nearly became the first petrel in space. My heart leapt, my shoulders had no pain, adrenalin flowed like it was wave time day one, my mind saw the Archangel Gabriel, the oars vaulted out of the water and the ocean was unimpressed. I stifled a grunt of surprise, one of those out of breathy, low-pitched sounds like a boxer being winded. God, I got a fright! Who frightened who, Hamill or the bird?

*

On the next shift Phil thought he saw a flare go up at 3.45 a.m. It went up and down, no parachute. This was to the east of us. Phil woke me early and asked me to set off a hand-held flare and to look out for a response while he continued to haul on the oars. He was in some doubt as to whether it was a flare or maybe a shooting star. If it was a flare there was very little we could do to be of practical help. The flare was upwind, making it impossible to make any progress in that direction.

We briefly talked about setting off our EPIRB and then letting it drift so that at least some outside help would come. Eventually we settled for watching out for a second flare and then we probably would release our EPIRB. Had we set it off because we were in trouble, our race would have effectively been over. We would have sought outside help and that would have been that. However the race rules permitted the emergency device to assist another competitor in trouble, without penalty.

No second flare was seen and we rowed on.

*

After two weeks of rowing, I had come to the realisation that, I would probably have the shoulder problem the whole way. It was a matter of managing the injury as best I could with stretching and medicine but I ceased deep-friction massage on the area as I was not convinced this was helping. I thought about the two or three crews that might be in front of us. At the rate we were going we could be finished in between four and six weeks' time.

24.

Starkers

But even the President of the United States
Sometimes must have to stand naked.
Bob Dylan IT'S ALRIGHT MA (I'M ONLY BLEEDING)

OCTOBER 28 WAS THE third successive day with north-easterly winds and by now the following swells were over 2–3 m from trough to crest and rising. The swell lifted the stern first and briefly the rudder came out of the water. Unless we were square on to the swell we broached the first few metres of our surf down the swell. In an attempt to improve that initial moment of control Phil tried the longer rudder he had made in Los Gigantes.

It was great while it lasted, giving added control at the commencement of the ride, but unfortunately it only lasted two hours, then snapped at the bottom of the hinge. The stresses on the longer rudder were obviously far too great for the ply construction to handle. I watched the whole process while sitting out over the stern; the rudder was flexing, moving with the increased pressure, then crack. End of rudder.

A great idea, but we were back to the reliable shorter and stronger rudder before we had even begun to get used to our new guidance system. Getting the old rudder back on was rather difficult. It was the same problem I had faced at White Island, but this time around we didn't have a volcano waiting to ravage our boat. The advantage this time was the temperatures were high, but the changeover still demanded strength, patience and timing.

The heavy swell that we were experiencing created its own difficulties of pressure on the rudder. I waited for a swell to pass under the boat. As it did, the pressure eased and I was able to get both pins lined up on the rudder gudgeon. The two shackles securing the guide wire were next and we were set.

As the rising sea was astern, Phil decided to shift the life-raft to the cabin in an effort to get more weight in the stern. His reasoning was that we were getting assistance from a multi-directional following sea. There was a concern about collecting a breaking wave, perhaps beam-on, that could roll us. Phil reasoned that if we lightened the bow and increased the weight in the stern, then the bow should be more willing to swing around and follow the wave. This would increase our safety margin and lessen our chances of broaching. And if we did roll, the life-raft was with the off-duty person in the cabin rather than in the bow cabin. As a consequence the life-raft became our pillow in the very stern of the boat: rather too high for comfort, but better for safety.

*

Maybe it was because it was the third day of welcome seas but I had my first shave since departing from Tenerife. It felt so good that I had a vigorous wash and felt even better. Then I saw my first marlin. They are amazing. A long slender fin signalled the marlin's presence as it silently surfaced, slicing the water and leaving no wake. The fin rose a little further out of the water as the big fish came up on the starboard bow, over my left shoulder of course, then slipped under the boat, appeared off to port and then simply disappeared. Over in one magic moment.

Later I saw a ship in the distance, but basically this was a day we rowed. That night was the darkest yet. Dense, low cloud obscured the stars like a layer of concrete. It was an eerie, oppressive, morbid feeling, with little wind and a calming sea. Phil astonished me when he explained that he was having difficulty keeping awake on the late shift, mainly because of the interrupted sleep pattern earlier in the night. I had taken that problem for granted. I had felt that way since the beginning and taken it as a given of ocean rowing.

Phil had this wonderful ability to go to sleep anywhere straight away; his police mates had commented on it in New Zealand. Even on the *Kiwi Challenge* he could do it. One minute he would be chatting, speculating on the weather, the next he would be out to the joe. But now, after 16 days at sea, he was truly suffering from sleep deprivation.

I asked if he too had a constant dull headache and aching eyes.

"Occasionally," he shrugged laconically.

Pursuing the conversation I asked him what he thought about at night, did he dream or imagine seeing things that were not there?

"Rowing. You know me, I'm as romantic as a brick. My focus is on the job at hand."

I thought about a number of things, but you had to focus on the boat and as a consequence you couldn't concentrate on anything else to any depth. If you're looking for enlightenment on the meaning of life you are not going to find it on a rowing boat mid-Atlantic.

*

Elaine Thompson, *Yachting World*, March 1998

La Baleine, crewed by French husband-and-wife team Jean Marc and Marie-Christine Meunier, called for rescue when their water-maker stopped working and their boat began to break up. The Meuniers were said to be very distressed by their failure. They got [a] little involved in sailing the rescue yacht, and Marie-Christine sobbed for hours afterwards.

*

I thought a rowing shift was rather like a session in a first-class cricket match.

For a start the rowing shift and the session both occupy two hours. At the commencement of a cricket session players are not thinking about the outcome in three or five days' time when they hope to complete the match. Individuals concentrate on their goals for the first half-hour. When that has passed and if that goal has been achieved, the goal for the first hour is focused on. Then the goal for the next 50 minutes, then the last 10 minutes of the session, so the team can maximise their position at the end of the session.

The batsmen concentrate on how to establish themselves against the type of bowler(s) they are likely to face. The bowlers have a plan to get the individual batsman out, while fielders know what positions they are most likely going to field in and the specific skills a particular position demands.

Often, before a ball is bowled, you, the spectator, can see the players visualising how they will play a shot, field a ball, throw, bowl and so on. Batsmen have the first goal of playing each ball on merit, then the next goal of getting off the mark. The next is probably the first 10 runs, the next 10 runs, and finally what they want to achieve in the first half-hour.

The fielding side have totally different goals; the right line and length to bowl, the field setting for a particular batsman and so on. The details have been considered, each goal has been planned, the whole team has discussed what they are trying to do together. At the end of a session there is an opportunity to reassess, regroup and plan the next one with the knowledge of what has happened in the just completed session.

And likewise with rowing. Back in New Zealand we had refined our ideas, our skills, our set pieces, our course, our routine, our game plan. But once we were on the ocean, the focus was on the here and now. Methodically we set out to achieve an attainable mileage goal in conditions involving the ocean, weather, boat, and crew. The checking of our position each morning with the GPS satellite navigation aid meant that we were able to confirm (or be forced to adjust) either our shift or our daily goal. Thus we focused on a shift at a time, a day at a time; beyond that the goals were too far away, too difficult to think about when struggling with the immediate conditions.

*

The morning broke calm, the sea was dying down and the north-east trade winds disappeared for the day. Now, as we rowed, we waited to see from which quarter the wind would get up. Please don't let it be another headwind. They are morale-sapping energy busters, those mothers! On a calm day, like this day, we could see into the water better and there appeared to be an awful lot of plastic bottles and containers, wrappers and light plastic sheet products floating in the water. I knew you have more time to examine the sea when it is calmer and perhaps we would see much more.

*

Consistent with other aspects of this voyage was our minimalist approach to clothing. We each had one long-sleeved Sunsmart cotton shirt, two pairs of rowing shorts, (I had an extra pair of black shorts I put on after rowing), cap, a polypropylene set (top and bottom) and a wet-weather jacket. Apart from this we had a couple of athletic singlets and T-shirts and nothing for our feet.

Our rowing shorts had merino lambskin sown in to ease the wear and tear on our bums. In these temperatures they felt more like wrap-around woollen nappies. We had both suffered for a couple of weeks before I decided I had to do something about them. For several days my mind had been playing with an intriguing idea. I decided to try it out, but I was damned if I was going to do it when Phil was around.

I rowed in normal attire for about 10 minutes to let "Sleeping Beauty" go to sleep. I then stopped, stood up and did something that would eventually be reported and commented upon by the media of the world — I removed my shorts!

I then placed the wool directly on the seat and sat down again, flipped my privates up on top of my inner thighs, and rowed. It was much cooler. Ever conscious of the effects of the sun, I still wore a hat, sunnies, long-sleeved T-shirt, gloves and sunscreen on unusual places; that was what the comfortably dressed rower was wearing this ocean-racing season. I rowed my shift. Then, 10 minutes before waking Phil, I put my shorts on again. I mean to say, two blokes in a boat mid-Atlantic, one rowing naked. It's not a good look, if you know what I mean.

I repeated this the next day. Again it worked. It was a hell of a lot cooler and more comfortable. This was definitely the way to go. The problem was, how to tell Phil?

Anyway, on the third day of experimentation I decided I had to let him in on the secret. After all the poor chap was still suffering in his naturally heated shorts.

I practised the lines in my head to make sure I didn't cause unnecessary concern.

"Hey Phil, I've got something to tell ya."

"Yeah, what's that, Rob?" was Phil's imagined response.

"Well mate, it's like this ... um ... the last few days I've been rowing naked."

"Listen, mate, I've got something to tell you, too," continued Phil's imagined reply, "This is not the time to come out of the closet."

No, that wasn't the way to do it. Finally I figured out the one argument that would make such behaviour acceptable to Sgt Philip Stubbs.

"Phil, I've made a discovery that could make the difference between winning and losing this race."

"What's that, mate?"

"We must row naked."

The conversation went as about as smoothly as one could realistically expect. For sure, Phil was at first apprehensive about rowing in his birthday suit, but once the rationale was explained he agreed to give it a shot. After a day or two of the new rowing regime he agreed it was indeed an improvement. So for much of the remainder of the race the *Kiwi Challenge* crew rowed buck naked.

*

As I began the dusk shift I suggested that Phil take a video or photo of the naked rower with, for decorum's sake, a strategically placed drink bottle in my lap. Phil was not interested. I suggested that we could swing the boat 45 degrees to get a better angle away from the sun. Phil failed to see the funny side, saying we were here to race not take photos. Okay, a fair enough comment and I suggested that we drop the matter.

Phil, however, went on. "What if we lost the race by 400 m because of a full-frontal with a drink bottle. How silly can you get?"

He rambled on about other things that could arise from not concentrating on the race. I lost patience. "Look, you can't help yourself, can you? Once you begin you get verbal diarrhoea and dribble on."

"Okay. That's it. I won't talk for two days!"

"Oh, don't take it too seriously. It was all a little lighthearted fun. Forget it, Phil."

Silence.

Another unnecessary tiff. I thought about it for the rest of the shift. Our communication had deteriorated at sea. We both had our opinions, but in this situation we had to communicate better. I knew I shouldn't have said what I did. Somehow I had to put it right before this thing jeopardised our chances of winning. I should apologise.

"Together" was the word written above the well hatch. This we had to focus on while rowing. This was how we could succeed. This should symbolise our effort. Good communications were crucial to how we worked "Together".

On the changeover I hesitated. I couldn't spit it out, but just before going into the cabin out it came. "My apologies, Phil. I didn't mean what I said about verbal diarrhoea."

"It doesn't matter what you say, it doesn't worry me. I'll just shut up and row harder."

I wasn't going to leave it there. I wanted to explain.

"I just feel that to be fast we need to be having fun and enjoying what we do. That was the idea of doing the photo session in the first place, to have a bit of a laugh. You recall we had talked about this in Auckland. I had said to you how I felt Mike Rodger and I screwed up the Atlanta Olympics because we were over-trained. We didn't enjoy what we were doing, the fun, the enjoyment went out of the training rows and we didn't perform. If we are having fun and enjoying what we are doing, we are more likely to succeed."

Silence. Then came the breakthrough.

Phil looked directly at me. "I accept your apology." In that instant his body language changed. His expression relaxed and the tension in his muscles faded.

I had learnt a lesson. The importance of eating the proverbial humble pie was brought home to me. It was a thoroughly enlightening moment to have buried my ego for once and to have been rewarded with a really positive response from Phil. The moment left my scalp prickling. An apology shouldn't have been a big deal, but somehow it was. I nodded and went into the cabin.

25.

Night Life

The last refuge of the insomniac is a sense of superiority to the sleeping world.
Leonard Cohen, Canadian singer.

DUSK, THE MOST PLEASANT time of the day. Then the glare of the sun, now long past its zenith, would reflect off my back. As the temperature dropped I would begin to feel better, the permanent headache would almost disappear and a freshness in the air was invigorating. Then, as the sun's orb touched the horizon, cutting its power by half, one sensed the impending darkness loom like a prowler in the back yard. Reality was that another long night was ahead. For the moment I enjoyed the spectacle, glancing over my right shoulder observing brilliant colour changes from bright reds and yellows through the spectrum to shades of violet and, eventually, darkness.

Sometimes when the cloud cover was dense and low the *Kiwi Challenge* would plunge into a total blackout, leaving only a red glow from the compass light as the night sky's sole luminance. At these times my imagination would take over, making the universe as small or as big as I so desired. Sea monsters lurked, then appeared through the darkness, serpents with multiple heads and darting tongues. It was a game I sometimes played to make myself more alert to the surroundings and, hopefully, more aggressive on the oars. I wondered if such monsters really did exist. John Ridgway saw them on his Atlantic crossing with Chay Blyth.

One thing I definitely did see — on two separate occasions — was some kind of brightly-lit craft hurtling across the sky at a speed far in excess of any aircraft. I wondered what these could possibly be; other than a UFO. The best explanation I could come up with was that they were military weapons. I knew from listening to the radio that there were new tensions in the Gulf. Could they be rockets streaking in the direction of Saddam?

*

Steve Boga, *The Oceanrowers*
Jan and Daniel [mother and son team] were prepared for squalls and huge, aggressive seas; what surprised them were all the calm, glassy seas.

"So many of the nights – especially in the second half of the race – were windless and calm," says Jan. "We began to call our ocean, Lake Atlantic."

She recalls one of the many nights: while Daniel slept … Jan rowed on a satin sea beneath a full moon. She wore only a bikini and her Walkman earphones. Classical music – Debussy – echoed through her head. With each pass of the oars through the water, she churned up glittering bioluminescent creatures. "Like scooping up millions of emeralds," she thought.

Occasionally a shooting star plummeted towards the horizon. A dozen dolphins suddenly appeared around the boat, cavorting, gliding effortlessly through the water, their backs glistening in the moonlight. It was possibly the most beautiful moment of her life. One she would cherish forever.

*

Let me take you through a couple of night shifts. On the night of October 28 — the night of the day I had first rowed naked — I came on at 8 p.m. when there was little natural light. Later on there would be a new moon, but it had yet to rise. My eyes were a little sore from the bright day just gone, resulting in me not being able see the compass easily. I slid right forward on the trolley seat, got my bearings and was away.

A swell came through and lifted the stern so with a little extra effort on the oars we swished, gurgled and slapped along, surfing a smidgen. When we were in the lowest part of the trough I would put in an extra couple of quick strokes, a little more effort to get us moving before the next swell caught us sitting in the water. I was pleased, as I knew I was working with the boat, but the early evening shift was never a problem. The temperature and brightness were lower and the colours were enhanced, a great time to be on the ocean.

"That's better, Rob," I thought. "That will get us home a little quicker." The shift was uneventful, and I had kept a steady three knots with the assistance of a light easterly astern of us, 6.5 miles for the shift.

The midnight to 2 a.m. shift was a gutbuster for me. We thought at that time, after 16 days, we were a quarter to a third of the way through the race and I was getting worn down at night. It was a struggle to stay alert. I rowed, but I wanted to sleep. When the sea is demanding you are awake and concentrating, but this night was as regular as it got and I had my eyelids closed, rowing by sound and feel. If I slept, I didn't stop rowing.

WHAM! I felt that!

I was wide awake in a flash, looking for the sea monster and the monster seas arriving with it, wondering what the hell was happening. Out of the west a tiny 10 cm flying fish had hit me in the middle of my back. A juvenile with learner's licence overcooked the glide and arrived, blat, in the middle of my back, and flopped in the boat. The fish, still a little stunned by its exuberance, slid towards the gunwales as I slipped my foot out of the rowing shoe to guide it through the scuppers back to mother sea.

I was sure it would have a whale of a tale to tell its mates. It gave me a fright; three times on the journey I was jolted by a hot shot flying fish, twice in the back and once in the neck. Yep, each one brought me to life with a start, just a minor adrenalin rush, although nothing compared to the mother of all frights I got when that storm petrel attempted to land on my shoulder.

Just as I thought everything was back to "normal", an unexpected cross-wave from the port side lapped ever so accurately into the stern cubby cabin, wetting the bedding and Phil. Even at night the temperature was in the mid-20s; so we often had the stern hatch open. In the half-light of the new moon I couldn't see the following sea and sliding up the stern a crest could flop into the cabin all too easily. Then for good measure another cross-wave did it again, just to remind us who was boss.

Thank God Phil had grumbled and shut the hatch after the first gentle splash. Throughout the middle part of the journey we had poor light at night, simply because of the phase of the moon. Under those conditions it was difficult to see the waves coming. Occasionally I could hear waves, but I still wouldn't know where they were and, apart from bracing myself, there was little I could do.

Thus it was always the unexpected and at night, the unseen, which caused chaos. This shift I hauled the boat 5.5 miles.

*

If the midnight shift was a gutbuster, the 4–6 a.m. shift was a gutbuster plus a headshrinker when my eyelids felt like sandpaper. The Sleep Monster remedy helped but not nearly enough for my liking. Waking the other person up became increasingly problematic. To begin with I had to call three or four times before an answering murmur would signal he had heard the wake-up call. Then as the days passed I would have to call louder. Loud, four to five times calling Phil's name whilst I was rowing, occasionally (the occasional became regular at the end of the odyssey) shouting when I got no response.

Likewise when I had been sleeping and then heard Phil's voice, I could tell from the tone and volume that this was not the first time he had called. In addition I had the sporadic difficulty of dreaming the wake-up call. I would wake up thinking, "Shit, Phil must have called me."

I would lie doggo for a little, waiting to hear Phil's, "Come on, mate, rattle your bones. The time is five minutes to four, your shift!" If this didn't happen I was asleep again.

At least half a dozen times, maybe more, I awoke and thought something along the lines of, "Damn, I've gone back to sleep," so I called out, "Yeah, yeah. I'm coming."

I would struggle into my shorts, put on my smelly, cold and damp rowing T-shirt then stagger out of the hatch to confront a startled Phil.

"What are you up to, Rob?"

"What do you mean what am I doing? You woke me up. Didn't you yell at me to go on the next shift?"

"No. No, it's only 3.25, mate. You've got a good half hour to go yet."

I turned and flopped back into the pit, totally brassed off with myself.

*

Another annoying factor was the effect a sleeping person had on the trim of the boat. I guess I had a similar effect but when Phil slept at night frequently he would sleep chest down, head tucked into the stern corner on the right-hand starboard side. This unbalanced the boat, making rowing more difficult. Generally I waited for 10 minutes or so when this happened. Sometimes he would automatically centre himself, sometimes he wouldn't. If he didn't, I would have to stop rowing, clamber down the deck, open the hatch and tap him on his feet.

"Phil, could you centre yourself, mate?"

He would shuffle back to the middle, "Thanks, mate."

Quite often he would not recall being woken.

*

While my body was taking the rhythm of the rowing, my mind was attempting to estimate time. I had a goal of going for 75 minutes without looking at my watch. Counting stokes was too mind-numbing and stupefying.

Instead I would look at the compass bearing, a star on the horizon, the wind on the water, the wake, the wash, anything but the watch! I would try to fathom the ocean's mood, but my mind would lose the plot, so I'd begin an intellectual medical, going over my body minutely, checking responses from my neck, shoulders, arms, back, butt, thighs, privates, knees, ankles. Later, as the race progressed, I would notice that my heartbeat was getting stronger and stronger.

I'd listen to the rhythm of the row, watch a cloud form, move, dissipate and reform. Then I'd go through the same process again through the water, the sky, the body, the boat, the second haul on the water bottle. When I felt reasonably sure that the 75 minutes was long gone I would row for another "10 minutes" and then check my watch. Damn, only 40 minutes. Try as I might to increase my 75 minute accuracy I hardly ever made it.

Chocolate bars were one of the staples to help our energy levels up at night. In the middle stages Phil had a philosophy that worked well. One bar of chocolate had seven pieces or knobs in it. Phil would watch the log like a seagull and the moment he completed a mile he would have a knob of chocolate, row another mile and have another knob of chocolate. This would spread a bar over the entire shift. Not a bad idea, eh? Invariably he would have a chunk or two left over to celebrate the completion of his shift.

*

The phosphorescence in this part of the world was unique. In New Zealand waters the phosphorescence seems to be evenly spread, but here it was patchy. When you hit a patch there would be almost an explosion of light. On an ill-lit night, irregular pools of phosphorescence would well up at the tip of the blade, quickly bloom in intensity and then equally quickly dissipate. I would think, "What is that?" Another exhausted bird about to land on an equally exhausted human, or another "L"-plate flying fish playing shark with the boat? No, nothing dramatic like that; it was just the plankton playing.

*

The night settled in long and hot. The head wind faded. It was funny watching each other go through our get-up routine at night. It was a huge struggle. I had to will my eyes open; they refused, my brain short-circuited. I thought harder, the eyes opened, but they didn't seem to be part of the rest of me. My brain re-attached, I then got the rest of me to shuffle to the hatch, hitting my head on the ceiling joist in the process, hit the light switch and rummaged around for the smelly, sweaty shirt that I had been wearing only two hours before.

The shirt dried in the day, but never at night. I pulled it on, usually bumping my head on the hatch while exiting to get my drink bottles and occasionally bumping it going back inside. Now that I had my drink bottles I had to put the powder in. I stepped outside, bumping my head again, clinging to the bulkhead with one arm to stabilise my body, twisting to the right and pumping the water, then filling the plastic water bottles with water. Shaking the bottles was not a difficulty and neither was the inelegant collapse into the cabin, while bumping my head again.

Nearly awake now I would climb outside again, bumping my head, and stand up, wobbling from side to side, struggling to catch up with the roll. Standing in the outside well I stretched for two minutes, then had a scratch and a grizzle about the calm, the head wind or the tail wind. The ritual proceeded as I wobbled and rolled up to my rowing position. I then applied silicone barrier cream to my bum, sat on the woollen seat, positioned the drink bottles in their individual holders and placed my feet in my shoes. I would now be ready to row although still half asleep. I took a couple of strokes with Phil and forced myself to wake up. I began to stiff-arm the Atlantic again.

*

One clear night I decided to make a huge effort and try and find a few constellations in the night sky. My father went to sea on a merchant ship during the war; transporting arms across the Tasman Sea and up the coast of Australia. He ended up as second mate and navigation officer. He had lent me a battered old star chart that had all the Northern Hemisphere's constellations laid out, with lines drawn connecting the stars and names for each one.

I used this map to identify the constellations one by one. There was the Great Bear (or Ursa Major), with two of its stars acting as pointers to the Pole (or Northern) Star. Then there was the Little Bear (Ursa Minor), Pegasus and the brightest star, Sirius. The most distinctive constellation — for it is also found in the Southern Hemisphere skies — was the Greek god Orion, with his sword ready for action.

And then I spied a huge shooting star. It was as if the string holding Sirius in the sky had been severed and the star left to drop into the atmosphere to multiply a hundredfold in brightness, streaking across the black night looking for anonymity on the other side of the world. Then it was gone, leaving only its blinding flash etched into the back of my retina for a few moments.

*

Until we rowed naked, the Walkman was often clipped onto my shorts at night and so was Frank Sinatra. I have always enjoyed him, most of all "New York, New York". Great song, great song. I learnt to row in sync with it. That is one tremendous advantage crooners have; they go well with scullers. To be successful at either you need unrivalled timing. In an endurance race we synchronised really well.

There was "New York, New York" of course, and "I Did It My Way", which incidentally is the first song on the tape, most appropriate. "*Regrets I've had a few....* " Sinatra was fun and fitted well with the 4 a.m. shift, and I genuinely enjoyed "New York, New York". "*I want to be a part of it....*" Anyone can see the appropriateness of "For Once in My Life", "The Best Is Yet to Come" and "They Can't Take That Away From Me". Here was my own concert, in my own theatre. It was warm, I kept to Frank's rhythm, we were working well together.

The music was my consolation and my inspiration. Phil never understood this.

*

Later in the journey, when we were further westward, the sun rose on the 8–10 a.m. shift. The faint purple hue over the stern registered the imminent arrival of another day. The water began to change from jet to ethereal black, a little later to dark grey, followed by a yukky grey-blue. Likewise the sky lightened to reveal few clouds and signal a thirsty day ahead.

Quickly, very quickly, the sky would lighten right through the colour spectrum, and day would come racing. Then came the golden blind. Horizontally, unswervingly targeted into my eyes. The shafts of the first rays sought you out, as though to register back to the sun, that you were still here on the sun's planet, still sitting on the water, still paddling away, still present. My lids were screwed up under the sunnies to shield my eyes from the sun's laser probe.

The intensity of the rays precluded much else other than being forced to acknowledge the dominance of the new light over the old dark, watching the sea with peripheral vision, acceding to the assertive power of the full-on, high-beam light still coming right into my eyes. "Ah yes," my mind would say, "but we are further around your planet, we are making miles away from you."

Rowing within myself waiting as the sun rose a little and the light beam dipped a little, but then quickly the reflection off the sea twinkled to torment me for a while. The warmth of the sun began to register on my shoulders, then chest and waist, while my eyes did battle with the light of this new day.

*

We did not alter our watches during the Atlantic crossing, which meant the shifts altered in real time for the longitude we were at. For example, the first of the night shifts at 8 p.m. watch time became 6 p.m. real time halfway across. Although our shifts stayed the same sequence on our watches, the light intensity appeared to increase as we progressed westward. Unconsciously it gave us the perception that we were rowing out of the night and into the dawn.

"Yeah. We really are making progress around the girth of Earth. We are doing it."

26.

Doldrums

There is nothing so desperately monotonous
as the sea, and I no longer wonder at the cruelty of pirates.
James Russell Lowell

THE NIGHT WAS CALM, the next day a doldrum-like Karapiro calm. A small pod of dolphins hung around curiously then disappeared on their journey; we were just too slow for their interest. It is amazing how much noise rowing the boat actually makes. The seat wheels roll, the axle rubs on the plastic, the oars clack in the gates. The oars rip the water, water drips as your oars exit the water, the boat shifts water in front of it, the sea closes in behind and around you, each making a differing swish, gurgle and fizz.

In the dark hours of the morning it was incredibly humbling sitting on a plastic bucket in a plywood dinghy on an endless ocean. Just before dawn, sitting on the throne, an audible still pervaded, the sounds silent, I could hear the blood rushing through my eardrums, a deafening quiet. I felt out of place, like a fish in a desert, a pollutant in an ocean stadium intruding on Mother Nature's turf. Would she tolerate this irritant? I hoped so but at the same time I wondered about the bigger picture.

Would she tolerate the prolific problems we humans thrust upon her daily? The self-cleansing environment that is our planet has long since been overloaded by a variety of pollutants causing change. It reminded me of the boiled frog syndrome: a frog placed in a pot of hot water will immediately jump out. But place that same frog in a pot of cold water and begin to heat the water slowly over an element and the frog will happily remain, unable to detect the gradual change in temperature that reaches the point where the frog will be cooked alive.

As individuals, we cannot detect the subtle changes that are occurring as nature tries to balance out the polluting intruders we create and thrust into the air, soil and water. It is only our instruments that tell us that the average global temperature is rising or that our ozone hole grows bigger with every passing year, yet we still fail to act with a sense of urgency. Like the frog, our senses are unable to pick up these subtle changes on a daily basis to constantly remind us that, should we fail to act soon, it would be to do so at our peril. Ultimately our apathy could lead to our extinction.

Adding to the problem, I chucked the bucket contents, swirled seawater in the bucket, chucked again, cleaned the inside, stowed it, picked up the oars and rowed.

We are a species of Kermits.

Phil checked the hull late that morning. I thought it was quite courageous, really. During the previous night, as he was washing his hands in the sea after a crap, there was a flash of phosphorescence below his hands and he had then seen the outline of a really big fish 2–3 m long. Now, the next day, he was about to enter the water with a reinforced nylon scrubbing pad 20 cm by 20 cm in hand, scouring the hull.

I grabbed the video camera and began to record the event, then felt suddenly guilty. "What am I doing here with the camera when you are going in with the sharks, Phil?" "You kind of volunteered for the camera, Rob," he replied good-naturedly.

He held onto the grab line (the nylon safety line strung along the outside hull just above the water line) with one hand and scrubbed with the other, slowly working his way around the boat.

Brave Rob stood guard, looking out for intruders. After Phil had completed the job and was back on board, he said there were even baby barnacles attaching themselves to the hull. I got the *Kiwi Challenge,* now clean and shiny on the underside, under way again and this time Phil was happy to take a photo of me, naked but equipped with a Sunsmart drink bottle. It seemed as if we were trying to have some fun at last. But I still couldn't figure out the Adam and Eve brain-teaser.

*

Colin Quincey, *Tasman Trespasser*

I think there is a very thin, very precarious line which separates the uttermost striving to achieve something and obsession with the achievement to the exclusion of common sense. To survive it is essential to maintain sufficient mental faculty to know where to draw this line.

*

The last day of October, the 31st, had been another long, hot day, the third in succession. During the day we had our second big food dumping session. I dumped the contents of 14 day packs. That took us down to 56 days' supplies. The packs were torn apart, we kept the plastic bags and wrappers and dumped freeze-dry meals, energy bars, fruit bars, milkshake mix and cereals. I was particularly tough on the honey soy chicken. I guess we lightened the boat by 10–14 kg, maybe more.

I was taken aback by the energy required to stay out in the boiling sun, opening the bags and deciding which to dump. It took only 20, 30 minutes maximum, but it sure was a tremendous drain on energy, or a huge cutback in recovery time. Whatever, it amounted to the same outcome; I was stuffed. The last time we dumped food the weather immediately changed and we had that three-day storm. This time I hoped it was not going to be a harbinger of adverse weather.

*

Neil Hitt, *Hospicare*, July 1999

We were rowing along after about three weeks when the ocean was totally flat. Both of us were rowing and it was about two hours before sunset. We were both aware of a rumbling noise gradually getting louder. Pete was rowing in the bow seat and looked over his shoulder to see a large cargo ship coming straight towards us.

They had cut their engines some time before and had been coasting towards us, trying to work out what was causing the small blip on their radar screen. They passed so close to us that we were able to shout across at the crew and say that we were fine and rowing to Barbados. As they were still moving we were soon out of earshot and the VHF radio didn't seem to be working.

We sat down and started to row again, putting about ¼ mile between the two boats. It looked as if they were altering course, but they continued to turn their ship. They were coming back!

"Ships don't stop," said Pete. "They certainly don't turn around for a chat!"

The ship came back and stopped alongside us. We were tiny compared with the mass of this cargo ship. We got the VHF working and chatted with the captain. He invited us aboard for a meal and a drink but we said that we were in a race and couldn't accept outside assistance. Two seconds after I had said that I regretted it but after a couple of hours when the ship had gone we were glad that we hadn't got on board. We may not have wanted to get back off.

The ship was from New Zealand, bound for Europe. The captain's parting words were, "Only MAD dogs and Englishmen…."

Little did he know there were two Kiwis out there as well!

*

Sometimes, once the shift was under way, all I could think about was when it would end. And the worst thing I could do was to keep checking the time. This had the effect of slowing time down, making two hours drag on for what seemed an eternity. And when the wonderful moment arrived when I could call out to Phil for his shift, I would then hawkeye the watch, making sure he did not fluff around too much.

When I noticed Phil was between one and three minutes late on some shifts I made a point of being one to three minutes early on all my shifts, or at least I thought that was the case. However, in the middle of the day I was four minutes late as I was adjusting the solar panel to maximise incoming solar radiation and greasing the seat axle. Phil just stopped rowing, in a slight huff.

The next morning I accidentally woke Phil one minute earlier than usual for the 2–4 a.m. shift so he woke me two minutes early for the 4–6 a.m. shift. That gave me an extra two minutes' stretching time and I used them. Then the irritation Phil felt came out. "Jeez, mate, I think you need to start your shifts on time, not a bloody minute late each and every shift." Not a major, but it was interesting to note how we were watching each other like hawks. The nights were so tough it was easy to get annoyed like that.

27.

Racing Life

The wonder is always new that any sane man can be a seafarer.
Ralph Waldo Emerson

TALK ABOUT ROUTINE. I don't know why, but whether I was going forward or aft I always went over Phil's left, the starboard side. This was part habitual and part sensible, putting my weight into the oncoming swell and assisting in the rowing regime by being consistent; the boat should react in a similar way each shift change, making it easier for both of us. And the boat did react; being a light boat it always rolled.

Once I had reached the well, I would also stretch. Here I could stand and use the solar panel and cabin roof for purchase and holds. I would stretch my calves, thighs, shoulders and back. Stretching completed, I would retrieve the plastic eating utensils down in the port hatch at the side of the well. I'd dig out the breakfast bowl, spoon and milkshake maker, automatically dip them in the ocean, clean and dry them and mix the milk.

In New Zealand we had batched milk powder in airtight packets that would last four days. In total we took 3 kg of milk powder. The low point would be mixing the milk with fresh water at sea temperatures, temperatures that normally were around 28°C. This made for slightly warm reconstituted milk. It was no use even thinking about cooler temperatures.

Next I'd attack the opened day pack in the adjacent watertight hatch. Labelled day packs contained enough food for two rowers for one day, with a twist. Breakfast cereals were included in every second day pack, obviously one flavour/type cereal for two consecutive breakfasts. Phil would have opened the pack when he had breakfast at 8 p.m. Hubbard's supplied our cereals and they were great.

Most mixes I really enjoyed; my favourite being Oat Bran muesli. Berry Berry Nice ran a second and Outward Bound was a close third. Into the plastic bowl would go the cereal of the day with half a cup of milk on top. Then I stood, braced in the well against the pitch and roll of the boat. I would ignore Phil rowing right in my face and watch the sea, the horizon, the sky over the bow. I would stand alone and munch my brekky. Eating completed, it was dishes in the sea, wiped, and returned to the hatch.

The breakfast production-consumption routine would take seven to eight minutes. Then I'd climb into the cabin for a rest. Here my mind would often drift back to the races that I had won and lost.

*

World Rowing Championships, Indianapolis, 1994
Final of the Men's Lightweight Double Scull

It wasn't easy. We had to go through the repêchage to make the semi-final after Italy, seemingly everybody's pre-race favourite, beat us in the heat. In this semi-final we met Italy (again), Spain, Poland, Japan and Hungary. Upsets occur, and crews often get knocked out of the final by "suicidal one-race wonders" whose main goal in life is to simply make the final, only to finish well out of the medals. Crews often wet themselves while waiting in the starting blocks — this one was an exception (Phew!).

We started okay but quickly fell back to fourth place. Still fourth at the 1000 m halfway mark, we were one length behind Spain and Poland with Italy a further length in front again. To qualify for the final we had to place third or better, so we increased our intensity to near-maximum pressure and upped the stroke rate. Another quarter went by and we hadn't made an impression (doh!). I felt awful; every muscle fibre screamed out for relief, my head hurt, my vision was blurred; the pain was too ugly to describe but I realised that if we didn't do something quickly we were going to miss out on the final. I became angry.

With 500 m to go we made our last move and somehow, almost miraculously, our muscles responded, nearly lifting the boat out of the water, (well, that's how it felt), and took back the length plus a half to finish just behind Italy. I was furious and elated; furious for having to pull out all the stops to qualify, elated because we did qualify! I learnt more about myself and my limits in that one race than in any previous race. The euphoric feeling is just as hard to describe as the ugly feeling I had felt 90 seconds before! The fury, the elation, the euphoric overrider. I was a little stuffed!

However, Mike Rodger and I had made the final. The warm-up seemed a waste of time (we had been warming up for months); now was the time to get on with it and do the business. Sitting in the blocks we knew we were ready to go to the death. We went through our checks, we were ready.

The starter went through the lanes during the starting procedure:

"Germany, ready?"

An acknowledging nod from the crack Germans, world champions in '91 and always good.

"New Zealand, ready?"

Stupid question.

"Switzerland, ready?"

Second last year and looking good again in '94.

"Italy, ready?"

Third last year and undefeated so far this year, count on it.

"Great Britain, ready?"

No problem.

"Spain, ready?"

They robbed us in the final last year. Can't let that happen again, ever.

The starter's flag up,

"Set?"

Believe it.

"Go!"

We came out of the blocks last but were back up in front with Italy within 15 strokes. The boat was singing. 500 m gone. Switzerland half a length back on us, watch them! Spain, Germany and Great Britain a further half length back — adios, dudes! 1000 m, halfway home and Italy moved. We did a "power 20" as planned but they inched ahead. Switzerland remained half a length back. 500 m to go, the Italians had clear water on us, two boat lengths, had they done too much too soon? Last big move and Switzerland fell back slightly. They wouldn't be back.

We dug in to take on Italy. The pain was bad but we were gaining; they were feeling the pain, too — worse perhaps. We torqued the oars, made the boat sing, only our speed was important. Ignored everything outside the boat, leant on the sculls and stood on the flamin' foot stretcher! The finishing hooter sounded, but not for us. We picked up more than a boat length but still finished second. The pain flooded back and dejection accompanied it. I slumped forward, desperately trying to get my share of oxygen.

*

Listening to the radio while dozing between 10 a.m. and noon was my favourite relaxation. We weren't able to get clear reception in the afternoon and we attempted to sleep at night, and so the hours between 8 a.m. and 2 p.m. were radio time. I enjoyed lying on my back, radio on my solar plexus listening to another world, alternatively fading and re-gathering volume to clearly tell me items of little consequence then fade or crackle at critical times.

Like the weather, the radio sound would evaporate into the ether, only to return with the threats of tropical storms, or a gale warning for the "crackle crunch zzzip of the Atlantic". Outside, "our" weather would be calm with a clear sky, but I knew I would be spending the rest of that day at my oars searching for that elusive tropical storm or "crackled crunched zzzipped" gale.

Sports results were equally vexatious. The Kiwi cricket team, not yet the Black Caps, were in the traditional position of beating up the Aussie cricketers on an equally traditional cricket tour of Australia. I did hear that through some present-day miracle the Queensland state side had defeated our gallant team, but subsequent to this never heard the outcome of the tests. I would hear encouraging position statements, then the next day we might have poor reception, or some ephemeral factors conspired to mean the results never got through to us.

Mind you, I had been known to doze off and miss the information I was waiting for. It was rather like listening to the radio for the weather forecast and losing concentration just before your region's forecast is given.

*

It was a similar fate listening to a tremendous play on radio. I would hear the beginning of a play but then have to go away from the world of radio and out into the harsh reality of an Atlantic rowing seat. Or I would hear episode two of a three-part play, not knowing when the final episode was going to be broadcast and probably not being able to receive it anyway. Nevertheless, after enjoying what I heard, I would spend some of the time during the next shift thinking through the plot and the characters, then end the play in my mind, to my satisfaction.

I thought about one radio play for many days and I still ponder on it. The plot involved a mother and daughter. The daughter informed her mother very matter-of-factly that she was to going to take her own life. At first the mother thought this was more of a tantrum than a threat. As the play evolved the mother realised her daughter had not feigned a melodrama; she was going to do it that afternoon. It was fascinating to hear only the half the story. I never satisfactorily solved the conundrum those two confronted, and still wonder about its conclusion.

Another interlude revolved around a play concerning a "hands on the car" competition. You know, the competition where the last person left with their hand on the car wins it. It was actually a play that had been produced in New Zealand. That was also inconclusive as we hit the Atlantic byway once again halfway through.

Despite these frustrations the quality of the radio programmes was outstanding and it took my mind away from my real world outside the cabin. Khazakstan village life daily routines and an analysis of why French truckies were on strike and blocking roads in France were certainly psychological breaks from the battle within ourselves and with the Atlantic.

Very definitely, life, from my perspective flat on my back on the Atlantic, was in danger of becoming a kaleidoscope of irregular, fragmented, disjointed weather, news, sports events and radio plays. However, one thing was not fragmented. I knew that in 90 minutes or so I would have my next rowing shift. That schedule was known, was remorseless and would not fade away.

*

Rob Hamill's diary, November 1, 1997

Jim Rohn wrote, "If you share a good idea long enough it will eventually fall on good people." P. He is "good people", especially for a race such as this. Sure, we have our differences, but that only increases our potential for when we harness our diffs in a positive way. I believe we are!

*

I stretched in the cabin for several minutes before writing up my log. I would use the roof joists as a fulcrum to stretch my torso, tease out a little flexibility and ease the pain of repetition on a restricted portion of my body. Both were therapeutic. Stretching was different; it served as a service check on my body, allowing it to either warm up or cool down without parts seizing up. Writing up my diary in the morning was to relax and release tension, even if this was sometimes difficult when I was tired — which was all the time!

I lay on my stomach and, as concisely as possible, recorded the events of the last 24 hours from a very personal perspective. Writing the diary eased frustrations. The frustrations I confronted with myself, my own body, Phil, the weather, the lack of communication between us or about the race. It also gave me a forum to express my concerns, delight, pleasure and joy. Phil was a very private, detached, unemotional person and the diary gave me an outlet to express my highs and note my lows.

As I wrote I was always aware that there was no place on the boat for me to lock away my written thoughts. When I was rowing they were right there in the cabin for him to read if he ever chose to do so, although he knew that that wouldn't be cricket. As the voyage wore on and our relationship became more strained, I wondered if he was doing so anyway. I even started popping the odd entry for his benefit, just in case. Crazy, I know, but the sea does strange things to your mind.

*

Generally, although not always, the stern hatch was left open, allowing a little air to circulate through the cabin. The difference between not being able to open the hatch and having a little movement of air was huge. And that was an understatement. Here, around 15 degrees north of the equator, the cabin was stuffy and humid, with the temperature constantly hovering around 35°C and it stank of exhausted humans.

If weather conditions allowed, we would have the hatch wide open. Otherwise it was raised only as far as the first latch. If seas were rough we increased the size of the opening at our peril. We would rather sweat it out in our little Calcutta than put ourselves at any real risk.

*

On the changeovers we adopted a minimalist approach. We didn't want to waste any time, or miss a stroke, thus neglecting an opportunity to pull

Kiwi Challenge through the water. Once seated I would join Phil's rhythm and we would take two or three strokes together. Then he would drop out, ship his oars and move out of his seat. That's how finicky we were about not wasting time.

You can imagine the time loss, the distance loss, if at every shift change I stopped rowing and moved out of the seat. Then Phil would have got into the same rowing position, the sliding seat, settle bottles and feet, pick up the oars. The boat would have lost way, or a good deal of speed, and Phil would have to put that extra effort into strokes to get the *Challenge* back to the average speed.

*

We had to ration our chocolate bars to two per person per day. We had been eating up to six per night. We had three flavours and it was interesting how we changed our preferences over the row. At the start we both favoured Fruit and Nut, but that was later demoted to third. Dairy Milk ranked second preference, while Energy chocolate was tops. The peanut chocolate bars had long since vanished but the Mother Earth fruit bars were plentiful.

*

So that was what living was like on the *Kiwi Challenge*. Repetitious, predictable, very basic but never boring when we were rowing.

28.
The Long Silence

The sea speaks a language polite people never repeat.
It is a colossal scavenger slang and has no respect.
Carl Sandburg TWO NOCTURNES

MY BACK AND NECK were starting to play up again. The whole left shoulder, shoulder blade, rhomboid and attachments to my spine were inflamed. I massaged the area constantly but found the old whiplash injury was giving problems. It looked likely that I might need to hit the anti-inflammatories again. But for the moment these and other aches were not slowing me down, although they were making life pretty uncomfortable. Phil didn't seem to suffer the tendonitis problems to the same extent. He suspected it was his history as a kayak competitor that strengthened different muscle combinations in his shoulders.

Perhaps sitting in the bow seat also meant that I had a slightly higher crossover with the oars than Phil did in the stroke seat. Perhaps height was a consideration, too. Phil was longer in the body and that gave him a little height advantage in rowing as well. I wondered how other competitors my height were getting on with muscle problems. Mind you, their rowing positions would have been set up differently to ours anyway. Regardless of the reason there was a difference, but I could live with that.

For the second time Phil tried to contact another ship as it passed across the horizon, to no avail. I asked if he was recharging the VHF battery between attempts, but Phil reckoned it was hardly worth it as none of them ever listen to it anyway. Foolishly, as it turned out, I deferred to his judgement on that one. Phil's port-side gate had been squeaking for the last three days and he still had not greased the thing. Even though he continued to row further than me, these things showed me that he was also feeling the strain.

*

I was having skin problems from welts, blisters and sesame seeds. It's true. I don't know where they came from but I definitely had the sesame seed problem. On the backs of my hands, on my feet, on my shins, they were most unusual. I opened one up and it appeared to be a skin deposit, or some sort of congealed skin, that didn't seem to be doing anything. These sesame seeds stayed with me until I got back onto dry land, then disappeared. I haven't a clue as to what they were but they didn't seem to be a serious problem.

But the welts around my anus were. They had formed after the first week and caused a considerable amount of discomfort. Only applying copious amounts of either silicon barrier cream or Vaseline before each shift eased the pain. Sometimes I had to stop mid-shift and freely slap more around before I could continue. I guess they were salt water sores that threatened to get infected. After every bowel movement I would take a bit of time out to wash the area and rub in an iodine-based ointment.

*

The sun's heat on November 2 was extreme. Even before sunrise the heat was oppressive. I had dreaded the evenings but now the days were becoming difficult to cope with too. The temperature on deck was in the 30s. Sometimes I would start off a day shift by dumping my hat in a little fresh water before throwing it on. Each time the hat dried out I'd repeat the process.

But this day I frankly didn't think I would complete my 12–2. p.m. shift. I suggested to Phil that we take one-hour shifts in the heat of the day — for the four hours from noon till 4 p.m. — but he was not receptive. This I really wanted to try. We had done such shifts when we were in trouble back in New Zealand. I felt this was a problem situation; it wouldn't last for long, and we could perhaps make better progress with a strategic change.

Oh well, we were both getting a little shitty and desperately needed a break in the weather. We had only hauled the boat 56 miles in the last 24 hours; not a great performance, but not a bad one either, considering we were still doing the longer shifts.

There were huge, towering thunderclouds around at night but they appeared to be all threat and lightning flashes but little else. It was strange that we did not hear a single clap of thunder. The whole ocean would be lit up with multiple bursts of lightning. "Bugger the lightning," I thought. We were experiencing a five-knot sou'westerly, right on the nose. I wanted a wind change.

*

Rob Hamill's diary, November 3, 1997

Even more affected by the heat today. Even though it was perhaps slightly cooler. The sun on my skin too much. 12–2 p.m. shift I rowed well for 75 minutes but then died in a big way. I keep saying to myself, "Feeling good, Rob, feeling good." If I say it often enough, I will. "Feel I could take on the world but today I will settle for the Atlantic." Well, today it didn't work.

*

The next day was almost an action replay of the one before. Again the noon shift hit me hard. The first 75 minutes were okay, but then I lost it. Something was happening with the weather though. The wind was slowly getting up but — give us a break — it was still the flamin' sou'westerly.

Phil put out the sea anchor at 3.30 p.m. as the wind got up to 15 knots with the sea proving as difficult to battle into as the wind. He then took the opportunity to give the hull another clean even though it was only five days since the previous scrub-up. Again there was growth. I was a little irritated when he suggested that it could be my fault the growth was there. He felt Bror and I must have sanded the hull too much back in the Los Gigantes Marina.

*

Pauanui, 1993

I remember going to my brother's place one Christmas holiday break to rest for a few days and earn a few extra dollars at the petrol station he owned. I had just returned from the rowing training camp at New Year, a fatigued figure, longing for rest. While staggering about in my brother's petrol station, desperately trying to look alert, I noticed a flyer announcing the Pauanui King of the Mountain race to be held the next day.

Cool! Wicked! Gotta have a crack at that one.

I began my sport-specific training there and then by running to the next car as it pulled up to the petrol pump for a top-up. I knew I wasn't ready for such an event. The last time I had put my running shoes on was five months before. It didn't matter. I was certain I could win regardless of my current state of exhaustion or lack of recent running. And so a short-term dream and adventure had begun.

The next morning I stood at the start/finish line at one end of Pauanui Beach. In front of me lay 1500 m of innocuous green grass that led to the beginnings of a very steep hill. The sheer climb would take about 20 minutes and was guaranteed to cause considerable leg and lung pain.

I began fast but settled quickly into a rhythm with a bunch of 20. The remaining 60 runners fell into line behind us like ants returning to their nest. The thick grass felt soft and springy under my feet.

The bunch soon spread out into a similar ants' trail as we approached and entered the narrow track at the foot of the hill. I was in tenth place at this stage but quickly worked up to fifth, sometimes scrambling on hands and feet, then to third as people fell away. The steep grade was taking its toll.

Two-thirds of the way up I sensed the leader was weakening and, chancing my legs and lungs, pushed my way past the two in front, put my head down and climbed like hell for five minutes. I felt the lactic acid fill my legs like water in a bath. The bath was beginning to overflow so I eased up slightly and looked behind to see how far back they were.

Nobody. Nothing. A beautiful sight!

I eased over the crest and went to say, "G'day," to the official. My lungs were screaming for oxygen, but I did my best to sound like I was sitting in the local pub having a quiet beer. "Gaah," was the sound that came out.

I ran along the undulating ridge for five minutes before dipping over the edge down a narrow track with overhanging bush. I had descended about 100 m when the track came to an abrupt halt.

"Shit," I muttered.

Wrong track. I doubled back up to the ridge, losing a minute or so to see the next runner approaching.

"Do you know the way?" I asked.

"Sure do," he replied in a mocking half-laugh.

I sat in behind and ran another 200 m along the track. I was fuming. How could I make such a fundamental error? The earlier extra effort had all been in vain. Would I now pay for that burst of speed?

"Now it's my turn!" broke a confident voice ahead of me that derailed my train of thought.

He was off and obviously loved running downhill. I hung in there with him but by the time we hit the bottom he was about 50 m ahead of me. We ran along a road for 500 m before getting back onto the familiar grass. My legs were weak and weary and my lungs hurt. The steep, aggressive ascent and jarring return had taken its toll.

Just when I thought it was over the other chap drew to a halt and proceeded to fertilise the grass with his vomit. I scooted past, suddenly feeling better. This was turning into a very memorable race.

That last 1500 m seemed to take forever. The grass seemed to grow before my very eyes, every blade doing its best to slow me down. I looked back to find the 50-m lead I now had was beginning to shrink. I dug in deeper. My stride increased in cadence but got shorter in length. It felt as if my legs were shortening, or was it the grass growing even longer? The same soft, springy grass of the race beginning now felt like knee-deep old porridge! Every step required colossal effort.

With 100 m to go I had a 10-m lead. A final burst of energy and I ate up the metres. The line approached, but not soon enough. As I dipped my head, an arm and torso lunged past me. I was beaten by a bee's willy.

The race had been in my grasp before taking a wrong turn. It was then handed back to me when the other fellow lost his breakfast. How could I lose it twice?

The winner strutted around like a rooster. I hated losing that race but it taught me an important lesson. If you want to win, you must do sport-specific training, know your route, plan your strategy, keep to your game plan and be alert for the unexpected.

*

We rested for six hours and needed all of that. We woke and agreed to have a crack at the damned headwind together. We hit the deck at 9.30 p.m. and rowed for an hour but we weren't making any progress. So we called it a night, hefted-over the sea anchor and collapsed into the cabin. We repeated our effort at 5 a.m. to attempt to shift the bloody boat towards Barbados, but at 6 a.m. anchored and rested again.

*

Rob Hamill's diary, November 6, 1997

As soon as P came inside I started to fart. Oh yuk, they were wicked, and just kept coming. Had to risk opening back hatch to clear the air each time. I was embarrassed and initially felt stink for P but then remembered overnight on the training row putting up with shocka farts from P which he let off with glee and gusto!

*

Weird, we both awoke at around five o'clock in the morning. We had that abortive crack at rowing together, to find our hands had clawed. Neither of us could straighten our hands; our fingers and thumbs had curled up into the palm of our hands. Beginning with the index finger we had to stretch each finger individually, massage it, straighten the next finger and repeat the exercise. The muscles and tendons were very sore.

Gloves were worn sometimes, but that was to save our hands from blistering and to stop the skin cracking along folds, not to stop this cramping finger lock. The gloves had done their job; our hands were by now callused and cracked but not painful. We had expected our hands to be like that. But this clawing was an entirely new phenomenon. I wondered if it was from a lack of blood flow to the extremities during rest time. Oh well, better keep rowing, I guess.

Day 23, November 4. We only achieved 16 miles over the last 24 hours. We were determined to do better.

*

Howard Croker, rowing oar manufacturer, Australia, April 1997

"And how are you going to protect your hands, Rob?"

"We will wear gloves some of the time. I don't think they will be a great problem, Howard."

"You need to peace on them, Rob."

"Peace on them?" I was not sure I understood Howard and his Ocker accent.

"Yeah, peace on them, it toughens them up. I always used to peace on mine before I had a shower, mate."

"Sorry Howard, I don't understand."

"Peace on me hands, mate," he repeated. "I used to peace on me hands before havin' a shower. Toughens up the skin!"

"Oh, piss on my hands!"

"Yeah, peace on yer hands!"

"Okay, thanks for that advice, Howard. Now these oars – the length and the spoon need to be different.... "

*

The headwinds were the cause of serious frustration. I knew I was tired, but in these conditions I had set myself a target of two miles in the hour. I would crank along nicely at 1.8–2 miles an hour only to strike a steeper wave that would send the boat up through the crest at the same time as the wave disappeared underneath us. The boat would fall with a whoosh, water sprayed out sideways and we were brought to a virtual halt. I then had to spend the next 20 stokes getting the boat back to target speed. That was very demoralising stuff, and bloody hard work.

In the middle of the day Phil spotted a large orange-and-black object out to port and woke me up. I couldn't identify what the hang the object was either, but I conjured up the idea that it was a life-raft. I gave a blast on the fog horn, but there was no response. Phil didn't want to waste time to find out what it really was so we ploughed on, Barbados dead ahead.

"The bloody Admiralty charts showing the prevailing winds to be north-easterlies at this time of year are a scam," he announced as he arrived for an early morning shift, this time rowing into the ever-present south-westerlies.

"Yeah, agreed, and I reckon the Americans never did get a man on the moon."

Phil laughed and eased what had been a terrible night shift. We had been blown upon, waved upon and rained upon and had only managed to progress three more miles. Phil lasted only 45 minutes before the sea anchor went out and we rested until dawn. It was Guy Fawke's Day.

*

I remember it clearly because I was listening to the BBC and heard that Jim Bolger had been forced to step down. Fancy that, burning old Jim on Guy Fawke's Day! There was also an interview with Sean Fitzpatrick at the start of the All Black tour of the UK.

I was back working at the office around 9 a.m. Phil took over at 10 a.m. and we were in sync again. I spent my downtime giving my body a deep massage and stretch. I noticed that when I was giving the oars a good tweak, I would occasionally get a sharp, almost electric shock down my hamstrings. I'd ease off a little, build up again and, if the sharp shock returned, I would take a minute or so to give the hammy a good stretch and massage.

The wind changed at dusk, changed to the south-east and we were off.

The best night in a week; these were still not the north-east trade winds, but hey, we'd settle for some assistance.

*

"What will we do to bring the boat up to weight if they weigh the thing in Barbados?"

"We're okay, Phil. You know I checked it out in Tenerife with The Challenge Business office. Teresa confirmed the 150 litres of water is included in the minimum weight of 410 kg."

"Well, the other crews at the marina had a different view. The 410 kg dry weight meant the water was not included. It would be criminal to come all this way to be counted out on a technicality."

"For fuck's sake, Phil! We've been through all this." I felt my temperature and voice rise. "I don't know what the fuck you're on about. This is bullshit and it's not worth worrying about, let alone talking about it!"

I was angry but immediately regretted my loss of composure. Phil had been fixated by the weight issue, wondering whether we were within the rules. He said not a word as we changed shifts. Now I was pissed off with myself. Damn it! Why did I fly off the handle? Why couldn't I have bitten my lip and explained in calm tones my point of view? Phil prepared a meal, ate it in silence and retired to the cabin. This was the last time we spoke for two entire days.

It was a terrible period for me. I simply didn't know what was going on in his mind. He withdrew totally, his expression morose and I actually began to question his sanity. I went over it again and again. The weight wasn't an issue. Why couldn't he see that? Or had I made some terrible mistake? Could he have been right? Could we still be disqualified? Was I losing my sanity, not Phil losing his? I tried to make conversation, but all I got out of him were grunts of affirmation or rejection.

I remembered one of the interviews we had with "60 Minutes" where the interviewer requested us to please turn on our video camera when we were having a blue. Phil joked, "If I arrive in port alone without the camera, you'll know we had an argument."

At that moment it didn't seem so funny. I was starting to fear for my physical safety. For two days I actually feared that he might throw me overboard.

*

Ranulph Fiennes, *Mind Over Matter*

This determined concentration to drive out mental demons, whether by mantras or other such means of controlling the brain, can be difficult for even the strongest of characters.

*

The break came on November 7.

When I began my 4 p.m. shift it was calm. The light easterly had dropped right away and it was hot and humid, and I had no strength. Out of the north-east I could see a horizon-wide line of cloud advancing on us. The sea colour was changing from clear, picturesque holiday blue to a darker "working overall" blue. The surface was changing from a passive slop to an active slap. I quickly checked the barometer on my watch: the pressure wasn't dropping; it remained high around 1014 millibars, so there was no danger there. A dark line in the water approached, signalling a squall.

It hit. One minute we were in calm neutral conditions, the next we were being buffeted by 35-knot winds and 2-m swells. But believe it or not, it was a north-easterly. We were on our way. I quickly put on a life-jacket and safety harness. Awesome. Cruising at four knots and surging up to six on the crests. My mind was alive. The lethargy I had felt an hour ago had dissipated with the front. This was sheer fun. I was energised.

This was living! I started hooting and yelling!

Phil popped his head out of the cabin. He didn't join in, but the silence was broken. It was good to be talking again. By the end of his shift the wind was gusting at well over 40 knots. Phil suggested we tie the oars down, stow the life-raft in the cabin again and hunker down until the wind and seas eased. The chances of capsizing had increased to danger point. We rested in the knowledge that regardless of our inactivity we were still heading for Barbados, a wonderful feeling.

Phil got up to seven and even eight knots regularly on his shift and it certainly felt rugged in the stern. By the morning the wind had dropped to 10–15 knots, but stayed right on the stern. What a great feeling. The front coming through had two additional positive effects. All the water sloshing around had cleaned the boat and cleared the air between Phil and me. Now we could measure the miles!

*

Another thing stayed with me that day. I was so relieved that the weather and the silence had broken that I fetched the video camera, did a quick self-filmed intro piece and then came out of the cabin to catch Phil. He was at his post, rowing easily, stark naked.

"So, tell me how are you going, Phil?"

"Well, I'm having a great time, actually."

We never discussed the silence.

29.
Speeding Up

A new beauty has been added to the splendour of the world — the beauty of speed.
Tommaso Marinetti

DAY 28, NOVEMBER 9, 1997. Evander Holyfield beat Michael Moorer; we heard the results, but not the fight. It was very difficult for us. Here we were fighting the ocean but hearing no results. We were well aware of many sporting contests by others, but unaware of our own. Obviously we were not making big enough waves. Oh well.

*

Conditions were now nearly perfect. The wind was directly astern at 15 knots. It appeared that we were well and truly in the north-east trade winds. In these conditions we literally surfed the Atlantic.

I would start watching a wave when it was 50 m out, trying to anticipate exactly how this one was going to break and where. If it was going to break after passing the boat, it was a beauty. All I had to do was to make sure we were square on to it, kick in a couple of big ones for acceleration, and it would virtually do the rest. If it was going to break before it reached us, life got a little interesting.

Being square on became absolutely imperative. If I failed, the boat would immediately kick sideways and I would have to let go of the oars and hang on for grim death. If I got it right, by contrast, the boat would hurtle down the face of the wave and for a heart-stopping moment I'd wonder if we were going to nose under. Then it would lift and we would surf for 100 m or more.

Exhilarating! Wicked!

We were cruising at 2.5 to 3 knots and surging up to 6 knots on the swells. In comparison with what we were doing earlier on, these were incredible speeds. I had reversed the previous trend where Phil was rowing greater distances per shift. I was delighted to be clearing 6 nautical miles per row against Phil's 5.5. This, coupled with current assistance meant that I was doing around 7 nautical miles per shift, 3.5 per hour. We were now averaging around 80 miles per day.

*

David Stubbs, mariner, August 1999.

One of the significant advantages that Phil and Rob would have had over the other rowers would have been their ability to handle the seas at night. Others who may have had ocean-going experience as yachties would be able to handle the night sea. Secondly, the unique surf-boat experience of Phil should have meant that the Kiwis would come to grips with the trade wind seas sooner than the others, thereby maintaining their advantage.

*

In fact, Phil's mileage had not increased as much as I would have expected, maybe because he had altered his technique. He had developed a style that required the regular, long, easy pulls on the oars to be broken up with a movement, not unlike the action of a grinder on a racing yacht, as he surfed down the waves. There was some sense in this. It gave the rower a breather when the craft was decelerating down the back of a wave.

The problem was that Phil was using it more and more, meaning the number of full-length strokes he was putting in decreased. I could hardly complain. He had spent the entire journey to date kicking my bony arse. The positive mental spin-off of our improved mileage was that I was now able to churn it out on a regular shift regardless of the state of mind or body. The metronome stroking and the deep subconscious mindset that says, "Keep at it, another stroke, Rob, now another, and another," was being reinforced by the sea log.

*

Rob Hamill's diary, November 9, 1997

Where does Carolyn fit into the picture? Would she support my decision? She's a great woman. We get on well. She seems to know me better than I do and everyone I intro her to likes her. What common goal could we work towards?

*

Day 29, November 10. We made good some 92 nautical miles; over 170 km, or the distance from Mount Maunganui to Raglan, Christchurch to Timaru, Wanganui to New Plymouth, Auckland to Whangarei, whatever. This was a great distance to cover in 24 hours. I was buoyed up; the "just do it" philosophy was working to a T. We had only 1000 nautical miles to go! Definitely this was an attainable target at this speed. Up until this time I hadn't dared to think about the finish. In my past sporting experience I had been so close, so often, only to just miss out on success. Now the big target was within grasp, if only we knew where we were placed! When I finished a shift, once again I felt satisfaction had returned. We had made miles.

*

What was anything but satisfying was that the short-wave radio was drowned that afternoon! I was resting in the cabin with the rear hatch half-open. My head was comfortably tucked in towards the stern bulkhead as I lay on my back; the radio resting lightly on my stomach. I was just relaxing, half listening, feeling at peace with my world. Quietly, stealthily, no drama, certainly with no warning, but suddenly splodge, a salty wet bloop. I was dumped on by a wave.

It had happened to both of us before, and it would happen again, but this bucket of ocean targeted the radio. Our receiver died, instantly silent. That was it. The world outside snuffed out by a sloppy wave. The tenuous umbilical cord to other realities was rudely severed. I swore. Phil inquired what was wrong. I opened the cabin hatch and told him, evidence in hand. Dumbfounded, we both stared in silence at the muted radio.

Phil stopped rowing, his body language and facial expression telling me he was also upset. Wordlessly, he dipped the blades, pulled on the left oar and our journey recommenced in brooding silence. Later he would tell others that he was furious with me, something I sensed at the time, even though he said nothing. I was ready for my 4 p.m. shift well before he called.

*

Yachting World, March 1998

Late on November 11 an EPIRB was set off from the *Spirit of Spelthorne*, rowed by brothers Matthew and Edward Boreham. *3 Com* went to investigate, but found nothing in the position the EPIRB had reported. After a long search pattern they were sure they were searching for bodies.

A Hercules was sent from Lisbon and, nearing the end of their endurance, her crew spotted the *Spirit of Spelthorne*. After returning to *3 Com* they guided the yacht directly to the rowing boat and neatly plopped down two smoke canisters, 20 ft on either side.

The Boreham brothers had given in. They decided to set off the EPIRB and be rescued. After reading the instructions they tied the device to a piece of rope and trailed it over the side. But the line parted and the EPIRB disappeared, crying into the wilderness.

Yet when their rescuers turned up a few days later, they found the brothers oddly subdued. They took them on board, then cautiously set the boat on fire with petrol and flares.

Once on board, the root of the Borehams' problems became clearer: Edward had been taking anti-depressants. In despair he had jumped out of the boat and tried to swim ashore. But the nearest land was hundreds of miles away. Matthew, mercifully, managed to grapple his brother back on board.

*

It was now that I threatened Phil with the ultimate sanction. The days during which I feared I would be thrown overboard were still playing on my mind. I thought long and hard about what I would do if something like that happened again. What was the worse retaliation I could take in Phil's eyes? How I could protect myself, or better still buy some insurance in advance? And I had figured out the answer.

When he jokingly said to me that if I did so-and-so he would hit me, I looked him straight in the eye and said, "If we ever come to blows Phil, I will throw the distress switch on the EPIRB." Both of us knew what that would mean. The end of our race.

*

On the 11th I did the third food rationalisation. My reason for another dumping was the excellent progress we were now making. With less weight on board we should go even faster. I was a little anxious doing this. The previous two times I had done a food rationalisation the weather changed, for the worse.

The first food dump on day five was followed by the south-westerly blow that shackled us for three days; the second rationalisation on day 19 was followed by three days of doldrum calm and energy-sapping heat. Surely this was tempting fate, or was it going to be third time lucky? I broke open seven of the daily ration packs and discarded the main meals. The favoured Greek moussaka remained, the less favoured honey soy chicken and sweet and sour lamb hit the water to feed those waiting mouths. I knew that while I was yet to see a shark, they were down there somewhere.

Next I had a minor assault on the snack bars. Apart from the Mother Earth fruit bars I had no preferences, so one third of the remaining bars were cast to the deep, along with a quarter of the milkshake mixes. I reckoned to have 70 kg of food left enough for, say, another three weeks of full-time rowing, but more importantly leaving us about 15 kg lighter. It took me an hour and a half to operate on the food store and the next shift I really felt the missed rest time. Once again the importance of rest and recovery was driven home.

*

The strange thing was that — all the tensions notwithstanding — there were still moments of pure hilarity on board. Before we had left New Zealand, Kim Webby — who had done the "60 Minutes" documentary — had asked that we shoot some footage for her at sea. Specifically, she had asked that we get a shot of one of us squatting on the bucket. This is TV One current affairs, you understand. Phil decided that we should do it, and that it was his turn to play the role of cameraman. Now, in case you have never done it, it is not easy to go to the dunny knowing it is going to be viewed by a million people. Phil was laughing so hard at my efforts that the skin of his face stretched, his enormous grin stressing his face so much that the bridge of his nose turned white.

*

The wind dropped a little and this allowed me time to play doctor. Either side of my anus was badly chafed. There were a few zits on my cheeks. These little narrow elongated slivers of hard flesh have a little residue of pus under them, and required a little surgery to lift them off. A good scrub and iodine treatment and an hour lying flat on my stomach allowed the area time to dry. I then had a good massaging session on a huge (well, to my finger tips it felt huge), knot in the rhomboids between my shoulder blades.

My left shoulder had been playing up after a particularly strenuous session overnight. With my right hand over my left neck/shoulder area and holding onto my right elbow with my left hand, I dug my fingers into the knot and worked away at relaxing the muscle. I would rest for a couple of minutes and try again, rest, massage, rest, massage until the muscle was feeling a little better. Vaselined up and with generous dollups of Sunsmart screen smeared all over, I was ready to face the noon shift.

*

The wind rose a little and instead of the noon sun I could see a towering thundercloud heading right towards us. It did its dance above us and rained on me quite heavily, not once, but twice. I slipped my wet-weather jacket on. I had had a cough over the last few days, and now I was hacking up rather biggish greens. Still, it could be worse. Phil had lost a tooth filling during the night as he was chewing a fruit wrap.

During the afternoon there came a moment that made a shift memorable. We had seen flying fish nearly every day of the voyage, but on this day I saw the leader of its species; the chief of the Indians, the Ayatollah of the Muslims. I saw him coming, a larger fish, mature, controlled, elegantly skimming the crest of a wave by mere millimetres, gathering speed as he came down into the trough towards the *Challenge*. Unlike the others, which flapped wings furiously, this monster glided across the surface.

He came on a parallel course, aligned to the boat, and we eyeballed each other. He was in the peak of condition, at one with his environment. I wondered what impression I would have conveyed to my inquisitive flyby companion; a fat creature with frail wings that did little to make its cumbersome body move. The next wave was coming more from starboard. I swung on the left oar, aligned the boat, hitched a 40 m ride, slid off into the trough and rowed on.

There was no time now for sitting around and pondering about brain-teasers.

*

November 13 and 14, 1997. I took Augmentin for my cough and partly because of that I managed to sleep for a total of four and a half hours last night, roughly in three 90-minute drop-offs. What a difference both the regularity and quantity of sleep made; I felt so much better that day. I didn't remember any dreams from the previous night and that added to an increased feeling of wellbeing. A great feeling and it was registering on the distance covered.

There were two concerns this morning. Phil had an ulcer inside his mouth that was irritating him. It was interesting that the physical wear and tear got to him differently from me. The second concern was the water temperature outside the boat. It was a smidgen over 30°C. Apparently hurricanes generate in waters of 28°C, and are self-sustaining in water over 30°C.

I knew this was very late in the hurricane season; June to September is usually the worst time, but the season can continue to the end of November. It would be our luck to strike the late-season, rogue hurricane. Phil and I had a chat about it. He wasn't worried unless the barometer dropped below 1000 millibars as the north-east trade winds were tolerably consistent. Nevertheless I had a few uncomfortable cells in my brain that morning.

30.

A Danger More Sinister

The maddening proximity of a too-familiar face may be torture in itself. The clash of personality has always been a danger more sinister than climate or terrain.
Ranulph Fiennes MIND OVER MATTER

THE FIRST OF THE MORNING shifts. A full moon watched over us and was ideal in helping us to see the following sea. The midnight to 2 a.m. shift went well. Off the *Challenge*'s stern, in the general direction of east, there was a dark, spreading blob. A little later, way over the horizon, the sky began to periodically light up with flicks and flashes. Then around 1 a.m. a brilliant lightning storm played to an audience of one.

As always I watched with fascination touched with a little fear, wondering where this storm was headed. After I concluded it was moving in a south-westerly direction and would not imprint on our bowl of ocean, the little knot high in my stomach relaxed and soon disappeared. But nature's light show didn't disappear. The show altered its style. It was far enough away that I was unable to hear any sound and there was no noticeable effect on the sea and wind, but the flashes had changed to "witches' fingers". Lightning initially strode out parallel with the horizon, then split into finger-like streams of angles and twists that plunged into the ocean.

No two flashes in this scintillating performance were the same; the lightning arching over a seemingly small piece of water. While I was glad that we weren't in the grip of any of those "witches' fingers" I was genuinely entertained with one example from nature's basket of virtuoso productions.

*

There was plenty of light from the moon, although high clouds were coming out of the stern sky and overtaking both the moon and the *Challenge*, leaving the boat in the black for a few minutes before we re-emerged into its torch-like probe again. But the sea was being reasonably co-operative, coming regularly from the east-nor'-east and I was rather enjoying myself. The midnight to 2 a.m. shift was an hour and a half in before I noticed light as I came up on the crests.

It was there with each crest, obviously something relatively large and, as it wasn't moving at an angle to us, it was definitely heading our way. This was just the third ship we had sighted on the entire voyage. I watched as slowly a supertanker appeared out of the moon's back-lighting; still a considerable distance away.

"Phil. 2 o'clock, mate."

Again, "Phil, it's 2 o'clock!" A reasonable shout, that.

Muffled mutters from the cabin, a change in the *Challenge*'s trim as Phil moved in the cabin. Thirty seconds later he unhurriedly opened the hatch and came out.

"Phil, there's a tanker over there. Off the port side."

"Hmm, there is."

"Why don't we try to contact it?"

"What's the use? Those cowboys will be on auto-pilot and asleep. They won't be listening to their radio. What makes you think they will be any different from the other two?"

"Nothing Phil, I just want to give it a shot."

"It's a waste of bloody time."

*

Phil mixed his cocktails and got into his rowing seat in the middle of the boat. I stopped rowing and moved past him and into the cabin. I switched the light on and lifted the VHF radio out of its holder. I flicked the set on, made sure channel 16 was selected and attempted to contact the vessel.

"Large container ship, large container ship. This is rowing boat *Kiwi Challenge*, do you read me? Over."

No response.

"Large container ship. This is rowing boat *Kiwi Challenge*, do you read me? Over."

I paused, listened, then came the response.

"I read you, over." A foreign accented voice.

I clambered out the stern hatch and sat on the transom. Phil had heard the response also and was yelling something at me. I was going through all the usual things ships say to each other when they made contact at sea.

The accented voice asked me to change to channel 22.

Phil was getting impatient. "Here, give me the radio."

"No, hang on, I'm changing the channel."

I made the change as instructed.

"Large container ship, large container ship. This is rowing boat *Kiwi Challenge*, do you read me, over?"

Silence. I tried again. Silence. What the devil had happened?

"Large container ship, large container ship."

Eventually they responded. Their concern was that they might capsize us. I could see them already beginning to slow. They still couldn't see us visually or on radar.

Phil didn't understand. He was shouting at me to give them the single side band frequency for *3 Com* to find out where we were coming in the race.

I was getting pissed off. Five minutes ago he hadn't even wanted to try the call.

Phil had had enough. "Give me the radio."

"Shut up and keep rowing." I turned back to the radio. "We have no mast light but you are okay." I released the speaking toggle and waited for a response.

Nothing. I glanced at the instrument face.

The illumination had gone.

Blast! And damn it!

"The fucking VHF is dead." I yelled.

*

Michael Calvin, *Daily Telegraph*, July 22, 1995

Rowing is an inherently aggressive sport and anger and disturbed sleep patterns are a time-honoured recipe for conflict.

"The big issue is how to avoid arguments," [Sir Chay] Blyth said. "When someone flares up you have to get away from the dispute, sustain your equilibrium. If you respond to conflict all it does is exacerbate it."

*

The batteries were flat!

I turned, dived into the cabin and plugged the VHF into the recharger. Nothing happened. I looked at the fuse and tried again.

"Shit, I've just blown the fuse."

I knew our chances of finding out where we were coming had gone. Phil was yelling at me. I didn't know what he was saying but I was bitterly disappointed. Why didn't he shut up? The anger was building up inside me, and this time I couldn't control it. Didn't want to control it.

Pretty soon we were abusing each other.

Phil leapt from his rowing position and screamed at the top of his voice, "Do ya wanna punch in the head?"

I froze. I could see him now and I knew he meant it. I couldn't believe this was happening.

Time slowed down. My reaction to his challenge would govern his next move. I imagined my aggressive response and saw him coming at me. I saw the ensuing fight and my likely defeat. At best, win or lose, our race would be over — I would set off the EPIRB as I had threatened. At worst I might have got thrown overboard.

His face was a mask of fury.

I made my decision.

I lifted my hands in a gesture of pacification.

It was a fight to get my voice under control.

"No, Phil. No. It's okay."

I waited a few moments for things to settle then turned back into the cabin. I picked out the screwdriver on my Swiss army knife but my hands shook wildly as I tried to unscrew the electrical box to replace the fuse. My rage was so near complete that I had trouble controlling my movements. My body was ready to take Phil on in a knuckle-up; every muscle fibre was taut and expectant, readied for action. My heart had said attack but, thankfully, my head had said withdraw.

*

Rob Hamill's diary, November 15, 1997

Really upset at the moment. Big set-to at 2 a.m. this morning (10 a.m. now) over contacting a ship. It doesn't have to be this way. I have learned that I should have given complete leadership of boat to P from race start. Naïvely thought we could co-exist as equals. Doesn't work like that on a small craft such as this. I feel so humble.

Later P really peed off, saying it was a lost opportunity. I felt terrible. P: "As from here on things have changed."

As I started 4 a.m. shift, sea changed to come from all over the place. Was as disturbed as I have felt. Got picked up by two waves combined as one. Steep front face and planed about as fast as we have so far. Jumble of confusing seas scared me with impending change in weather??!

At 10 a.m. I told P the opportunity had not been lost last night, but long ago when battery either not fully charged or capacity not big enough. Either way that part was not my fault, but the inter-personal part was!

P should be official skipper….

2 p.m. – Told P he is official skipper. Said I'd do whatever he says but draw the line at sex. Also have right to make suggestions and to mutiny, whereby I dare say I'll end up in the life-raft.

*

When Phil realised that the VHF battery may not have been fully charged his countenance changed. An apology was not forthcoming but his mellow and relaxed attitude more than anything made me think his mistake in not keeping the battery charged was understood.

*

Rob Hamill's diary, November 15, 1997 (6 p.m.)

P & I are in really good spirits. Incredible from how it was 12 hours ago! Some things happen for the best. Crisis brings change!

31.

Blaming Pavarotti

Going to the opera, like getting drunk, is a sin that carries its own punishment with it.
Hannah More

ON COMING OUT INTO the fiercely sharp sunlight for the noon shift, I swapped seats with Phil and borrowed his sunnies. My eyes were really getting sore from the intensity of the sunlight during the day and today was no exception. Of course there was the direct overhead sunlight, then the added reflected glare, fierce off the sea surface, plus the twinkling flashes from the cusp of a wave that were thrown up and shafted into your eyes.

I had left Los Gigantes with two pairs of sunglasses; one pair escaped me somehow, somewhere. Commencing a shift my eyes were okay, I'd have my sunnies on from the moment I left the cabin and for the first hour they would be sweet as. Then the deterioration would set in. The very back of my eyeball, the retina, would ache. Rowing with eyes shut as much as possible provided some relief, but the last 20 minutes or so were difficult.

To avoid any possible permanent eye damage I borrowed Phil's glasses and wore both sets at once. His bigger ones fitted over my designer jobs quite comfortably. They were of considerable help. Two sets of glasses gave a darkened vista. A downside was the difficulty I experienced in seeing the compass clearly, but my eyes appreciated the added protection.

The thought crossed my mind as to whether the eye problem was related to the slowdown of my organ performance elsewhere. For I had also noticed that my hair, nails, and beard weren't growing any more. Could it be that the eyes were feeling the race intensity also?

I got my Walkman functioning — at least that still worked — and listened to Pavarotti while my mind wandered back home. Mum had a knee replacement operation the day I flew out from Auckland. I was anxious about the outcome of the operation and wondered how her mobility would be this day. I then slipped off into thinking about others in the family: Dad, Peter, Sue, Kerry and John. In particular I wondered where Kerry and John were. What would they think if they could see me now?

God, here I was sitting in the Atlantic, rowing a boat 850 nautical miles from anywhere, sunnies hiding the fact that I was crying, my mind half a planet away and I blamed Pavarotti.

*

Day 36, November 17. As if we didn't have enough problems, despite our greatly increased mileage each day, the water-maker had started to play up again.

Phil had changed the water filter a few days before but the improvement was minimal. The real problem was that there were air bubbles getting into the high-pressure filtration system. The intake was near the centre of the boat, halfway between the bow and stern, a little hole drilled in the hull of the boat to which a plastic pipe was securely connected to our water-maker. It was up this pipe that we were sucking water.

The motor was working fine but only a small dribble of fresh water was being produced. After three days our fresh water reserves were down to 40 litres and it was clear that we were in real trouble. In the hot, humid conditions we were using 25–30 litres a day of reserve water. So we were forced into rationing water.

There was nothing I could do to fix it. This was Phil's territory and, just as I had had to do with my shoulder injury earlier in the voyage, he was going to have to come up with an absolutely original answer. Phil would have to find his Hillary Step.

He jury-rigged a funnel, plastic bottle and tube to the water-maker. As he was doing so I once again watched, feeling a bit useless. There were pieces of plastic piping everywhere and, for some odd reason, I remembered the advice of a friend before we left New Zealand. He had kindly explained to me how one gave one's self a salt-water enema. The point of doing so was to get water into the body, leaving the salt in the bowel. It involved the use of equipment very similar to that which Phil was discarding on the deck.

"Well," I thought. "If Phil doesn't pull this one off, we'll have another use for that."

Thankfully he found his Hillary Step and I was saved a most humiliating — and no doubt painful — procedure. Phil's jury-rigged system worked, but it was a far from perfect solution. We had to manually fill the bottle with seawater, monitor the water in the bottle whilst we were rowing, stop every eight minutes or so to make sure the bottle was refilled and repeat. We did this for six shifts each per day, 12 hours per day.

*

We had posted 90 nautical miles in the previous 24 hours, so we certainly needed that water. We sighted a tanker, but could not make contact with our newly recharged VHF radio. Then just before the 6 p.m. shift we had the wickedest ride yet. I caught a 5–6 m wave as it was about to break and we really took off. The only trouble was I wasn't exactly square. As we accelerated in the little curl the *Challenge* began to broach to port; it rolled with the shape of the wave. Water began to pour in through the scuppers on both sides, then over the starboard gunwale. By then I was up and clinging to the port gunwale, doing a very good imitation of a human barnacle.

By the time I remembered to look at the log to see how fast we were travelling, we had slipped over the crest and I was spread-eagled on the deck with a good portion of the Atlantic trying to escape back to the ocean through the scuppers. It was another little race between the ocean and me to see who could gain control of the *Challenge* first. Heaving on the oars, I swung the boat square on to the next incoming swell, it lifted the boat, the remaining water drained off the deck and we were away again. A few quick arm wrestles with the bilge pump and Phil was presented with a clean *Kiwi Challenge* progressing through the Atlantic chop.

I could tell from the adrenalin pumping through my weary body that I really had very nearly capsized the boat; tiredness and inattention could yet undo us!

I was keenly aware that in 1966 the rowboat *Puffin* was found at sea in the northern Atlantic and its crew lost. I have no doubt that they were tired and perhaps inattentive. I knew that I must remain alert in these seas; one mistake now could spell disaster for us. As happened at times of danger throughout the trip, my mind turned back to my parents again. Back to the time when I decided to tell them that I was going to risk my life for a boat race.

*

October 1996

On the advice of Graham Dalton I had informed the Sunday Star-Times *of my intention to row the Atlantic and that I was looking for a partner. Andrew Sanders interviewed me by phone and at the end of the interview said, "This is great Rob, we are going to put the story on the front page of the sport section."*

It was then that I realised my parents, both avid readers of the paper, would hear about my intentions to do the race. Up until then I had intentionally avoided telling any of my family what I was planning. Peter Montgomery had interviewed me on Newstalk ZB the previous weekend but I knew they didn't listen in and I hoped no one would tell them. I knew they would worry themselves sick about this project and I simply did not know how to break it to them gently. But I did know I had to tell them before Sunday.

I sat at my desk at work pondering my dilemma when the phone rang.

"Good evening, Rob speaking."

"Hi Rob, Dad here."

Dad? DAD. Oh my God!

"Um, oh hi, Dad, how are ya?"

"Good thanks, Rob. Look I won't hold you up," his pitch was higher than normal and he spoke a little too loud. "I have just returned from golf today and I was having a chat with a few friends in the clubhouse."

"Oh yeah, good round was it?" Come on Dad, let's talk golf.

"Yeah, not bad. Anyway, one of the blokes there reckoned they heard you on the radio last weekend talking about rowing the Atlantic Ocean!"

Oh my God.

"Isn't that the funniest thing? I told them they must have been confusing it with something about you at the Atlanta Olympics. Do you know anything about it?"

Oh my God.

"Rob! ... Are you there?"

"Ah ... Well ... Yeah." I stammered, "You may not believe this Dad but I was just contemplating calling you when the phone rang."

"Is that right?"

"Yeah, I was going to tell you and Mum that I am hoping to enter a rowing race across the Atlantic Ocean." I added hopefully, "Isn't that great?"

"Yeah, gee whizz, that's terrific, Rob." A nervous laugh followed and then a pause. "When does it all happen?"

"October next year," I replied, "In just under 12 months." I then told him the basic concept of the race.

"This is amazing. I'll put your mother on."

I spoke to my mother for two minutes and she seemed okay but I knew what she was thinking. This would be very difficult for them. Phew, I thought, that went okay.

About 10 minutes later Mum rang back, her voice a little more grave, "Robert, it is your life, you go for it." She said, "This could be the making of you, boy."

Unbelievable. I never imagined I would get such a positive and courageous response from them. During the campaign Mum often kidded with me, her soft voice and rich Irish accent becoming clipped, "I hope you don't raise the money, boy." She was joking, but deep down I knew she really meant it. Who could blame her?

To fully understand we need to drop back further in time.

August 1978

A 32-ft, double-ended sloop Foxy Lady *sailed into the Gulf of Thailand. The three crew had left the north-west Malaysian coastline several days before, bound eventually for Sri Lanka. The adventure they had discussed and planned for months was taking place.*

The day had been pleasant and restful for the crew as they headed west under full sail in a steady 10 knot breeze. As the sun dropped over the horizon, John went below to make some porridge while Kerry and Stuart took turns at the helm.

The twin-engine gunboat at first sounded like a horde of locusts in the distance but left little doubt as to the nature of the vessel as it rapidly closed in on the trio. Below deck, John was the first to hear the gunshots as the bullets ripped through the wooden mast, vibrating through to its base.

Stuart was the first to feel them. In the pandemonium, Kerry managed to throw a lifebuoy to Stuart who had been knocked overboard by the impact of the bullet. He then yelled to John below to get out and off the boat as quickly as possible. John emerged from below and the two went over the side of the boat for safety.

A spotlight from the gunboat lit up the Foxy Lady *and it wasn't long before the crew on board spotted two men clinging to a lifesaver. Canadian Stuart Glass was already dead.*

John and Kerry were hauled aboard the Khmer Rouge gunboat and were taken to Cambodia and on to Toul Sleng for interrogation. The camp was controlled by Kang Kek Leu, or as his "friends" called him, "Duch". Toul Sleng was a notorious internment camp that has been likened to an Auschwitz for Cambodians; a Pol Pot killing field camp. A termination point for thousands.

Two weeks later the remaining two friends, Englishman John Dewhirst and my brother, New Zealander Kerry Hamill, were also murdered.

Two years later my second eldest brother John Hamill committed suicide after fighting for years with his drug addiction.

*

When I had recalled earlier in the voyage what happened to my brothers, I felt selfish and egocentric for competing in this race. How could I blame Mum or Dad for being apprehensive about my adventure into the unknown? It was not only my parents but my brother Peter and sister Sue who were very concerned as well. As if our family hadn't suffered enough and now here was the youngest son doing a lunatic rowing race across some damned ocean. I'd felt an absolute shit.

At sea my emotions seemed to be more difficult to control. Tears rolled down my cheeks many times as I reflected on the loss of my brothers and what might have been. How would our family be if they were with us today? I wondered for the millionth time if Kerry and John were watching me now. I wondered how their premature departure had affected us. Life would have been all the richer if they were still here with us. It seemed so unfair. And yet here I was putting my life in jeopardy. Was this a selfish act, was I being unfair? Were they my motivation for doing the race in the first place? Whatever, they have always been a part of me wherever I am but more so than ever during this journey.

*

Sue Hamill, sister, August 1999

I thought you were mad. Why would anyone want to put themselves through all that gruelling rowing? Then I thought about the boat being mown down by a big tanker and your tiny boat being far too small and insignificant to be noticed. Even the wake of those things, Rob. I saw an oil tanker go through the Suez Canal and believe me when I say it was the biggest thing I have ever seen. Why should they notice you, or even bother with you? I don't think anything that huge is manoeuvrable, either. I was concerned.

Yes, I thought, I've lost two brothers. Am I to lose another now? How could he even think of putting us through this? There were reports about the likelihood of deaths during the crossing and I thought, just our luck! At some level I was hoping the whole campaign would fall over. But against all odds you managed to raise all that money and then I really felt for you because I know what it's like to come up against a wall of negativity, I know because I was feeling negative towards your passion.

It's true, if you really want to do something you can make it happen and you've been an inspiration to anyone who has seen what's been involved. I still think the hardest part took place before you hit the water. If ever there was an example where mental hardness took precedence I would say this is it!

Time has sifted out irrelevancies and left the very essence of my feelings about the race and your participation.

32.

End Game

It's just a job. Grass grows, birds fly, waves pound the sand. I beat people up.
Muhammad Ali, US boxer

I FIRMLY SECURED THE hatches. If we did capsize we needed the buoyancy in the cabin to right ourselves. I lay in the cabin gradually settling down after the action outside. Breathing steadied, I listened to the water fizzing along the plywood skin, sounding like Jacques Cousteau passing underneath, exhaling bubbles of breath that rippled down the length of the hull.

The eight-minute shifts, then top up the header tank would have to be our regime until we were close to landfall. Landfall! We were so close I didn't want to think about it. Once again we were trying to take each shift as it came, dealing with today before worrying too much about tomorrow. We were looking good to finish on the Saturday. By the afternoon of Thursday November 20, we had replaced the salt-water ballast with fresh water, so turned the water-maker off and concentrated solely on rowing.

We were still desperate to know where we were in the fleet but felt and hoped we would be winning, unless someone had had a superb run with the weather. We knew we were fast from the start when we rowed away from the fleet. This was confirmed the second afternoon when told by *3 Com* that we were still in fourth place having lost nearly six hours fixing the water-maker. But still we didn't know.

What say someone else was also closing on Port St Charles; someone who knew exactly where they and we were placed? They'd be rowing their hearts out and we knew that we must do the same. We gave it heaps and reeled in 93 nautical miles in 24 hours. Go on Peter Haining, beat that! As always through the voyage, the thought of beating Peter — or being beaten by him — drove me on.

*

By now the hurricane danger should have been well behind us. We were therefore both surprised and alarmed when we noted that the weather conditions appeared to be building towards a classic hurricane pattern.

We had a couple of torrential downpours — the only real rain we had

had for the whole race. The barometer readings dropped several points, the wind increased and the seas became dangerously confused. According to the Admiralty charts, another drop of two or three millibars, plus a wind shift to the north and a hurricane would almost certainly follow. Thank God the wind stayed in the easterly quarter.

We were desperate to get ashore. We found we were both thinking of people from home. Phil was wondering about whether or not his grandfather was still alive. I was wondering if Bror and Carolyn were in Barbados. Or whether we had made the crossing a little too fast for them to get there? Apart from friends and family was anyone even interested in what was going on?

*

We had now been at sea for 40 days. With the exception of our brief conversation with *3 Com* on the second day and the ill-fated talk with the container vessel — both of which failed to tell us what we wanted to know — we had spoken to no one. And then there it was. A big square rig off the starboard bow. Phil was on the VHF as soon as we sighted it.

He had only just made contact when a message came from a third vessel.

"This is *Wave Dancer* from Port St Charles, Barbados. We are looking for a boat rowed by two New Zealanders. Have you seen any vessel fitting this description?"

We leapt to our feet and scoured the skyline. No sign of any other craft.

"This is *Kiwi Challenge*, can you read me? Over."

"Read you loud and clear Kiwis. Great to hear you!"

"Great to be here. Can you tell us what our position is? Over."

There was a considerable pause. This was the moment for which we had waited 40 days, rowed over 1.3 million strokes and sweated over 800 litres. This was the moment of truth.

"*Kiwi Challenge*, you're 13 degrees 19 minutes north, 59 degrees 22 minutes west."

No kidding!

"Thanks for that, but what is our position in the race?" Phil called back, a bit frustrated. "Are we first? Fourth? Tenth? How are we going? Over."

"*Kiwi Challenge*, you are number one."

Wooohoo! NUMBER ONE! I liked that, it wasn't "first" or "leading", it was, "You are number one!" We hooted and yelled like lunatics and nearly fell overboard.

Phil gave me a big, solid, warm handshake. I returned it with the same feeling. A great feeling, a great moment.

"Hang on a minute, mate, we don't wanna be overtaken on the last hurdle." Phil ever the pragmatist. We were still 70-odd miles from the finishing line so could still be passed by a determined competitor. Phil was on the VHF again.

"That's fantastic news, guys. Can you tell us how far back the next boat is? Over."

"Yep. 560 miles."

We couldn't believe it!

For the first time Phil broke into song, "Whoa, we're going to Barbados. Whoa, on the sunny Caribbean sea."

I joined in, "Whoa, we're gonna have a party."

We laughed and sang it over a few times until we became embarrassed.

After a two-minute break I was back on the oars.

*

During my next break I spoke to one of the boats on the VHF radio and caught up on a little of what had been happening in the race. I talked to the skipper of *Wave Dancer*, Thomas Herbert, who turned out to be the CEO of the main race sponsor, Port St Charles. He gave me a few details of some of the other competitors. I couldn't believe that we had such a lead, and that so many top teams had come to grief. I was delighted to learn that *Carpe Diem* and its crew were still hanging in there, albeit 1960 miles behind us. After separate shifts we ate dinner at dusk and then put in a shift together.

*

Not surprisingly, getting up for my shifts was the easiest I had experienced in nearly seven weeks. And to cap it off the ride from 4–6 a.m. was one of the most exhilarating I had had during the race. I think having two boats with us, knowing that we were so far in the lead made us take a few risks we may not have taken alone. Out of the dark this flamin' huge wave broke into the back of the boat. The *Challenge* surfed and I hooted like a kid, a very relieved kid, actually. And, while the water around the northern tip of the island was dodgy, once in the lee of the island we were fine. We headed for Port St Charles.

At 10 a.m. (6 a.m. local time Barbados) Phil did his final check for distance covered in 24 hours. We had done 92 miles, very nearly matching our best effort of the voyage.

*

Bror Muller, rower and friend

The morning you arrived Chay and I went out on one of the Port St Charles boats at about 4 a.m. to start to try and find you. It was still dark. I had had the romantic notion that after having been the last person you saw from the start of the race I might be the first person you would see at the end of the race. But I knew by then you had spoken with someone on another boat and therefore you must understand you were in an unassailable lead. It took us a long time to find you that morning.

The light was grey and the sea was far from calm (I would guess a 12-ft swell). It meant we would be high on the crest of a swell, bewildered we couldn't see you then way down in a trough unable to see much at all. We would call back to Teresa Evans (on land), who would relay your latest position and we would race to where you were supposed to be. There were several reiterations of this process before we found you.

I will always remember that morning. Apart from the communication about where you were supposed to be, the people on that boat were very quiet. I suspect we were all thinking a similar thing. We are about to see two men who have been alone for six weeks, achieving what will always be recognised as one of the world's most gruelling challenges. It was very humbling to reflect upon how we were now both in the same physical place on earth but how different our journeys had been to get there.

When we finally found you and I saw you I have to admit I couldn't say anything. It's embarrassing to say but I found my throat constricted and my vision blurred by an excess of fluid. Even now, recalling that moment to write about it brings tears to my eyes. It was very emotional for me.

The skipper of the boat was honking his horn so you knew we were there and I finally composed myself enough to yell at you. At that moment you were rowing. I can't remember what I yelled but I do remember thinking whatever I said or could think of saying in the way of welcoming you seemed pathetically insignificant compared to what you were achieving. Phil and you swapped shortly afterwards and, I'm not sure if you remember, but you had a shit. We pulled back far enough to give you a modicum of privacy but we saw you throw the waste overboard. We all groaned and laughed at the same time.

It was actually a great moment because it felt like we were getting a real insight into your regular routine and at the same time brought us all back to reality. The superhuman status we had subconsciously given you was given a more realistic perspective. You were, after all, still just human beings with the same basic needs as the rest of us. For the people on the boat that day I would say it was a very powerfully motivating experience. People who breathe, eat and therefore shit, just like themselves, could achieve seemingly unachievable things.

*

In fact, while Bror and Chay Blyth were on the vessel, Carolyn was not. I was deeply disappointed not to see her there. In fact, the reason was simply that we had travelled so fast in the closing stages that she had been unable to make the airline connection. She would arrive two days later. Her absence was the only blemish on a perfect day. Mentally I reviewed what we had accomplished.

*

We had crossed 2757 miles of lonely and often dangerous ocean. We had rowed, virtually non-stop, for 41 days and nights; averaging 2.8 knots for each hour at sea. We had survived not only the angry waves, but also our own equally tempestuous relationship. We had left some of the finest rowers and best-prepared ocean campaigns ever mounted in our wake. Those who struggled on were now strung out over nearly 2000 miles of seascape. In the final stages, urged on by following seas, we had several times come close to covering 100 miles in a single day. After 101 years, a two-man crew had finally rowed the Atlantic faster than the legendary Norwegians, Habro and Samuelson. And now I didn't want the journey to end.

33.

Barbados

The problems of victory are more agreeable than the problems of defeat, but they are no less difficult.
Sir Winston Churchill

TWO SUPPORT VESSELS — ONE of them a media boat — both to starboard, one astern, flying a New Zealand flag, accompanied *Kiwi Challenge* as we made our way towards the leeward coast of Barbados. In stark contrast to the blue of the sea, Barbados with its coconut trees fringing the shoreline was a welcoming green. What a great colour.

A nasty rain squall from the south hit, sending us off course for 20 minutes, before departing just as quickly as it had arrived. Once again the vocal cords were given a tune-up.

"Whoa, we're going to Barbados."

Phil joined in, "Whoa, on the sunny Caribbean sea. Whoa, we're gonna have a party."

We corrected our course and rowed together for Port St Charles. A fleet of curious well-wishers joined the fray. It was strange getting such attention after nearly six weeks of social isolation. It would be fair to say that it wasn't altogether unpleasant; quite exhilarating in fact. It galvanised us into action, sending the boat along at a tick under five knots.

The vessel flying the Kiwi duster made a move and came right up on our stern.

"It's Chay again," said Phil, "Now we're going to get a blast of Scottish philosophy!"

"Lads," that voice could cover miles, "Lads, if you can make port in the next half hour and get there by 8 a.m., we will make CNN live. So get going."

Their vessel dropped back to its station astern.

Phil chortled, "I really don't give a shit."

We looked over our shoulder,

"Bit bloody far for half an hour." I guestimated.

"Oh well, let's give that old bastard a run for his money. He doesn't think we can do it." Phil dipped his oars and really gave it the juice. I laughed and joined in. Another flamin' challenge.

*

We entered the Port St Charles harbour a fraction before 8 a.m. — local time but noon our time — 41 days, 1 hour and 55 minutes after leaving the island of Tenerife. We dropped off the mail bag and continued to South America ... No, just kidding.

I don't know if we ever made CNN, but we made port in that half an hour. This was one of the things I had visualised. When I crossed the line I was going to reward myself by standing up and raising my fist, you know, "Yes, we did it!" Just revel in the moment was my attitude that day. I wasn't going to be a dull automaton. So as we entered the harbour entrance I stood up and raised both fists to the cloudless blue.

"Yahoooo! Whoooa!"

"Sit down, ya mug, the finish line is up there off the jetty," Phil said jovially, "Give me a hand or do I have to do it by myself?"

Doh!

The support boats had already moved into the harbour ahead of us and had berthed. The harbour and resort were still being constructed, and along the piers, jetties and nearly completed condominiums, workers were watching and offering encouragement. There was a steel band playing. I drank in the atmosphere.

I had imagined this moment right from the beginning of the campaign: piers lined with gorgeous women, throwing their clothes at us. It was a wonderful thought and actually very motivational. We pulled into the finishing jetty, and there before us on the pier was a line of ugly men! To the forefront were Chay and Bror who proceeded to spray expensive champagne on us. They threw the bottles of bubbly and we both took a long, hard drink. I nearly fell overboard again.

*

Actually, I thought getting off the boat and back on steady land would be difficult but at first it didn't seem too bad. Armed with our passports we walked along the pier unassisted and were ushered into a room where two men sat behind school desks armed with a pen and reams of paper.

"Are you going to stamp my passport?" I wanted the stamp for nostalgic reasons.

"Yah, mon. Welcome to Barbados, mon. I hope you have a good time," the customs officer replied. His delivery reminded me of a joke that I'm not going to tell.

Then there was a short awards ceremony. There was no prize money — after all, sometimes, the rewards for having done something well is simply to have done it. However, we were presented with a miniature oak barrel containing about five litres of Mount Gay rum, the famous local brew.

"You've also won a 55-gallon barrel of rum which we will get to you in the next few days," said David Myers, the CEO for Mount Gay. "Don't drink it all at once," he cautioned.

"Not likely."

We were then shifted to another room where a crowd of people, including press, gathered to meet us. The way they were looking at us made me feel like an alien, as if one of the UFO-like objects I had seen at sea had landed and we had stepped out. When we had set out from Tenerife we were just another couple of blokes in a boat. We still didn't feel any different, but heh, we now seemed to be celebrities.

*

A photographer by the name of Jon Nash flew from England to Barbados specifically to see us finish and send shots back to the British daily newspapers. He arrived 30 minutes after our arrival and asked if we would mind getting back into the boat to stage a couple of cork-popping celebration shots for his records. We obliged and consequently the photo that *The Times* of London used on its front page showed us waving the New Zealand flag, Phil dressed in a green rowing suit, me in black shorts. *The Daily Telegraph*, having sourced their photo from Jon that same day, showed us popping a bottle of champagne wearing clean, white collared shirts emblazoned with our sponsors' logos. As Kiwi band OMC put it, "How Bizarre".

*

Following interviews we were served our first meal as per instructions e-mailed to the organisers from Jeni Pearce: cold skinless chicken with fresh fruit and vegetables. I was looking forward to getting home to a good old-fashioned Granny Smith apple and a feed of feijoas. When queried during the interviews Phil said he was keen to get into a cold and frothing Guinness.

Before we ate anything we both got on the scales to see what our respective finishing weights were. Phil was 85 kg and I was 70 kg. Phil had lost 8 kg and myself 14 kg. A fair bit to lose in 41 days at sea. Fourteen kilograms is roughly 32 pounds; imagine that number of pounds of butter stacked up one on top of the other! Bror commented that it was the skinniest he had ever seen me. Ironically Chay, perhaps enjoying the good life that I had observed in the Taihape restaurant, seemed to have put on a few extra pounds in the same time.

All joking aside, I was keenly aware that without Chay there never would have been a race. He had taken some stick one way or another, especially just before the start when half the crews damn near mutinied. There had also been a fair bit of criticism of the boat design. Some of it in Marten Marine's workshop. But the fact was that it was a very good design indeed. And a safe one. One of the great fears had been that some crew would be lost at sea. It hadn't happened.

Chay had given us all the opportunity to tackle a unique challenge. From there on it had been up to the individual teams to accept.

*

We slept solidly for the afternoon, six hours on a wide, soft, unmoving bed with genuine sheets, with a pillow and not a life-raft under our heads.

That evening Chay, Bror and The Challenge Business staff took us out to dinner. Chay bought the wine; Church Road Cabernet Sauvignon all the way from Hawke's Bay, New Zealand.

"Great choice of wine, Chay," Phil complimented.

"Not bad, eh, considering I couldn't organise a piss-up in a brewery?"

Chay couldn't help himself.

*

For breakfast the next morning the local cereals were being served up when Phil piped up, "I've got something better than this chaff." He disappeared and returned a few minutes later with four vacuum-packed bags of left-over Hubbard's cereal. It was another Oat Bran Muesli start to the day and I for one wasn't complaining.

*

And what of all the others? How did they fare?

The French entry, *Atlantik Challenge*, with Joseph Le Guen and Pascal Blond, arrived eight days later. All of the jokes that had circulated in Tenerife, like the one about the *Atlantik Challenge* arriving in Barbados minus Le Guen, proved to be ill-founded. Pascal would complete his most unusual celebration of freedom after his incarceration, and in doing so wipe the smiles off a lot of faces.

I realise now that he was a very smart choice of rowing companion; for a man who had spent 14 years in a cell, 49 days at sea in a two-man boat was positively liberating. He would go off to become a physical training instructor. Joseph would come to New Zealand in early 2000, determined to row from here to South America.

A further six days back would be the husband and wife team, David and Nadia Rice in *Hannah Snell*. Dorset firemen Steve Isaacs — the practical joker from the Harbour Lites — and Mark Stubbs in *TocH* would come in three days later and be placed sixth. Neil Hitt and Peter Hogden, the club rowers from Exeter in *Hospicare*, would follow them in what amounted to a day-long sprint finish, only to be pipped by less than 40 minutes after nearly two months of rowing.

The next day would come *Commodore Shipping* with just half its original crew. Early in the race John Searson relayed a message saying that Carl Clinton (he of the suturing lessons) had sustained a serious back injury. Carl was taken on board *3 Com* suffering from a prolapsed disk and was later airlifted out by MRCC. John refused to give up. He would row on alone, he said; nobody was going to burn his boat. And that was exactly what he did. He finished in 55 days, which would have given him eighth place; a superhuman effort. Carl flew out to Barbados to meet him.

The Golden Fleece of Rob Whitaker and Daniel Innes was another three days back. But Rob would not be on it. You will recall that the shoulder problem which he had been suffering from in Tenerife had deteriorated to the point where he could not start. His place had been taken by another rower. He observed the race aboard *3 Com*.

Next would be Graham Walters — the carpenter who had still been knocking his boat together in Tenerife — and Keith Mason-Moore in *The George Gearry*. Keith celebrated his finishing by getting married in Barbados. Then came Jock Wishart, who had fancied our chances at the start, with Duncan Nicol, in *Mount Gay Rum Runner*.

Cellnet Atlantic Challenger came in the following day. Incredibly, they had spent no fewer than 20 days on the sea anchor. Had they had similar weather to us we estimated they would have finished within three to four days of us.

Key Challenger had activated their Argos beacon on October 15. David Mossman had also suffered from food poisoning. He had been taken on board *3 Com* and later returned to land. David Immelman spent the next two days remaking the *Challenger* into a one-man vessel, then set out in an attempt to break the solo record of 75 days set in 1970. This he did, completing the voyage alone in just 65 days. His success may have owed something to his unique technique for cooling off at sea; he lashed himself to the boat and dived down 5 to 10 m. I'm damned if I would have done it.

Roger Gould and Charlie Street, the policemen from Middlesex in *Sam Deacon*, came in on December 17. The UK Army captains Martin Bellamy and Mark Mortimer — whom I had initially thought arrogant, but came to admire — arrived on Christmas Day.

The last boat to complete the voyage — *Carpe Diem,* rowed by Dan Byles and his mother Jan — would reach Barbados on January 21 after a crossing of sheer serendipity. The crew had not exchanged a single cross word and had found time to share a gin and tonic each evening. Anything more different from our own experience would be difficult to imagine.

*

Roger Gould, *Sam Deacon*, October 1999

As for falling out of the boat, I did do that. TWICE in fact. Third night out, Charlie at shift change dropped an oar overboard in the storms. I leant over the side to reach it. I wasn't dressed at all, middle of the night, no life-jacket on or nearby, not strapped on, just out of the cabin looking my best. As I leaned over, we were hit by a broadside wave and I went into the foaming water.

Grabbing the oar as I landed, I turned to get back on board. The boat had disappeared! In the distance, I could see it over the next wave. Decision time, Rog. Which piece of wood (our oars were wooden, remember) do I need the most? The bit in my hand, or the one Charlie is sitting on? Difficult as it was, I let go of the oar and swam like fuck for the boat!

In the half-light of the storm, I could see Charlie struggling to get another oar out of stowage. When he eventually got it out, he tried in vain to turn the boat around for me. I could see him every now and then as I bobbed up to the top of the waves holding water one side and pulling like crazy on the other. Nothing was working! 45 minutes later, I was finally back on board.

Two weeks from finishing the race I fell out again at night. The good thing about humans is they learn from bad things happening to them. This time I was strapped on! Still had no life-jacket on, but, hey, who needed it. I was attached to a big old lifeboat wasn't I? Charlie had just finished the midnight to 2 a.m. shift and I could hear him in the cabin. Headphones on and joining in with Pink Floyd singing loudly. *"I, I, I, am comfortably numb"*! I knocked on the side of the boat because I could not find the strength to climb back on board. He didn't hear me though. Settling in for a two-hour drag beside the boat in nice warm water seemed quite appealing.

I think I must have started hallucinating a lot because I remember trying to climb back on board several times and not managing it. All of a sudden though, I looked up and, leaning over the gunwales were my four children. Arms outstretched, they said together.

"Come on daddy. Get back in the boat."

Next thing I recall, I was lying on the deck of the *Sam Deacon* crying like a baby, soaking wet. Charlie thought I'd lost the plot completely. Perhaps I had but the mind is a strange thing. Very powerful images can create powerful strength.

*

In retrospect I can see that one of the really stupid things that Phil and I both did during the crossing was to ignore the safety factor far too often; in particular the use of the safety harness. The harness was definitely an impediment to rowing, but we should have worn them more in training and then we would have known that. Barring this we should have tried to fashion some kind replacement while at sea. I'm amazed and thankful that our luck lasted to the finish.

*

A number of the crews that had set out from Tenerife had all fallen before (and sometimes into) the mighty Atlantic in their different ways, although — thankfully — nobody had died. The first to quit had been Ian Chater and Nigel Garbett in *This Way Up* who had returned to Los Gigantes Marina under their own steam; arriving the morning after the start. They had already realised there was no way they could make it.

My old nemesis, Peter Haining, and David Riches had contacted The Challenge Business on the second day — October 13 — by satellite phone saying that David was suffering very badly from food poisoning. They also got caught in the tail end of the storm and the boat had taken a battering. They were rescued by helicopter from the MRCC *Tenerife* and the boat was towed back to land. I had spent over six weeks in a mental death struggle with a competitor who was no longer in the race.

The following day, Tori Murden and Louise Graff had also been rescued by the MRCC and returned to Tenerife suffering from food poisoning. Both women were taken to hospital. They had a second attempt a week later, but because of electrical problems they were towed back to land again. The following year Tori would attempt to row *American Pearl* solo from North Carolina to France, failing magnificently and writing a lyrical account of her voyage entitled *Will You Walk With Me*? In late 1999 she would finally became the first woman to row the Atlantic solo.

Le Baleine, rowed by husband-and-wife team Jean and Marie Meunier, had activated their Argos on October 29. Their boat had been damaged in storms and was taking on water. Marie had been thrown into the water, but Jean managed to drag her back in. They were taken on board *3 Com* and their boat then burned at sea; a Viking funeral.

Perhaps the most remarkable story was that of the demise of the *Spirit of Spelthorne* rowed by Edward and Matthew Boreham. They disappeared off the radar entirely. For three weeks they were rowing in circles without power and lived on emergency rations. Then Edward — suffering from severe depression, which was hardly surprising — lost it completely and set out to swim for land! His brother had to reel him back in. They were eventually rescued 900 miles south of the Azores. Their boat was also burned.

Most of the ill-fated incidents occurred on Wednesdays; this must have been a unlucky day. I might add that we were not the only crew to have inter-personal problems at sea. We all knew that this was going to be a difficulty for some and so it was for many of the crews. Rowers who had been best mates for years — far closer than Phil and I had ever been — went through the same kind of hell.

The Atlantic Rowing Race, Final Positions Ocean Rowing Society, www.oceanrowing.com, April 6, 1998

Place	Boat	Crew	Distance covered	Date Finished
1	Kiwi Challenge	(Hamill/Stubbs)	2757	November 22
2	Atlantik Challenge	(Blond/Le Guen)	2907	November 30
3	Hannah Snell	(Rice/Rice)	2931	December 6
4	Spirit of Jersey	(Blandin/Cassin)	2933	December 8
5	Christina	(Kavanagh/Kavanagh)	2847	December 9
6	TocH Phoenix	(Isaacs/Stubbs)	2875	December 9
7	Hospicare	(Hitt/Hogden)	2939	December 9
	Commodore Shipping	(Searson)	3046	December 10
8	Team Ryvita	(Callaghan/Welford)	2893	December 11
9	Keider Atlantic Warrior	(Bryant/Lee)	2892	December 12
	The Golden Fleece	(Innes/Lowe)	2861	December 12
10	The George Gearry	(Mason-Moore/Walters)	2948	December 13
11	Mount Gay Rum Runner	(Nicol/Wishart)	2984	December 14
12	Bitzer	(Reid/Watson)	2970	December 15
13	Cellnet Atlantic Challenger	(Chalk/Rock)	3012	December 15
14	Endeavour	(Gavey/van Katwyk)	3016	December 15
15	Boatcom Waverider	(Jackson/Shekdar)	3013	December 16
16	Sam Deacon	(Gould/Street)	2878	December 17
17	The Cornish Challenger	(Elliot/Hunkin)	2883	December 17
	Key Challenger	(Immelman)	2861	December 18
18	Star Atlantic	(Bentsen/Hoff)	2938	December 20
	Salamanca	(Bellamy/Mortimer)	2861	December 25
	Mistral Endeavour	(Duckworth/Fraser)	3058	January 4, 1998
	Carpe Diem	(Byles/Meek)	3044	January 21
	Spirit of Spelthorne	(Boreham/Boreham)		DNF
	La Baleine	(Meunier/Meunier)		DNF
	American Pearl	(Graff/Murden)		DNF
	Wabun	(Renzelmann/Wedmeyer)		DNF
	Walter Scott & Partners	(Haining/Riches)		DNF
	This Way Up	(Chater/Garbett)		DNF

*

I was unaware that — while we were rowing the Atlantic — a debate was raging on the Internet which then spilled out into the other media. They were actually questioning the validity of our performance. When we stepped ashore at Port St Charles I was taken aback at the suggestion that what we had just accomplished was considered by a few to be suspect. At the outset I thought reporters were joking; when I discovered they were not, I was disappointed and annoyed.

We could prove that we had not cheated. Consider this. First, during the times in the doldrums — approximately a week — we still rowed further than all the other crews. Second, on our best day we had covered 93 nautical miles. This was admittedly an incredible performance and that had triggered the doubts. But they should have been silenced on our last day at sea when we came within an ace of bettering that distance. On that day we were with the official Port St Charles craft that were shadowing us to the finish line. I rest my case.

Did anyone cheat? Well, it could be said that *The Daily Telegraph*, using a staged photo, certainly did so. But, in some way or another, we all did. We cheated on sleep, fresh food, comfort, the company of other humans, information about the race and we took advantage of the sea, we surfed.

I suppose you could say John Searson and David Immelman cheated: they rowed alone without any help. Roger Gould cheated. He actually left his boat, the *Sam Deacon* twice; both times were quite involuntary, but nevertheless he left his rowing partner, Charlie Street, alone on the boat. The way that *Hannah Snell* came home suggested the Rices most likely cheated using their ocean craft knowledge gleaned from sailing the Atlantic. Mark Stubbs stitched Steve Isaacs' head gash on board the *TocH Phoenix* with neither anaesthetic nor medical assistance, so by my book they cheated the National Health Service.

And, of course, we all repeatedly cheated death.

What the 24 crews that finished at Barbados didn't cheat on was pain, deprivation, relationship stress or success. Every crew member was, in my eyes and — to use Roger Gould's apt expression — a bloody hero.

*

Jan Meek, *Carpe Diem*

When I checked my diary for the 20th day I saw that I had written that we picked that *Kiwi Challenge* would be winning. Around the 50th day we heard that you had won. We were just closing on halfway. By then you were probably back in New Zealand!

34.

Going Home

Going home must be like going to render an account.
Joseph Conrad LORD JIM

WITHIN A FEW DAYS I was putting weight on again. I was eating quality food and not spending the enormous energy output and so my body was recovering at pace.

The following weekend the annual around Barbados yacht race was held. A great guy, Bizzy Williams — one of the partners in the Port St Charles development — owned a yacht called *Silver Bullet*. It was a super cat, a ripper of a boat, a 9-m catamaran that produced startling speed. It could do close to 30 knots. He invited us to crew for him and his son. They controlled the *Silver Bullet* while Phil and I stacked out on the trapeze. It was a handicap race around Barbados, and we were the final contestants to start.

The others had at least an hour on us. There were maxi yachts and a mixture of other types and sizes. Man, it was exhilarating. We beat into the wind, hard work but good fun. As we circled the island we ended up with tail winds. We were out on the trapeze. Every now and again the windward hull would go over one swell but dive into the following one. At one stage Bizzy was lost over the stern. He held on to the mainsheet rope and with much advice from the other three of us got himself back on board. Hell, if he had let go, God knows how we would have got the cat around and back to him.

For virtually the whole race — 4 hours — we hung in space, overtaking boat after boat, but those other two men could control that cat. It was just unreal, going along at 25 knots. We were coming up on this beautiful maxi, we were chewing into their lead, but they hit the finishing line just before us. We didn't get line honours but we broke the record by an hour. A great buzz. Mount Gay gave us a barrel of rum — as you do when in Barbados — which Bizzy shared among friends.

I remember that day for another reason. It was the same day the French — who had rowed 150 miles further than us — came into the port and we went sailing past them in this race in the super cat. We thought it was quite funny although I doubt that they saw it that way. They, too, had broken Habro and Samuelson's record. We chatted afterwards, then I took a look at their boat. They had two batteries on board; big mothers weighing a total of around 70 kg, probably more. Ours had weighed 23 kg. Incredibly, the boat was also still loaded down with tinned goodies. They like their food, the French. I wondered how much tinned food they had at the start.

Had they travelled lighter and taken a more direct route we might have had a real race on our hands.

*

The awards ceremony was four days later. Prince Andrew met with us in a private room before the presentations. I don't know why, but for some reason I had it in my mind that he was Prince Edward who had spent some time as a tutor at Wanganui Collegiate, and in a private conversation with Andrew I jokingly observed that, "The Barbados weather is almost as good as the weather in Wanganui, isn't it?" He gave a blank look and moved on. Half an hour later the coin dropped. "Oh God, not again, Hamill!"

The ceremony was low-key and pleasant. I was surprised at the number of people there and concluded that they must have been there to see the prince. We were awarded a trophy and commemorative plaque. We were stoked. Still, 50 grand for first prize wouldn't have been a bad idea. Listen up, Chay.

*

After the awards the local radio interviewer spoke with us. She was a thoroughly pleasant person and afterwards I congratulated her on her style of interview and discovered that she was standing in for her husband who was busy with radio elsewhere in Barbados.

"Gosh. What on earth do you do for a regular job?"

"Oh, I am the Barbados marketing manager for BWIA. The British West Indies Airways." She responded smartly.

"Well, that's interesting. We haven't got tickets back to the UK and we might end up flying with you guys. We have to get to London to get our Air New Zealand connection back to New Zealand. Otherwise we're stranded here."

A quick, direct discussion ensued as she ascertained our financial and logistical position.

"Look, I am sure BWIA can assist you here."

"That would be really helpful if you could," I responded honestly.

"Rob, consider it done." Now, that's my kind of interviewer!

*

The 55-gallon barrel of Mount Gay rum that we won for the rowing race was another story in itself. We hardly touched a drop of it. Bror had arranged a cell phone with free local calls for us, but by the time we had rung home, rung friends, rung the media — we rang every sod we knew and a few we didn't — we had a gigantic international phone bill. The Mount Gay rum company agreed to pay us the equivalent of what it cost them to produce the rum, which virtually covered the bill. Thanks, Mount Gay.

*

Air New Zealand upgraded us to first class for the flight back home. On landing at Auckland we were whisked through formalities to be interviewed by the media. I was more interested in my family. I searched the crowd, saw Mum at the back of reporters and made a beeline for her. It was great to see her, Dad, Peter and Sue. We had interviews and a few photos for the Sunday papers and prepared to leave the airport.

It was only then that I realised I had left my bag with the video camera, logbook, photos and other precious belongings in the main welcoming foyer. I dashed back to collect them. They were gone! Nowhere to be found.

Five days later — the day before a civic reception in Hamilton organised by radio reporter Kay Whittle — a message was left on my answer phone: "Oh, Rob Hamill, I have a bag of yours, I wonder if you could give me a call.... "

Yahoo!

A group of New Zealanders returning home had gone through the airport after us and some diligent soul had gathered up all camera bags, etc. and bundled them into their bus. It was only after checking with the individual travellers that he opened the bag and discovered it was my missing records.

*

Our boat was marooned in Barbados. We had no way of financing it back to New Zealand. Kay Whittle, the Hamilton radio journalist who had tracked our row and kept the Waikato informed of our progress as well as supplying Radio New Zealand with information, got into action and rang the Blue Star Line. Kay has an incredible, assuring and unstressed voice, which is very difficult to argue against or say no to. She persisted with the Blue Star bureaucracy and got through to the general manager, by which time any discussion was going to be no contest. Blue Star agreed to transport our boat back to Auckland.

*

Kiwi Challenge arrived back in Auckland just before the Halberg Awards evening. The Halberg Trust had asked if the boat could be a centrepiece for their awards that evening. We were delighted that they wished to have the boat there and readily agreed. Phil zipped off down to the wharf to collect it. Blue Star had met all the return costs to that point. Now there was a small matter of duty and GST to be paid on the boat returning to New Zealand!

This was not unexpected, but we didn't have the sum required. And of course we were in the usual situation. No money, no boat. Phil argued, but many great and powerful people have argued against Customs and lost. A mere police sergeant, wanting his boat back for an awards ceremony, stood little chance. In frustration Phil suggested that they set light to the boat, right there on the dock and leave it at that.

Dave Currie of the Halberg Trust stepped into the breach, negotiated with Customs and paid for our boat to be released.

*

This incident had an unintended positive outcome for us. It alerted the Auckland business community to the fact that we were broke and were not kidding.

That night at the Halberg Awards, Dave Currie offered to run a silent auction to sell the boat, and they put a piece of paper on every table on which individuals or companies could bid. The written bids would be collected and the Trust would adjudicate and sell the boat on our behalf. At the awards ceremony, Paul Smart from Sky TV discussed the idea that a number of companies should get together and purchase the boat to eliminate our outstanding debts.

A number of prominent New Zealand companies all contributed to purchase the boat and clear our accounts. Whew, one more monkey off our backs. Grant Hirst — the CEO of Westfield, the management company for the St Luke's Group — was one of the participants and, as part of the deal, suggested a tour of their shopping malls in Auckland, Hamilton, Wellington and Christchurch over a period of 10 weeks. We were about to hit the road. Together.

*

The Right Product
The Right Team
Came from Nothing
NOTHING, but a dream
Rob Hamill

*

You might wonder how it was that Phil and I — who had come so perilously close to blows at sea — managed to go on working together when we returned. Had our relationship suddenly become all sweetness and light when we reached Port St Charles?

Well, yes — up to a point. Relieved of the pressures we felt at sea we certainly stopped bickering with each other, but we still carried the baggage of all that had happened in those lonely days and nights at sea. In some ways the speaking sessions were therapeutic. The dross was gradually being tossed overboard. We started doing motivational presentations.

We described how we had planned, prepared, paid attention to detail, were consistent and worked hard. We explained our short- and long-term goals, how we broke tasks into small, easily attainable bites to progressively build our boat, our finances, our race. Along the way we had to change and adapt. We both found that very difficult, but adapt we did.

We talked about decision-making and commitment, but above all we gave our audiences the message that I first noted on the back of a Mainfreight truck plying State Highway One. *With Passion Anything Is Possible*. And, yes, we spoke about teamwork. Because ultimately we were a very good team.

*

Our friendship was undergoing a rebirth. We were starting again to appreciate those qualities that we had seen in each other that had led us to accept the challenge together in the first place. We also learnt that many people didn't want to hear about our problems. They wanted to believe that we had been the best of mates; before the race, during and after. That had not been the case. But we were involved in a process of growing understanding, both of what we had been through, and of what we could still achieve together.

Indeed, we started planning for the next challenge.

Wisely, perhaps, we decided that we would not row together, but that we would conduct a two-boat campaign next time. We would fundraise together, boat-build together and train together, at all times building on the wealth of knowledge we had gained from the 1997 race. But we would not ultimately row together. Phil would row with Steve Westlake. And I would, of course, have to find some other partner. Or so it seemed at the time. But — as so many have learnt at sea — fate has a way of dramatically interfering in the affairs of men.

A Eulogy

Because I'd sooner die with memories than dreams.

76-year-old trans-Tasman microlight pilot

WANGANUI, DECEMBER 20, 1998. It was around 9.35 in the evening. The end of another long day of multiple testing and rowing sessions was nigh. The Sydney 2000 Olympic Training Squad had assembled three days earlier for intense testing and training. I was walking back to my sleeping quarters — feeling that intense but not unpleasant weariness one gets following a good day's training — when my cell phone rang.

"G'day, Rob here."

"Hello, Rob, I'm with the *New Zealand Herald*."

"Oh g'day, howzit?"

"Good thanks, Rob ... Rob, I was just wondering if I could get a comment from you regarding Phil Stubbs."

"What about him, what's happened?" The tone of the reporter's voice more than anything else had alerted me that something was wrong.

"Oh, ah, you haven't heard ... look, I am not in a position to say. You had better ring this number."

He gave me the number of a police officer in Auckland who — in a very policeman-like manner — informed me that Phil Stubbs had been killed in an air accident. Apparently the plane he was piloting crashed on Karekare Beach on Auckland's wild west coast soon after take-off late that afternoon.

I stopped walking, stood stock still. I just couldn't believe it.

We had delivered a presentation on our success just five days before. It had been a heap of fun, doing a tag team talk, bouncing off each other and taking the mickey out of each other. Afterwards we had talked about what each of us was going to do for Christmas, about working together on the two-boat campaign. We had joked, wished each other all the best for the Christmas break, and parted.

Now Phil was gone. I was deeply shocked.

*

Later I would learn the details of what had happened. That afternoon, Phil had flown the restored 1959 Piper of which he was a part owner — it was the same aircraft that he had flown to Hamilton when first we met — from Ardmore to Karekare Beach, putting her down on the hard sand.

He had taken a couple of members of the local surf club for a joy-ride and then spent the rest of the afternoon swimming among the rocks, kelp and surf. Then, with his brother-in-law — Mark Gusse from Nebraska — on board, he had climbed into the cockpit and taken off down the beach. The take-off was perfect, the plane banked gently and then — to the horror of the surfers and others watching from below — it nose-dived down into a stream that crosses the beach.

By the time rescue workers reached the craft, Phil Stubbs was already dead. Incredibly, his brother-in-law was still conscious and would survive.

*

I informed my rowing colleagues I was leaving the next morning and went to bed but got little sleep. I was out on the water early for an hour and a half; rowing hard, remembering, trying to make sense of what had happened. Then I drove up to Auckland to Phil's mother's home, none the wiser about the meaning of death. It was a long drive, but it was one of those where many miles are blank; the rubber was on the road but my mind was dull and disoriented.

I reached Joy Stubbs' home to be met by Graham Dalton.

"Geez, mate, you look a right mess."

He'd summed up my feelings perfectly.

Joy's living room was packed with friends of Phil's. The television news was just starting. Seeing David, Phil's father, reminded me of our journey together across the North Sea: father, son and friends.

Then came a TVNZ tribute to Phil midway through the news. Seeing him fist raised at the race finish and joking with the TV reporter broke me up. Joy, who was sitting across the room from me, threaded her way through the grieving friends and held me. All the while Phil's tribute continued.

It was an unbelievably selfless act. She seemed more concerned about my welfare than her own. She absolutely loved Phil to bits and would have gone to the ends of the earth to support him in his every endeavour. I knew how much she was grieving, having seen my parents go through it twice. I felt ashamed of my weakness, when compared with her strength.

*

Albert Camus (while crossing the Atlantic en route to South America)
As usual I finish the day before the sea, sumptuous this evening beneath the moon, which writes Arab symbols with phosphorescent streaks on the slow swells. No end to the sky and the waters. How well they accompany sadness!

*

On the day of the funeral service I arranged to have the *Kiwi Challenge* placed outside the church. Most of the mourners paused as they passed it. I was privileged to be asked to offer a eulogy. Here's what I said ...

> Phil and I have teamed up at a number of speaking occasions this year. We formed a bit of a tag team and had a lot of fun doing it together. Speaking can be difficult, however, and this is easily the most difficult and trying talk that I have ever given.
>
> As you may know I did not know Phil for as long as most of you here. I'm not a brother or family member or an old school buddy for that matter. Circumstances brought us together for the challenge and adventure of a lifetime. If ever you were to row an ocean, Phil Stubbs would be the man to team up with. I remember five days into the Atlantic rowing race we were hit by bad weather and had to take cover in the cabin of the craft, which is no penthouse apartment, as you may have seen outside the church. We stayed in that cabin for three days.
>
> During that time I discovered several things about Phil. Firstly he was obviously passionate about his work with the police and he took it very seriously. I remember one evening being woken by Phil thrashing around the cabin and grappling with structural joins on the cabin ceiling. He awoke from his dream and told me that he had been chasing some low-life down the street and had finally apprehended a man who was now resisting arrest.
>
> The next morning I heard some interesting news on our short-wave radio receiver. The BBC presenter announced that in Christchurch, New Zealand, inmates of a prison had rebelled. The prisoners had taken guards hostage and were making demands for reform to prison conditions.
>
> "Ya see, mate," said Sgt Stubbs, "Look at what happens when I leave the country!" We decided it would be a good idea to make the crossing as quick as possible before anarchy erupted back home.
>
> Mid-Atlantic and it came time to clean the boat. Algae and barnacles were causing drag and had to be removed. After several futile attempts, I realised I could not get in the water. Somewhat embarrassed, I admitted this fact to Phil. He just shrugged, chuckled and said, "Fear ... a wasted emotion."
>
> In truth it was Phil's courage that helped overcome any fears he had. As Mark Twain said, "Courage is resistance to fear. It is the mastery of fear. It is not the absence of fear."
>
> Phil always backed himself. The day before the race finished, a welcoming party from Barbados informed us that we were leading the race. Phil remarked, "Ya' see, mate, I told ya we would win!
>
> To many of us Phil was indestructible, almost bullet-proof. When things were going wrong and getting a little out of hand, Phil would somehow appear to have a semblance of control. When he was around, you somehow felt safer.
>
> I have received many faxes and e-mails from many people, some of whom did not even meet Phil. One such message from Barbados, where we

finished the race, reads as follows:

Dear Rob
This is Kate. I don't know if you remember me. (Thomas' daughter?) I heard the news of Phil's death this morning. It has hit us all very hard. He had many friends here in Barbados – probably more than he realised. He's almost a legend here and I know memories of him will be cherished by all. Uncle Bizzy and I took Silver Bullet *out today in memory of Phil. He loved that boat, I know. I think that is what he would have wanted us to do. That's what he did, live life to the fullest, seeking a thrill in every moment. I know we didn't know him well, but he touched our lives, and that can never be lost. His friends must be in shock at this huge loss. I wish them strength, and hope that they remember Phil, his laid-back attitude, his ready laugh, and know that his spirit is still with them, and he would want them to smile and make the most out of everything they have.*

I don't think there is a proper way to end this e-mail, at least I can't think of one. I guess there are just some things that words can't express.
Kate Herbert.

I continued …

It is not what you are given that matters, it is how you use it that counts. Phil Stubbs was the epitome of making everything count.

And I concluded my words with a poem I had written on the night before (it appears at the beginning of this book).

*

Dost thou love life?
Then do not squander time.
For that's the stuff life is made of.
Note under Phil's photo at his funeral

*

Phil's ashes were scattered over the sands of Karekare Beach.

A few days after the funeral I was at home listening to the radio. The DJ was inviting listeners to try and solve a brain-teaser.

"Did you hear about the two archaeologists tramping in the mountains of Iran? They came across two frozen bodies at the foot of a glacier. On close inspection one said to the other, 'My God, it's Adam and Eve!' How did they know that?"

I felt oddly numb. Once again Phil was tying up the loose ends.

"They had no belly buttons."

I finally got it.

Author's Note:

Next

It's never too late to be what you might have been.
George Eliot

SOMETHING WAS GNAWING AT my soul.

Somewhere the endless swells were still rolling, the fish were jumping, the trade winds blowing. And every day that passed was another day that I wasn't out there to see and feel them. Gradually I found myself longing to feel the ocean oars in my hands again, and to smell the tang of the ocean in my nostrils.

I knew that I must make a decision. Either I would challenge the Atlantic — and those who dared row her — again or I would not. I debated the issue in my mind for several months, but in truth the outcome of my deliberations was never seriously in doubt. And next year another chapter in the story of the ocean rowers will be written.

When the hooter sounds for the start of the second trans-Atlantic rowing race in October 2001, there will be 50 crews and craft on the Canarian waters; among them an as yet unnamed boat with a Kiwi crew on the oars. One of those rowers will be Steve Westlake — he who my heart described earlier in these pages as "some scumbag imposter" who would take the glory that was rightly mine! The other person in that craft will be me.

God willing, we will paddle into Port St. Charles around six weeks later, hopefully ahead of the fleet. If we do so we will dedicate our victory to Phil.

Is this sufficient reason to go through all of the pain and agony again? To raise the funds? To build another boat? To put in the endless hours of training? And then to risk our lives rowing a race with no prize? For Steve and I it is, but to you it might well seem as misguided as Phil's and my endeavour seemed to the man who told us that there were easier ways to pick up girls. If so, then all I can do is to repeat the words with which I began this narrative.

"Make voyages. Attempt them. That's all there is."

Race Acknowledgements

"Together" was sign-written both inside and outside the cabin of *Kiwi Challenge*. To help identify with what the word would mean to us, I made a list of descriptions both specific and abstract. For example: interdependence, shared destiny, communication, "united we stand — divided we fall", 1 + 1 = 3 (the business equation where the whole is greater than the sum of the individual parts), PRIDE (Personal Responsibility In Delivering Excellence), and TEAM (Together Everyone Achieves More).

If ever I felt doubt or concern the word "together" helped me focus on the positive and work on the process rather than be preoccupied by the outcome. After all, it was only "together" that the team could win.

Behind every success story there is a team of people supporting the effort — like mission control sending an astronaut into space. Our team was literally hundreds, perhaps thousands strong. The following are some of those, not already mentioned in this book, who gave either their time, advice or financial support (in the form of money, or discounted products and services). My apologies if you have been missed.

"Together" we made it happen.

TOSHIBA

Gold Sponsors

LEP International — Chris Dunphy
Lion Foundation — Brian Corbett
Power & Marine — Allan Dickinson
ECNZ — Ken Smales
SERCo — Warren Hodgson
Sunsmart — Iain Potter
Perry Holdings — Brian Perry
Air New Zealand — Hinemoa Sharmen-Salter
NZ Sports Foundation — Chris Ineson
DMW Trailers — Greg Dutton
BFA Marine — Axel Meissner
Pauanui Service Station — Peter Hamill

Support Sponsors

Adlite Signs
Horleys
Sony NZ
Merino NZ
Alliance
The Thoroughbred
Pinelands Motor Hotel
BWIA Airlines
Papakura Tavern
Bellbird Arms
The Grand Establishment
The Commercial Hotel
Clyde Tavern
Twizel Top Hut Restaurant
Mates Bar & Grill
Hubbards
Safety at Sea
Cadbury
The Photo Place
Weaver Marine
Spy
Courtaulds Epiglass
Mike Rodger Upolstery Services
So-Pac Group
Ngatea Lions
ROHO
Courtesy Car
Creative Sandblasted Effects
Amtex Holdings
Stitch-it Embroidery
Irie Blue
Vistec Prints
NZ Rowing
Dive NZ
Sea & Sea Marine
Waikato Rowing Club
Lifestream Spirulina
Wells Agencies
R & R Sport
Donaghys
Kodak
Tactel
Dunlop Foam
Plastic Wholesalers (Wto)
M & A Electrical
Uniden
Boat Haulage Ltd
Mother Earth
Rigtech Engineering
BP
Cellnet
Kathmandu
Sprout Man
Pub Charity
NutraZeal
Free Power
Capital Instruments
NZ Safety
The Waikato Polytechnic
Kiwi Innovations Limited
Croker Oars

Post Race Consortium

Sky TV — Paul Smart
Westfield NZ — Grant Hirst
Nuance/Regency Duty Free — Kelvin Ricketts
Buddle Findlay — Michael Dineen
IBM — Lynn Currie
Fisher & Paykel — David Henry
ASB — Ralph Norris
Lewis Holdings — David Levene
Thought Group & Racing Lotto Ltd — Berri Schroder

Supporters Club — Gold

WEL Energy
Alfred & Gisela Pallas
Joe & Elwyn Young
Cameron Bell

Supporters Club — Silver

Dr Steven Lillis
Don and Gaye McGlashen
Beattie Rickman
Chris Ineson
Ma Bakers Hot Bread Shop
Dave Harrison
Don Rowlands
Steve Krielan
Paul Dunlop
WD Saunders
Chris Thorsen
Martin Foster
Neil & Sarah Hyland
Chris Horton
Brian Dale

Supporters

Peter Rotgans
Monique Bjerkman
Richie Allen
Phil Oliver
Trevor Simpson
Brian & Dot McKinnon
Barry McCann
Ken Goody
Tracey O'Toole
Mandy Quantock
Sara Moulder
Max Hall
Mark Townsend
David Norrie
Mark Durling
Tony Steel
Bob Simcock
Don Putt
Kevin Sweeney
Christine Haughie
Colin & Betty Peck
Colin Sutherland
George Duncan
Dr Paul Judd
Dr Gordon Paterson
Gregg Dutton
Christine Wright
Nigel Cranston
Criss Strange
Bill Falconer
Gary & Amanda Reid
Nicole Cope
Mr S Koda
Thomas J Hartmann
Rosheen Whelan-Turnbull
Ken Smales
Bev Ngatai
Helen Broome
Andrea Lim-Sun
Kerry Williams
Howard Croker
Dave Moran
Andrew Sinha
Brett Smith

Simon Cope
Colin Quincey
Russ Rimmington
James Sheehan
Kim Thorp
Jeff Ross
Peter Wells
John Willis
Tracey Riley
Kim Thompson
Ross Jenkins
Ken Atkins
Ian Baserio
Mark Wheeler
Clark Abel
Jason Whaanga
Kevin Stewart
Art Lester
Bruce and Dolsie Laurenson
Dave Henry
Herman Kruetzmann
Rick Carlyon
Bruce Stevenson
Dean Edge
Marten Marine Staff
Clive Brown
Terry Jarvis
Dave Currie
Dame Susan Devoy
Beatrix Carrington
Stephen Clews
Tracey Kinney
Tracey O'Toole
Don Malcolm
Peter Masfen
Brett O'Callaghan
Tenby Powell
Duncan Reid
Dick Hubbard
Mark Callighan
Earl & Kathryn Austin
Dave Whylie
Nigel Cranston
Mayer Goldich
Jamie Whatman
Alastair Carthew
David Beatson
Jennifer Chadderton
Mike Harrison
Mr D Dearnley
Bob Faram
Mrs BL Hurst
Peter Leitch
Debbie Tawse
Andy Haden
Jim Hainey
Dr Steven Saunders
Bob Leveloff
B & P Lumley
V & N Morrison
Adelaide McLean
CK Pepperell
Chris & Lesley Saville
Scott Bevan
Chris Sharpe
Ross Southcombe
Dick Thevaward
Peter Thorburn
Hillary & Tony Ward
Loraine Wetherall
May Woodcock
Angela Griffen
Graham Johnson
Steve Shaw
Carl Emmerson
John Brakenridge
Kathy Cunningham
Kenneth Crutchlow
Tom Lynch
Rob Bristow